THE BEAU...
BY RALF HALEY

PROLOGUE

'Again!' the coach yelled at me. 'Again!' He seemed to know some broken English when angry.

I dribbled the ball as fast as I could, but was tackled again by the cone that had become my nemesis. I quickly retrieved the ball.

'Again!'

I zig-zagged my way through the cones set before me, the ball barely under control, and was tackled again.

'Again!' The Portuguese seemed to have little patience.

I tried once more, only to be felled by the cones.

'No! Again!'

Lying there face down on a pitch in the middle of the Pyrenees Mountains, I slowly pushed myself up off the floor, and went again.

THE BEAUTIFUL DREAM

CHAPTER 1: IN THE BEGINNING...

The happiest day of my life was without doubt was when I was 10 years old. Tragic when you think of it, that the peak of my life came in my childhood. On that day I won the best player award at a local under-11s football competition in my hometown of Hebden Bridge. The fact I won the trophy in the 'small' schools category didn't detract from the achievement.

To me it was the greatest thing ever. I was the best player out of 600 school kids littered across the countryside of West Yorkshire in the Calderdale region. Granted half of them were girls and therefore would take little interest in football, and from that number a fair old majority were under the age of 9 so they couldn't really challenge for the title simply because of being taken ill with Chicken Pox or that they simply preferred to play marbles, eat sand or wee on each other as a pastime as opposed to playing the game that I love. Those things didn't matter to me because on that day someone said to me I was good at football – I had been acknowledged by the football fraternity.

As I held that plastic trophy aloft and stood on that two foot high podium in a muddy field in the middle of nowhere, I'd never felt so proud, and I haven't since. That day I had my life mapped out in front of me.

I *was* going to be a professional footballer. It *was* going to happen.

Even then I knew it was an unlikely career path but nothing would stop me. I was going to train every day after school, do weights and learn new skills to accomplish the dream. My teenage years were going to see me train every day in pursuit of my ultimate goal.

I was going to win the FA Cup, the League and captain England to World Cup glory.

On the way home from that happiest of days my Dad didn't believe me but I was going to show him, I was sure. Still drenched in mud and glory I ran into my room, put the trophy above my bed and peered at the poster of Alan Shearer placed at an awkward angle on my bedroom wall. I had never been so sure of anything in my life. *I was going to be a professional footballer,* and nothing was going to stop me. That's what I thought anyway. Of course the dream never came to pass for one simple reason: I'm rubbish at football.

Truly truly rubbish. Horrible, ghastly, terrible, dreadful, turd. I am a mishmash of being very small, fat, slow, naturally unfit, weak and scared of physical contact with both males and females.

I never came close to making 'it' and I drifted away into being another member of society, forgetting the only dream and ambition I ever had in life. When I won that trophy I made a promise to myself that I would do all that I could to be a professional footballer but I broke that promise, spectacularly and quickly.

My teenage years went by in a flash of awkward facial growths, awkward approaches to girls, awkward retreats from girls and generally making a knob of myself. I was popular but never cool, smart but never clever – a middle-of-the-roader.

My College and University years went by in a flash of awkward facial growths, awkward approaches to girls, awkward retreats from girls, and generally making a knob of myself only this time fuelled by alcohol.

But despite not trying to be a professional footballer by training regularly or doing any voluntary exercise like any sensible person, I still hold the dream in my heart.

I am not sure what happened in these intervening years that took me from being a half-decent footballer to one that had no grace about him on a football pitch. I suppose everyone got bigger than me rather quickly, while I maintained the physique of Ronnie Corbett. But truthfully whilst I list thousands of differing contributing factors the real reason is that I had little talent and didn't work hard enough to maximise what little sporting prowess I had.

The discovery of girls, intoxicants and getting tubby, and thus not playing football every second were the potent cocktail that caused my failure.

By the time I had reached the latter part of my school years I was invariably the last person picked for the team during P.E. Team-mates would berate me for breaking moves down with my shin sliced passes into the echelons of the trees surrounding the training pitch and Teachers showed new depths in swearing and unprofessional behaviour whenever I came near the ball.

Of course many people reassess their dreams when they are growing up, change personalities, interests and switch ambitions and become very successful in their chosen line of work, but not me.

I remember a conversation with my careers officer when I was 17 that sums up my predicament:

'So Ralf, what is it that you want to be when you're older?' asked the bespectacled lady before me.

'Well I want to be a professional footballer,' I said, matter–of-factly.

'Oh, there's nothing on your file about that. Are you part of he youth team?' she asked, with wide-eyed enthusiasm.

'No.'

'Well do you play with a local side?' she asked, raising eyebrow.

'Not any more.'

'The school?' She raised the second eyebrow.

'Sometimes, if no one else turns up.'

'Right. Are you actually any good at football?' If she had three eyebrows they all would have been raised.

'No. Not really.'

'Okay. This could be a problem if you want to be a professional footballer, don't you think?' She scowled.

'I've never really thought about it, I just always thought it would happen.'

'Right. Okay. I er… I think we need to assess your options.' She pulled her chair up, leant forward, and looked at me sympathetically. She gave me some career options but I ended up drifting through a series of 'temp' and part-time jobs, ending up as an admin assistant for Manchester University.

My dream, and how I'd failed to chase it, was all I could think of, but I knew I had no chance of achieving it.

Football is the religion of millions of people on an over-populous rock in the Atlantic where every boy dreams of being a professional footballer, and furthermore its economy is still just about strong enough to attract the crème de la crème of foreign talent from all four corners of the world. Anyone brought up on these shores, talented or not, is going to struggle to make an impact or impression simply because of it being such a crowded market.

But then things changed beautifully, marvellously and wonderfully for the better.

During a restless night I had an epiphany. I sat bolt upright in the darkness of my bedroom and switched on my bedside lamp to bring light both physically and emotionally.

Why should I give up?

Football is a worldwide game after all, isn't it? Michel Platini, winner of the European Player of the Year award in 1984, '85 and '86 and now even the UEFA President says there are too many foreign footballers in this country. In that moment, I decided he was right.

At the inception of the Premier League in 1992, just eleven players named in the starting line-ups for the first round of matches hailed from outside the British Isles. However by 2000/2001 the number of foreign players participating in the Premier League was up to 36%. By the '04/'05 season the figure had increased to 45%. By my own calculations, that figure will have reached a staggering 147% by 2017. These figures cascade through the football pyramid in England all the way to the bottom preventing chances for home-grown talent. It was their fault not mine that I'm not a professional footballer, but what's stopping me going to their country and doing the same thing? Surely without them in their respective countries there was to be a gap in the market? Definitely so!

With these thoughts I felt liberated. I stroked my chin and paced around the room. By simply being a typical Brit and reasoning that my life was miserable because of foreigners, in a jovial way not the hatred kind, I decided that I *could* be a professional footballer. Who said it had to be in *this* country? 'No one that's who!' I shouted to the darkness.

I am not an idiot; I knew I wasn't good enough to actually make a career out of football. I'm *really* bad at it. But what about one game, anywhere in the world?

Surely someone, some club, somewhere, would be willing to pay me a pound or a Euro or a Lat or a Krone for one game of football so that I could finally say 'You know I used to be a professional footballer.'

Football is now a worldwide game, *the* worldwide game and there are hundreds of clubs and league systems all around the world, and each one of them is getting more and more professional, pumping more money into the beautiful game. There are 207 recognised countries in the world with FIFA. Surely one of these places would have a club that would pay me something?

I was going to try and be a professional footballer, and nothing was going to stop me.

One minute, one Euro, ANYWHERE will do.
'I am going to be a professional footballer!'

I am 10 years old again and life is great once more. Could I really be a professional footballer abroad? There was only one way to find out.

'You're going to do what!?' said Jamie pressing the pause button on his Xbox – a rare occurrence if there ever was one.

'I'm going to quit my job and try and be a professional footballer anywhere in the world,' I said, sat on his dirty sofa, scared of catching the plague.

'Are you serious?' He leant forward in his arm-chair, his bushy eyebrows questioning me as well as his words.

'Of course I'm serious. Look at my face, this is a serious face.'

'Well, no offence, but you're dreadful at football!'

'Well thanks!'

Jamie was right and I wasn't a man to argue with him. If anyone was ever able to pass judgement on my football skills it was him. At school he was one of our few football gods. He'd had trials with Huddersfield Town as a 15-year-old, but was deemed too slow, and so instead he had to make do with captaining the school football team and local side for seven years from the centre of midfield, running the show left, right and centre. If that wasn't enough he also was a long distance runner, and now works as a Corporate Healthcare adviser. I had visited his house firstly to break the news to him, and secondly to ask for advice.

'What honestly makes you think you can do it?' he asked.

'Desire. The fact that I am probably not going to give up until I can say that once, just once, I was a professional footballer.'

'But you won't do it, you need to be fit and have ability and aggression. Playing with mates and playing with professionals is a different thing entirely. Your ship has sailed, let it go like the rest of us.'

'Have you ever played football in Latvia?' I asked.

'No, of course I haven't.'

'Do you know where Latvia is?'

'Not really no,' he replied sharply.

'Do you know any famous Latvian players?'

'No.'

'Well, there you have it, how do you know how good people are in lower league football around the world when you don't know anything about it?' He was stumped; I had him.

'I don't know, but I do know they'll be better than you. That's a guarantee. You're like Darius Vassell without the pace.'

'But Darius Vassell without pace would be awful,' I said, questioning his metaphor.

'Exactly! Seriously, when was the last time you ran anywhere?' he said, starting to point out the holes in my foolproof plan.

'I don't know.'

'Go on think.' Jamie was probing, gesticulating at me with his games console remote.

'Probably when I was late to meet you in the pub a few weeks back.'

'And when you arrived it looked like you'd just escaped from fat camp.' Jamie threw himself back into his seat.

'Can you stop now please?' I pleaded.

'Alright.' He continued on his Xbox. 'I'm just trying to tell you you're probably making a mistake.'

'Well I'm not listening to you, but I do need your help. I was hoping you could draw me up a fitness plan, maybe give me some pointers on what I need to be working on, given your profession and all that.'

Jamie pressed pause once more and exhaled as if I was interrupting something frightfully important.

'Is this actually serious?' he asked.

'Yes, how many times do I need to say it?'

'Right, well I'll tell you what I tell everyone. 30 minutes respiratory exercise every day, make sure your lungs are working, and then you'll be on your way.'

'What do you mean that's what you tell everyone?'

'Well that's what everyone needs to be doing every day, so that's what I tell everyone.'

'What, regardless of how healthy they are?'

'Pretty much, yeah.' He shrugged his shoulders.

'Don't you get bored?'

'Oh yeah! I hate my job, I wish I could be a professional footballer, but I've faced facts, unlike some of us.' Jamie paused mid-sentence to assess what I was saying to him before coming to a conclusion. 'This is a joke isn't it?'

'Of course it's not a joke,' I replied.

'But you won't do it.'

'It's not a question of achieving, it's a question of trying,' I lied. It was all about achieving.

Jamie tutted. 'It's quite possibly the most ridiculous idea I've ever heard.'

This went on until the early hours.

Chapter 2: Pain

'Don't you need to be good at football?'

'I didn't know you were good at football.'

'I've seen you play football, have you got a lot better or something or are you still rubbish?'

'When was the last time you actually played 11-a-side football competitively?'

These were some of the many questions levied at me by friends, family members, loved ones and even strangers in the pub once word got out of what I was doing.

I admit the questions are viable; of course they are. Yes, it would help if I was good at football, and no I haven't improved markedly since my last outing as a footballer in an 11-a-side game, the mention of which invokes horrifying memories.

It was six years ago on a bleak January day. I was 16 years old and it was the morning after a particularly heavy night before. I was at that awkward age where you don't know your drinking limitations, and I found that a bottle of Jack Daniels certainly exceeded mine. After vomiting away every solid and liquid I had in my body, I hope you can appreciate I wasn't feeling well for the 11am kick-off in our Hebden Bridge Saints game against the Guiseley Gremlins.

Despite it being a cold day I rolled onto the pitch as a substitute with perspiration already dripping down my face, lost the ball several times in dangerous positions, threw up as part of a cunning plan to lose my marker at a corner and then subsequently rolled off the pitch again once my lungs and will had given way after a mere seven minutes of game time. Luckily there were just two minutes remaining and my team held on for the win, finishing off a 5-1 victory I had no part in other than to cause damage. Although it was the middle of the season and we had plenty of games left, I took the look of disappointment from our kind manager that perhaps my services were no longer required. I think its testament to how bad I am at the game that the biggest trophy the team won over seven years playing together came while I wasn't part of it at the end of that season, just three months after my final game.

I had played for Hebden Bridge Saints for all seven of those years on and off as a consistent substitute, starting no more than a handful of games and scoring no more than a handful of goals. I was a utility player, there for when the manager wants to protect the prize striker from the aggressive lunges of a mentally challenged brute when our team was winning 6-0. A sort of youth-team John O'Shea. I had played in every position other than goal by the time I left the team and have never had a specialised position. The manager would often look at me on those cold Sunday mornings, and I could see in his eyes he was visibly burdened by the thought he would eventually have to put me somewhere on the pitch or risk upsetting me.

The only reason I was part of that football team growing up was because I was willing to turn up every week and do what I was told, combined with the fact that no one could find it in their hearts to tell me that I was, quite frankly, shit at football.

Towards the end of my time with the team I adapted my approach to the matches to show that I still wanted to be part of it all, even if it meant not playing, as I didn't want to be to asked to leave the squad. My new approach to football saw me grow my hair into a curly mop as I became the comedy japer; a great character to have in the dressing room, the one who was willing to make an arse of himself for team morale without showing displeasure at not playing, even though it killed me inside knowing I wasn't needed.

I had the basics, being able to pass in a straight line and knowing the runs of other players but that was it. I was a very rounded player, unfortunately for me the roundness related to my physique more than my ability.

But that didn't mean I stopped loving football, far from it, I just stopped loving the physical exertion part. I've only fallen in love with the idea of playing and being a professional now that reality has dawned on me that normal life and work is not for me.

With my mind racing here, there and everywhere, I decided to divide the quest into a two-part action plan, thus:

Action Plan:

1) Pick the countries well, you have limited funds: I can't do this escapade forever, financially or emotionally. I've reasoned over a six-month period I could save £1500, when the money runs out, I'll give up. My targets for attempting to get a trial have been drawn up: China, Australia, Japan, Eastern Europe and perhaps Scandinavia. I might get lucky. They definitely have the passion for the game but I'm hoping the sport hasn't been around long enough over there for any half-decent young whipper-snappers to come through, so I may have a window of opportunity. There is absolutely no point going to France, Brazil, Germany, Italy or any other country that regularly qualifies for the World Cup. A six-year-old boy in the streets of Brazil with no shoes would run rings round me with a football. Seriously.

2) Be in the best physical condition you can be: Having no pace, no height (I am 5ft 7in) and no strength is a problem. I also have an aversion to aggression – violence just doesn't agree with me. I have never seen the attraction or advantage either socially or in sports of enjoying bringing physical harm to other people, especially in football. It's called the Beautiful Game for a reason.

My point is that I am not going to attempt to be a professional footballer by enhancing my aggressive tendencies, as it does not agree with my humanitarian ways and so that means I have to concentrate on my lungs, become an engine room of energy, constantly hounding and harassing in a pressing manner, and still being in my 20s, I should have enough left in the tank to be able to do this.

Unfortunately there is a drawback to this in that, like any sensible individual, I hate exercise. It makes me sore, tired and grumpy.

When it comes to exercise I am an OAP prodigy. I have the knowledge, skill and desire to do little exercise, I just need to wait for my body to age sufficiently enough so I can fulfil my unquestionable potential of being a world class old person of sitting down all day and drinking tea. That particular dream needs to be on hold for now as I need to be in peak physical condition to give me any sort of a chance. I am going to need to buy a pair of trainers and some shorts in order to achieve optimum fitness levels. I even have to go against every fibre in my body and go against the upbringing my parents gave me and do the unthinkable: join a gym.

In reference to action point 2 I have also drawn up some vital statistics to inspire myself to improve upon whilst I go on:

Height: 5ft 7in (taller than Diego Maradona).
Weight: 10.75 stones (lighter than Diego Maradona).
Fastest Mile: Unknown (but surely faster than Diego Maradona).
Sit ups done in a row: Unknown (but more than Diego Maradona).
Press ups done in a row: Unknown (but more than Diego Maradona).
100m Personal Best: 15.87 when I was 11 and not been timed since (I have slowed over the years, but I'm still faster than Diego Maradona).
Time spent at the gym: 0:02. I went in to get a drink (More than Diego Maradona. Probably).

You'd think when reading that I'd be better at football than Diego Maradona, but unfortunately technique plays a strong hand in football and my keepy uppy record of 72 leaves a lot to be desired. However, improving technique in just six months with a full-time job to pay the bills is a big ask. This is why I decided to concentrate on fitness while identifying those countries awful at football to visit. It's February now, so this gives me six-months leading up to Europe's pre-season, where clubs would be looking for new players and where I would hopefully be in tip-top shape, getting the jump on a lot of the competition.

With the plan in place, I decided to take my first steps of putting my dream into action, and what better way to start than by going for a run?

The first steps of this were going to be like the Apollo moon landing for me, venturing into a new world.

I can't remember the last time I went for a run voluntarily or part as a leisurely activity, probably in the late 80s, but now I'd have to get used to it. Donning a home made headband, combat shorts and my red plimsoll shoes I felt confident. Opening the door to the streets of Manchester before me I looked above to see blue skies all around. I breathed a lungful of nature's not-so-finest city air and attempted to stretch by trying to touch the ground with my hands whilst keeping my legs straight. Sadly that resulted in only reaching my knees, strained hamstrings and a spine that wasn't entirely happy judging by the clicking noises it made on the way down. The stretching was promptly aborted and the run brought forward in the schedule.

Starting to pound the streets in a leisurely fashion, as would any normal jogger, I felt incredible. Why hadn't I done this before? The fresh air and the sound of the tarmac made me feel alive as stresses washed away. Just me and the road. Me, my dream and the road. Every face I passed seemed familiar and friendly and every motorist let me cross the road; I was Rocky. But what's that? Just a short stabbing pain in my heart. It will be fine. Oh hang on, that's a stitch I feel coming on. Oh, and I think I've just pulled a muscle. Oh, and another one. Hmm, now I feel like I want to die. Ah yes the familiar feeling of exercise, how I missed you.

My legs were tense and I couldn't feel my hands. My face was so hot you could have fried an egg on it, and thick, sticky saliva was building in my mouth at an alarming rate. I found the nearest wall to sit on to recover.

As I sat there defeated by the stretch of road from my flat to the bus stop, an old lady pushing a trolley who I had passed mere moments beforehand effortlessly scuttled past my defeated body on her way to the post office. Grey clouds appeared out of nowhere above me. The heavens opened and rain began to batter down on my slumped torso. I refused to see this as a metaphor for the journey ahead.

It took me three days to fully recover from that run. A two-minute run had made me sore and achey for three days, a terrible ratio. Paired with the fact I haven't played football for a year, I had my trepidations when I met up with Jamie and another friend, Coop, for my first game of football in many a year, especially as there were many young, athletic men present, all taking things a bit too seriously.

Stood outside the maze of floodlit astroturf pitches I watched contemporaries and counterparts prepare for their respective games by lunging in all manner of directions. I thought to myself that if I attempted to do any of the stretches they were doing then I'd probably tear every fibre in my body and discover muscles I didn't even know existed.

Ironically, football has always made me a bit of an outcast. None of my family were into the game and so none would talk to me about the latest results. Friends and fellow players had an affinity with the sport mostly because of their dads, and they all had the latest boots, football shirts and the like. I never had any of that – my family never saw it as a priority, and so my unique kit of denim shorts and cheap boots often saw me come into conflict with opponents and team-mates through no other reason than them seeing a potentially weak target.

I love football, just not all the people who play it. I think if I'd been born in the Stanley Matthews era of baggy shorts, fags before, during and after the game, half-time pies instead of oranges and copious amounts of alcoholic rehydration. It's just unlucky for me that I was born when football was started to be consumed in a far more professional and aggressive way, where people who actually crack a joke when playing football in their mum's gardening shorts are cruelly cast aside.

The game I was nervously awaiting to play, with Jamie and Coop beside me, had been arranged through a friend of a friend as part of the local student leagues and we were doing them a favour by turning up so that the team didn't incur a fine.

The players littered around the pitch were either people like me – an out-of-shape slob who has a rubbish office job – or pumped up testosterone-fuelled morons with mullets, who have a rubbish office job but feel the need to show everyone just how much of a neanderthal they can be by playing football in a far-too serious manner of a Sunday evening.

I was happy being part of the slob brigade, but my ambition meant I would eventually have to join the ranks of the serious mullet boys.

Here before us was the graveyard of youth's ambition, the ghosts of dreams gone by, the product of the foreign football invasion. But even this felt great. The sound of the whistle, the smell of a musty luminous bib, the sight of the ball rippling the net – this was where I belonged, and I couldn't figure out for the life of me why I had banished myself from the environment I loved for so long.

The match was to be a game of seven-a-side and wearing a holey light blue t-shirt, combat shorts and a pair of boots I'd managed to borrow off Jamie that were a size too big, I was ready to take the first steps of a foolproof plan.

I was introduced to the people on our team that I hadn't already met from parties or pub outings and instantaneously forgot all of their names. They looked at my pot belly and tragic John McEnroe headband and probably thought some nasty things. They told me to go stand up front and do my best.

We kicked off our 20 minute game and after 7 seconds things were bad. We quickly fell behind one-nil and I immediately felt the need for a brandy to numb the physical pain I was already in. The goal conceded was nothing to do with me, the defence was just asleep. However, the fact that we couldn't score a goal or keep possession thereafter was wholly on me.

Passes to my feet were returned to team-mates faces at an alarming pace, and shooting opportunities were missed due to my inability to kick a ball harder than a toddler could achieve. I was running on sand and breathing treacle. I was pushed and torn from right to left, up and down, always several thousand steps off the pace. Every time I got the ball I lost it, often tripping over it in slapstick fashion before stumbling into the chest of the mightier, mulleted opposition. Soon it was two-nil, then three, and then four. My team-mates looked at me angrily and I cursed at myself under my breath. Jamie and Coop distanced themselves from me, pretending he didn't know me, like I was an embarrassing drunk at a party, however with full time fast approaching, my moment to shine arrived.

Our goalkeeper drilled the ball to my feet in the centre circle. With my back to goal, and in one swooping turn, I managed to manoeuvre myself between two opponents and curl a delightful first time left foot shot into the top left corner of the net from 15 yards. It was a peach. However, the celebrations weren't. I turned back to my team-mates finger wagging, gasping 'that's the goal of the game!'

It's an unwritten law that you don't celebrate in a non-competitive match, nor do you yelp something so ridiculous or arrogant to complete strangers in an icy atmosphere. But I did, and it ruined the goal. With that, the final whistle went. I stopped my impression of running, spat phlegm to the floor and doubled over, put my hands on my knees breathing as deeply as I could; oxygen had never tasted so good.

'Still want to be a professional footballer?' Said Jamie jogging over to me, looking so relaxed he could have easily just finished a nap.

'Yes… definitely… this fitness thing was…' I was struggling to talk such was my fatigue. '…only to be expected.'

'You look terrible.' Jamie handed me his water.

'Looks… can… be… deceiving.'

'Yours can't. You look like you need a doctor.'

'Why… do you know one?' I stood up and demolished the bottle of water.

'It's going to take a lot of hard work for you to do this.'

'Hang on. Did you not see my goal?' I pointed in the direction of the empty net.

'I did see it. But one goal doesn't make a professional footballer. 10 years of neglecting your body makes a bad one, and I know which you are at the moment.'

'We'll see.'

'We definitely will.'

I wasn't too disappointed with the result of the match, only with my performance. Yes I scored a goal, but I didn't contribute anything else other than illustrate new lows in physical fitness for an aspiring athlete. I needed to improve drastically if this is going to be pulled off.

Days later and fully recovered from the match I received a call asking me to play again that Sunday. I had obviously impressed enough with my lack of fitness last time around to warrant another game. That or they were short of players.

Obviously it was vitally important not only to train, but to get an idea of my level of skill on the pitch before letting the cat out of the bag at work, quitting my job, and going travelling in search of a team that may be willing to pay me for a match, only to find out that I am indeed not good enough. I may be crap at football now, but given a rigorous six-month training programme I could get potentially get to a decent standard.

I was confident in the plan: play plenty of football, get fit, and pepper football clubs around the world with requests of a trial. It was a good plan; all I had to do was play lots and lots of football.

12 minutes into the game and I was lying in a crumpled heap, writhing in agony whilst I watched my ankle swell to the same size as my head. I failed to see the irony of my situation. It had happened whilst intercepting a pass. At full stretch I managed to get my toe caught on the ball in a position where neither the ball nor the ground could move. Momentum had carried me beyond my body's limitations, and there was only one possible end result. My ankle fully rotated the 360 degrees around the football whilst admirably keeping contact with the ball, and I fell to the floor. What I did was certainly not natural. Nor was the reaction of my team mates, who despite my yelp and subsequent theatrical tumble, continued to play on.

'Coop, Coop! Can you come take a look at my ankle please?' I cried.

Christopher Cooper, a life-long friend, a qualified Physiotherapist and surely the man who could help me in a situation like this. He decided to ignore me and ask the referee a question.

'How long left Ref?'

'Two minutes.' Even the ref didn't care about my predicament.

'I'll be there in two minutes mate,' Coop said.

We lost the game. I can't recall the exact score, probably something to do with my ankle exploding to four times its natural size and my body going into shock. I turned a paler shade of white and felt the need to throw up. I had done this injury before as a teenager whilst playing football in my kitchen, much in the same manner. I had been pretending to be left back Roberto Carlos whilst holding a double fried egg sandwich, watching him strut his stuff for Real Madrid against Bayern Munich in the Champions League semi-final in 2003. Unfortunately I can't exactly 'strut' as well as he can, and so my attempts at dummying and stepping over the ball whilst running round the kitchen table resulted in me standing on the ball and my right ankle giving way. I remember my Mum entering the room minutes later seeing me flat out with a balloon sized ankle saying "You look awfully pale Ralf", not having noticed the fact that I was a) lying on the floor in agony, or b) had an ankle which had its own heartbeat.

As soon as the full-time whistle blew, Coop stuck to his sterling promise.

'Yeah that looks pretty nasty mate. Can't really do much about it now, just rest it, keep it compressed, elevated and on ice on for 20 minutes and off for 20 minutes and repeat, then come and see me once its calmed down and I'll try and get you back up and running. But you aren't going to be playing football for a while. That's not a sprained ankle; you've definitely torn something in there. That looks disgusting.'

'Thank you,' I said lacking all sincerity in my voice.

I started to panic that the quest would be over before it had even begun. If Marco Van Basten, winner of the European Footballer of the year award in 1988, 1989 and 1992, arguably the finest player of his generation, could be forced into early retirement in his late 20s with ankle problems then so could I, Ralf Haley, water-boy for Hebden Bridge Saints circa 1996-2002, and 1991 Colden School Easter Egg Competition bronze medal winner.

Three days later I sought medical advice.

'Does it hurt when I do this?' asked Coop kneeling on the floor of his apartment thrusting my swollen black ankle into unnatural positions.

'Yes!'

'Okay, what about this?' Another thrust from my 'friend'.

'Yes!'

'And now?'

'OW!'

Why do people in the medical profession do this? Is it some sort of sycophantic lust for power?

'Yeah it's screwed. I'd recommend not playing on it for a couple of months. Even then, for it to fully recover it will take seven months to a year,' said Coop.

'A year!' I exclaimed.

'Well, yes. If you were a professional you'd need an operation, but you're not a professional so, unless you want to go private, you're just going to have to let it heal on it's own, and in your case, for it to fully heal that would be a year.'

'A year!' I repeated.

'I'm sorry but ankles are very delicate, and once you've done an injury like this there's a 40% chance that you'll do it again.'

'Well I did it when I was 17.'

'In that case better make that 70%.'

Wonderful.

Coop continued: 'How's this going to affect your plans to travel?'

'I don't know, that's a pretty substantial bombshell. It's February now, if I can't play football until the end of March at the earliest or do any training then that only gives me three or maybe four months to train and even then it might not have fully recovered. I wanted to go in Europe's pre-season when squads were taking shape.'

Coop didn't look overly concerned for me; in fact he didn't seem to care at all.

'Well, its not like you would have made it anyway is it?' He said wiping his hands down with a damp tea-towel.

'What do you mean?' My eyes narrowed.

'I've seen you play football.'

'Well thanks a bunch.'

'I just think blind optimism is no substitute for talent, skill and physical attributes.'

He did provide a compelling case.

'But I'm going to train *really* hard.'

'But you can't train; look at your ankle, its black! You'd need a professional team behind you pushing you all the way, and you'd need five years, ten hours a day to get anywhere close; and you're doing it over the next six months with no plan beside an occasional kick-about with mates, and even that's impossible now.'

'You're a professional and you're treating me.' I responded in desperation.

'Someone to treat a gammy ankle doesn't count. In fact, my involvement in this is another reason why you will fail. You're already injured. You're like Darius Vassell without the pace.'

'Jamie has already made that joke.'

'I wasn't joking. It's an accurate description.'

Coop wasn't doing much for my mood. I had gone round to his to not only get treatment on my bad ankle but to also discuss my options, to talk about which countries and what levels of football in these respective places around the world I should be targeting.

'I played with guys who were a thousand times better than you at junior level and they never got anywhere near a professional contract.' He was saying it all in good jest but it was still hurting.

'Ha-ha yes, but what if they were only scouted for 30 minutes and were rubbish for those 30 minutes, have you thought about that?'

'That's a good point, however even then those 30 minutes in which they might have been rubbish they'd still be a thousand times better than you ever were or will be. You need 5 years.'

'I've got six months!'

'By the time your ankle has recovered properly you'll have two, three tops, and that's optimistic given the level of your injury.'

'So, I still can get fit in that time and improve my skills.'

'No you can't.'

'Yes I can.' I said presenting no evidence to back up my statement.

'You're not strong enough.'

'I'm joining a gym.'

'You need to be ridiculously fit.'

'I'm joining a gym!'

'You're not tall enough.'

'I can still grow.'

'You stopped growing when you were 13!'

'Diego Maradona is 5ft 5.'

'I can't believe you just compared yourself to Diego Maradona.'

'Why are you being so mean?' I pleaded.

'I just don't want you to be disappointed that's all. You're not Rocky, this is real life.'

I definitely am Rocky.

I continued: 'Look, thousands of people go travelling when they're our age; I'm doing the same thing, but at the same time trying to achieve something beautiful. Granted it's probably not going to happen but wouldn't it be amazing if I could say I once, just once, I was a professional footballer?'

'It would be pretty amazing.' *I had him!* 'Still won't happen though. Anyway have you even thought about how you're going to get trials?'

'Not exactly. I was going to do that later, probably write to them or call them on the phone. I can blag like no other.'

Coop's bottom jaw dropped at my lackadaisical attitude.

'When exactly?' he asked.

'When I'm fit.'

'So never then,' he said sarcastically.

I decided to ignore him.

'I can't afford to go away for ages, so they're going to have to rule their thumb over me in one or two training sessions, and then they'll know if I'm good enough to make it with them or anyone else in their country.'

'If you get any trials,' he responded.

'When I get the trials.'

It was optimism versus pessimism that evening, and it went on for a long time. Ten days after committing to my dream I had a serious injury and no idea how to get trials. I thought I had a plan, but right now it seemed scuppered. I couldn't wait another year to do this because the ridicule from friends was already too much, and I wanted to prove them wrong. To prove *hope* right.

My beautiful dream had just gotten a whole lot more difficult.

CHAPTER 3: FOOTBALL CVs

<u>Action Plan:</u>

1) Pick the countries well, you have NO money.

Let me get this straight, I hated my job, so much. People say the word hate is a strong word to use and should only be uttered under extreme circumstances, like when describing the Nazis or Marmite. But I *really* hated my job. The daily occurrence of assaulting my alarm clock at 7:30am in order to deal with obnoxious people in my cruddy admin job didn't do much for morale, for me or for them. As employees go, I was not the best.

Work was good to me. I hated it, but it was good. I'd say that in any given day I probably worked about 4 hours on average. The rest of the time I'd either be chatting to colleagues, chatting to friends over the internet or looking for jobs that I either didn't want or wasn't qualified for, and didn't want badly enough to get the qualifications.

Not doing any work whilst at work sounds like fun, but believe me it isn't. In fact it gets extremely tiring extremely quickly. Staring at a computer screen for hours on end and attempting to come up with ever more diverse ways to keep yourself entertained is a tough task, the lowest ebb being paperclip basketball, which after many hours of playing, I realised I didn't even know the rules, and I was the only one who played it. In the blink of an eye I'd lost over a year of my life to sitting in an office reading football gossip pages, inventing terrible games and reading about people who were better and more successful than me on Wikipedia.

I was hoping to put my hunt for trials on hold, until I had grasped if I could get fit enough to do it, and gauged whether or not my basic football skills would be enough to succeed anywhere. Unfortunately with a serious ankle injury restricting the chance of any football happening for a while, and nothing to do at work, I decided it was best to do what I could when I could.

The questions I had been asked about the project had been varied, but there was one consistent theme, delivered by two parties of people. The first group are those who know me and have seen me play football who ask: 'How are you going to get trials? You're rubbish.'

The second group are more supportive, simply because they haven't seen me play football: 'Oh my god that's amazing, how are you going to get trials with these clubs? Are you any good?'

Although delivered in different manners, the basic question is the same. How does someone who has no history of football (bar a few sorry appearances from the substitute's bench for his local side), as well as having no references from anyone involved in football, go about getting effectively a job interview with football clubs around the world?

The normal practice players go through in England is getting scouted playing for a local side whilst still young, signing terms as a youth player as a result and working their way through the youth system as a teenager. Often it doesn't work out that way for them, and they either get injured or don't progress to the club's liking and are released from their contract. Then they're either free to move to a different club lower down the football league pyramid, or simply have to get a normal, rubbish job like the rest of us. This process can start at any age, with many people signing terms as a youth player up until they are 15 or 16. Any time after that and clubs generally hold the view that, no matter how much potential they show, it is too late to imprint them with the basics to make it as a professional footballer.

Now in my mid 20s, I was never scouted by anyone when I was young, nor had I had any trials. Not one club showed an interest in me, and why should they? Apart from one sunny glorious day when I was 10 years old my football history is not the greatest.

Many discarded youth players will have an agent or a representative and a football CV; much like a standard CV, it lists everything they have achieved in their football career. They will also have a show-reel DVD that they can send off to prospective employers. Another avenue available to them is the week-long Football Association showcasing events each summer, where players between certain ages released from their clubs are invited to play football with other people who've been rejected from clubs, under the watchful eyes of scouts from across the country – a kind of footballer junk sale.

I obviously have none of this. No agent, no football CV and no glowing references from coaches. A youth player's ideal CV when looking for a new club would read:

Name: John Smith
Date of Birth: 17/06/1992
Age: 17

Playing Experience: Signed by Arsenal aged 10, played in the youth system for six years, making 98 appearances in Academy games and scoring 12 goals from a deep-lying midfield position. Patrick Vieira said when he was at the club that I was the player who reminded him the most of himself when he was young.

I also made 12 appearances for England Schools between the ages of 12 – 15.

References:
- Arsene Wenger Tel no: xxxxxxxxxxxx
- Patrick Vieira: bigpat@football-legends.com

Physical Attributes and fitness
Height: 5ft 11in
Weight: 178kg of pure muscle
100m Sprint: 11.67secs
1 mile: 5 minutes 11 seconds.

Other Skills: Can do kick-ups for 24 hours continuously before I pass out.

Other interests: The gym, girls and Playstation.

Reason for not making it: I didn't grow to be 6ft tall by the time I was 17 and was subsequently released.

My Football CV on the other hand would be slightly different:

Name: Ralf Haley
Date of Birth: 17/06/1985

Age: 23

Playing Experience: Hebden Bridge Saints ages 11 - 17, played 40(ish) games, 10 of those being starts when we only had 11 players. I once managed to kick myself in the nuts during a game.

References: My Mum.

Other skills: I make a mean Tuna Pasta Bake.

Other interests: Girls, sitting around, cooking, knitting and Scrabble.

Physical attributes and fitness: Will be disclosed at interview.

Reason for not making it: Will be disclosed at interview.

How on earth was I going to get a trial with anyone? I don't have the history or talent in order to achieve this. I don't want to lie; lying is not in my nature. Besides, quite a few people would question why someone who said they were on Manchester United's books has turned up at a third division club in Timbuktu hoping for a payment of three fags. But before all this I needed to figure out how I was going to open a correspondence with these clubs in the first place.

I considered cold calling all lower league clubs around the world and just simply explaining my situation, but that idea was dismissed pretty quickly when I realised that my phone bill would be extortionate, and also the language barrier with a Bulgarian over the phone might prove to be a problem. I also considered writing to them by letter, but again that would cost a fair bit, and would take a long time both to write and to get replies. Those two options would also have to be done at home, eating into any leisure time I may have. That left me with one option, and it was clearly the greatest one. The one I can do at work, all day, every day, with nobody any the wiser: email.

Yes the power of the internet was at my fingertips. Thousands of football club websites and hundreds of those willing people to contact them by publishing their email addresses. This was genius.

I began to spend a ridiculous amount of time trawling the internet for clubs who have published their email addresses on their websites. It was beautiful. Google, brilliant Google, even translated the foreign web-pages for me. Even better, Wikipedia lists every football club in the world, categorised by countries and by league standing, so I could roughly identify which clubs I should be emailing. All I had to do was go to the club website and copy and paste the club name and email address into a spreadsheet so I had them all in one place.

In total, and shamefully I'm quite proud of this, I managed to amass 1,044 email addresses of football clubs all over the world, but not from countries like Brazil or Italy or Germany or France. No I gathered them from those other footballing giants such as Luxembourg, Liechtenstein, Malta, San Marino, Andorra, Lithuania, Latvia, Estonia, Denmark, The Faroe Islands, New Zealand, Kenya, Ghana, Vietnam, Japan, China, India, Canada, Tahiti, Ghana, Macedonia, Slovakia, Slovenia, Poland, Cyprus, Albania, Sweden, Norway, Finland, Hong Kong, Singapore, Egypt, Morocco, Hungary, Belarus, Malaysia, Costa Rica, Japan, Moldova, Iceland and Georgia.

1,044 email addresses in one spreadsheet: it's a thing of beauty and something that I figured out, at an average of 4 minutes to acquire each email address once I'd navigated my way there and then copied and pasted the address, took me an incredible 4,176 minutes to compile. That's over 69 hours of simply looking at foreign football club web-pages and copying their email addresses into a spreadsheet.

The websites themselves varied in quality, quantity and content. One football club had a photograph of a dog as its site. That's it, just one picture of a mongrel dog. Bar this one peculiarity, however, the rest had one thing in common, and that was that they listed contact details, and so they were surely willing bad footballers like me to contact them asking for trials.

But what to write? This in itself took nearly as long as amassing the email addresses. As I have already mentioned, under no circumstances was I going to lie to them. I could, however, be economical with the truth. Many people confuse being economical with the truth with lying, but it's not the same thing, it's merely divulging information in a selective manner that could be interpreted to mean something else. After what I have approximated to be 7,023 different drafts, here is what I wrote.

Dear Sir,

My name is Ralf Haley, a 23 year old from England. In August, September and October I will be travelling the world attempting to be a professional footballer anywhere (even 5 minutes in one game will do).

I am requesting a trial with your club so you can pass judgment on me. It would only take a 1-2 of hours of your time. Of course if you think I am any good and want to offer me some more training sessions with you with a view to something more then I would be extremely interested.

I am of decent standard and was watched by a number of English clubs through my childhood but never offered a youth contract anywhere.

I am 5ft 8in tall (172cm) have a decent amount of pace, a good football brain, good technique, an iron will and desire to win.

I hope you can offer me some of your time to see if I am good enough to achieve my goals. I will travel to your club when it suits you. I am travelling all over the world to any club that is willing to have me for a couple of hours so please don't hesitate to say yes if you feel you are a long way away or too small a club.
Please let me know what you think. I really look forward to hearing from you.

Yours Sincerely,

Ralf Haley

That's it. I think it had the right balance of desperate grovelling and being economical with the truth. You may be questioning a number of the comments and I would like to put your mind at rest:

'I am of decent standard and was watched by a number of English clubs through my childhood but never offered a youth contract anywhere.'

This is not a lie and is in fact true. I was watched by a number of English clubs throughout my childhood. Granted they were there to see my far more talented team-mates and opponents, but that wouldn't have stopped them watching me for 30 or so seconds before reaching the concrete conclusion that I was not good enough at football. It's not my fault if the person on the receiving end reads between the lines.

The second truth I have been economical with is my Unique Selling points, all 5 of them:

'I am 5ft 8in tall (172cm) have a decent amount of pace, a good football brain, good technique, an iron will and desire to win'.

I am actually 5ft 7 ½ inches but rounded it up. The other things listed, such as pace, football brain, good technique, iron will and desire to win are all matters of opinion: my opinion. I do have a little bit of pace (the 11-year-old version of me did anyway); I do have basic technique, an iron will (who else in the world is attempting to achieve what I am from such a low starting point?) and a desire to win. You should see me playing Scrabble, it gets tense.

I actually haven't listed any facts and figures about my attributes and ergo have not lied. Furthermore with this section telling them of my skills I feel I have managed to cover all 10 outfield playing positions on a football pitch. I want to play right back, or as a striker, but I didn't want to put that in because I didn't want the reader to immediately dismiss me in the event of them already having several players in those positions. If they want to stick me at centre back against a 7ft giant up front for a game and pay me a Euro, then I am fine with that, but in terms of training I am going to attempt to improve my skills in those two positions which, given the injury, is now a small window of opportunity.

The hardest part was clicking send. I've never been proactive about anything in my life, too shy to ask for anything or to put people out of their daily routine by asking for a favour, I'm very much a people person and I hate not being liked. Clicking send when I am bothering people with an odd request, putting them out of their daily routine by asking them to write back to me – I was setting myself up for not being liked by a good number of people when I turned up to any trial offered to me and was predictably crap, letting down the person who had invited me to their club.

I had no expectations about how many people were going to reply and from that how many people were going to say yes. It could have been hundreds, or it could simply be two, but I promised myself that I would go to all the clubs that offered me a trial as long as my limited budget would allow it. Yes, getting to the far reaches of Asia or New Zealand may prove quite tricky, however, I could potentially blag a lift.

It took me two hours to build up the courage to click send. It was a fear of rejection, the kind of fear that stops you going up to a girl you've shared a moment with across a bar even though you've got nothing to lose. There isn't a job or career I know of that I want to do other than achieve this, just once. If I can get it out of the way and then return to a life of rubbish work then I'll be happy, I would have achieved my life ambition. But to be rejected before even being given the opportunity to achieve my dream and also have a once in a life time adventure that I have already mapped out in front me would kill me.

Someone once said that dreams should be kept that way, as they're what keep the mind sane. I was about to bring my dream sharply into the focus of reality and I was scared it would become a nightmare.

I sat down at the desk, I read the email again 100 times over, deleted and reinstated sentences several times, breathed sharply between my teeth and clicked 'send', and watched my computer melt under the strain.

I had a bad ankle, no football CV and seemingly no chance. My grovelling letter flew at thousands of miles an hour to computers of football clubs all over the world. All I could do was wait.

I returned to work the next day feverishly anticipating what would no doubt be dozens of replies from football clubs giving me permission to have a trial with them. My heart skipped a beat when I saw I had 106 new messages in my inbox. 106 messages, unbelievable! Could it really be that I, overnight, had inspired clubs to write back to me with offers of trials all over the world? Well no. Of course I hadn't. The 106 messages in my inbox were all of course "Mail delivery failed: returning message to sender" emails. But that's okay, that still means 900 got through, and out of those 900 how many had written back to me by the end of the week? None of them, not one, the bastards. That spreadsheet took me weeks to compile, this was my dream, did they not realise this?

Two months later and still not one response received. The time had passed by in the blink of an eye and my ankle had only just got to the stage of feeling strong enough to run on it again. Two months! The ankle still hurt, but at least I could run on it and thus begin the now much-shortened fitness regime. I had scheduled myself six months to get fit and healthy after years of neglecting my body but now I only had three. Not that this was a problem, as I still hadn't arranged one trial.

I continued to send the email again and again and again, desperately hoping to get an answer. Things had not got off to the great break neck speed start I was hoping for.

Chapter 4: The Real Beginning

Johann Mifsud, the brilliant man. Johann Mifsud, the visionary. Johann Mifsud, creator of dreams.

> **From:** Johan Mifsud [mailto:xxxxxxxxxxxxxxxx]
> **Sent:** 12 May 2009 16:23
> **To:** Ralf Haley
> **Subject:** Re: Football clubs of the world
>
> Dear Ralf Haley
>
> We will be more than glad to give you a trial with our club; you can come whenever you want to train with our team. The only problem is that here in Malta second division clubs and below can't register foreign players with their team.
>
> While wishing you good luck for your future
>
> Yours Fatefully [sic]
>
> Johann Mifsud
> Club Secretary

Did I care that second Division clubs in Malta can't sign foreign players? Nope. And you know why? Because 1st Division teams can, and once I am over there and wow them with my football skills, they'll either pass me onto another club who can sign me, or invest in the squad so heavily that they will get promoted and then invite me back to play because I am that good. I know I am rubbish at football, but only in *this* country. How can I be rubbish in Malta? It's a rock in the Mediterranean with a population of about 20,000. Malta's most successful sportsman of all time is Tony Drago. Tony Drago the Snooker player. Tony Drago the 25-stone, huge, hulking snooker player. If that's what they deem to be a sportsman, an 'athlete' in Malta, the most successful 'athlete' the country has produced, then I am onto a winner with this country. I admit I'd been having doubts, but now it was game on. Johann received an immediate response; I was going to Malta in a little under 3 months.

Chapter 5: The gates of Hell

Many people had touched on this next aspect when I first told them my plans – the sacrifices and the difficulties that I would face. In order to gain approval I simply batted away their concerns, saying that it would be easy, simple, a piece of cake, saying I was looking forward to the task, and that I'd be able to handle it. I'm not talking about the football aspect here, oh no, that part I truly was looking forward to – no I am talking about the most unholy of places: the gym.

I hate, yes hate, everything to do with gyms and physical exercise. I dislike the narcissists who frequent them, the narcissists who run them, and the narcissists who are so self-involved that they never bothered to get a decent enough education to know what narcissism is. Of course there are always exceptions, but in the most parts the world, gymnasiums are full of muscle-ripped mono-syllabic neanderthals who all enjoy physical aggression against teenage and adult versions of me as a pastime. The word 'gymnasium' comes from Latin and it means 'Home of Arseholes'.

It was a world that I had of course developed an opinion of through the magic of prejudice, and was something I would have liked to have kept that way, but unfortunately, sometimes you have to shake hands with the devil, and this meant joining a gym. Technically, I thought to myself, if I were to do this I should really get a nutritionist as well, but apparently – according to my research at least – they don't really pay true dividends unless you take it seriously over a prolonged period of time, and I love cheese too much to get a nutritionist. Plus I couldn't afford it.

Walking into the gym wearing my combat shorts, my trusty, holey, navy blue t-shirt and my newly christened 'Converse Trainers: Running Edition' I felt immediately at unease. I had a sinking feeling in my stomach that you get whenever you feel guilty about anything, or feel heartbroken. I was feeling both, guilty at betraying my code of never doing any voluntary exercise, and heartbroken that I had become a man I never thought I would. Sweat pants were invented for a reason, but that reason was Sundays.

I had thought about achieving decent levels of fitness elsewhere, by going for runs on the street and lifting weights at home, but the small part of my brain that reminds me of logic and common sense told me that if I were to follow that path then I would inevitably end up not timing how long I run for or how far, and at home with the weights I would inevitably just end up drinking tea and eating fried chicken followed by chocolate. At a gym you can measure everything you do with little distraction. I had three months to get fit; the gym was a necessary evil.

Whenever you see adverts for gyms you always see models with toned physiques, smiling with pearly white teeth as they effortlessly use the gym machines whilst listening to music through trendy headphones. The gym adverts or flyers you get through your letterbox want you to think that if you join the gym then you too could turn out to be young and beautiful like them. However, I was soon to find out that this was all rubbish and that gyms are not full of gorgeous young people, but more akin to the stereotype I had built in my head over the years.

I'd never been to a gym before so I tried to find the most inoffensive one to my morals as I possibly could. Thankfully the Manchester Metropolitan University Didsbury Campus Gym (catchy name isn't it?) is located a 10-minute walk from my house or, even better for me, a 2-minute drive. This was the primary reason as to why I chose this gym. The secondary reason was that my friend Adam went to Manchester Metropolitan University to do a film degree. He is not that sporty, so following this lazy template of a Manchester Met student I was hoping to encounter more of his type at this gym, rather than the sports obsessed kinds you would find at many of the countries leading establishments. Sadly I was wrong.

Like most gyms I received a free induction from one of their 'specialist members of staff'. I liken this to cigarette companies handing out free packets of fags to kids leaving primary school at the end of the day, get them reeled in and watch the profits soar. Either yourself or someone you know has probably been a member of a gym for a long time, paying a monthly subscription while never actually going, and making up all manner of excuses as to why going to the gym, despite the financial outlay, wasn't actually possible.

That wasn't going to happen to me, I was determined to make sure any subscription fee I signed was used to its optimum.

Not surprisingly my 'inductor', Marvin, was massive. He filled the room, not with charm or elegance, but with his 6ft-cube-like appearance. He took pride in showing off his 'guns' and other attributes by wearing what can only be described as a sleeveless vest, no doubt designed for a 6-year-old girl, and a pair of shorts that left little to the imagination.

'Are you Ralf?' he said in a voice that I'd only ever encountered in my head when reading the lines of the Giant in *Jack and The Beanstalk* as a child.

'Yep that's me,' I gulped.

If I had to hazard a guess I'd say his shaven head was literally four times the size of my own. His hands were like snow shovels.

'Follow me,' he said. 'You ever been a member of a gym before?'

'No, never.'

I'm pretty sure the ground shook a little with every step he took.

'Ever used a rowing machine?'

'No.'

'Weight machine?'

'No.'

'Running Machine?'

'I've walked on a running machine before.'

Marvin grunted, I think this is how he showed displeasure.

'Right well I'll have to show you everything won't I?'

His grunt was definitely how he showed dissatisfaction; I was obviously interrupting him from watching Deal or No Deal in the staff room or something equally as important.

As Marvin gave me the grand tour of the weights in the gym I couldn't get over how big he was and, as a consequence, I wasn't paying much attention to the words coming out of his mouth. He would easily fill a doorway, his shoulders were broad, his arms wider than my legs and he had no neck. His neck was long gone, so much so that only specialist archaeologists assigned to him would be able to find traces of one. His shoulders were pure muscle. As you moved your eyes horizontally from his shoulders to where his neck should be you gazed into his bulging eyes, that's how much his shoulder muscles were built up.

'So here you've got your peck deck, and over here you've got your bicep pump.'

With the introduction of each machine, Marvin demonstrated its use with total brutality. I felt sorry for the handles as he clenched his club fists and squeezed the life out them whilst lifting ungodly heavy weights.

Then came the humiliation, after each station I had to then have a go, the weight peg, dictating how much weight the user wishes to lift, was moved from his ridiculous, inhumane amounts to the second lowest level for me, which was probably put there for old ladies rehabilitating from strokes, but I didn't care. Well, I did, but I accepted that it was a suitably nerdy amount. In total Marvin showed me 20 various weight stations and boy oh boy was I going to feel stiff in the morning. But the most important thing he showed me was the running machine; this was what I was most interested in.

If you see a Premier League Footballer you don't see them weighed down by the amount of muscle my good friend Marvin has. No, they are lean and toned but fast. I had decided that this machine was going to be my best friend for the next 3 months, I was going to run miles on it every day, increasing the speed and distance and time over the coming weeks. Speed nowadays is what makes football tick.

I've always thought I have a good football brain, I understand runs, angles and what pass to make. My problem is I am never in the right position to do this not because I can't identify where I need to be, but because my tubby little lard-ass can't get there in time, or I simply pass out and give up on the way during the seven-yard run.

Once Marvin left me to my own devices I looked at the black behemoth running machine before mc. We were about to get to know each other very well.

I planted myself on the machine and began to instruct it with what type of run I would like to do today. Unbelievably there wasn't a 'gentle stroll option' built in and so I decided on a 5km run, with the machine deciding how fast and how slow I should run at intermittent intervals. I lasted 2 kilometres before deciding I quite liked not feeling disgusting, and stopped. It was horrifying. I stepped off the treadmill and suffered a seasick feeling that I'm sure at some stage has been christened 'treadmill sickness', as the solid floor beneath me wobbled right to left resulting in me planting my face against the wall as I desperately tried to regain my balance. Elegance and exercise do not go hand in hand.

Jamie, my fitness instructor friend, had told me that if I was going to achieve a decent level of fitness to be a professional footballer then I need to be able to run five miles, or eight kilometres, in 30 minutes. That's six minutes a mile. At the time that didn't seem like too much to ask, but I had discovered after just 12 minutes and one mile on the running machine that this was pure madness. Was Jamie serious?

'I'm afraid so mate.' I'd phoned Jamie to clarify the situation. 'In fact, you should be running a bit faster than that and that's only to give you a decent base. That's not including all the agility skills you need to be doing, and the weights as well.'

'A base?'

'Yeah, if you want to take it seriously, you need to be doing all that, then some stuff on a cross trainer, then rowing machine, and also the weights. In a decent session you'd be looking at an hour and a half for everything. That needs to be done five times a week with two rest days.'

'An hour and a half? Two rest days? Cross trainer? What the smeg is a cross trainer?'

'Weren't you shown in your induction?'

Jamie was clearly eating something whilst talking to me, and was thus not taking much interest in my despairing state of how much work was needed to be done.

'Probably, is it those up and down pedally things?'

'Yeah that's them.' Jamie continued 'Also…'

'There's an also?' I wanted to cry.

'…Three months to get the level of fitness you need is a big ask. You can do it, you can definitely get fit in three months, but it's going to take a lot of dedication.'

'What do you mean?'

'You're going to have to cut back on fatty foods.'

'I can do that. I don't even like fatty foods.' There was a pause. A long pause; a very long pause, of the kind only used by Doctor's when delivering bad news. 'Are you still there? Jamie?'

'You're going to have to give up beer too.'

'Beer! But I love beer.'

Never before has anything so true been spoke.

'I know. You don't have to stop altogether but you can't go on big nights any more, and you can't have one with dinner every night. It'll be like taking two steps forward at the gym and one step back with the beer.'

'What happened to 30 minutes every day? How did that become 90 minutes?' I felt like I was grieving for the death of my social life.

'What do you mean?'

'Well, when I first told you about this four months ago you said I'd need to be doing 30 minutes exercise a day and that would set me up.'

'Yeah well I didn't think you were serious. Besides that's good to get a half-decent level, or maintain a good one. You're not at either of those stages. You were dying the last time you played football, long before you did your ankle in.'

'I can't believe this. An hour and a half *every day*?'

'Yes, but you really need to do some agility work as well, and playing football from time to time might not be a bad idea, given that's what you're attempting to do.'

'I know, but my ankle is still gammy. Seriously an hour and a half a day?'

'Yes. But it won't be too bad, just go after work every day and you'll be fine.'

I'll be fine? I'll be fine my arse. I am going to die. I looked at my fitness action plan, the one I drew up when I first decided to do this and updated it for the first time.

Height: 5ft 7in
Weight: 11 stones
Fastest Mile: 9 minutes.
Time spent at the gym: Two hours. Two hours too long.

The offer of a trial in Malta had sparked wild celebrations. However, the idea of exercise and severe hold on my alcohol consumption meant that I was in a state of grieving. If I had known that I would have to work so hard in the gym then I may not have ever told anyone. But I had, and already had a trial, with many more possibilities potentially being mulled over or still floating around in cyberspace until it reached the correct receiver. There was no turning back, unless I got another serious injury. The advantage currently was that my one and only trial in Malta could be taken as holiday time away from work and if I failed I could return without financial ruin or the doom and gloom of a recession hanging over me.

I cracked open a beer and toasted the death of my social life.

CHAPTER 6: MIDGET COACHES AND MONTAGES

My advantage was gone. The potential of doing the trial on 'holiday time' was no longer an option. You wait three months for one trial, and then three come along at once.

From: xxxxxx@xxxxxx.com
To: ralfhaley

Subject: re: Requesting a Trial

Hi, no problem for trial but I can't pay you for your time here and can't pay for your accommodation here but if you are good enough we see.

SS PENNAROSSA

From: Justina Sveikyte [mailto:justinaxxxx@xxxx.com]
To: Ralf Haley
Subject: Hi from Nevėžis.

Dear Ralf Haley,

This is writing the journalist of FK Nevėžis in Kėdainiai , Lithuania . We are sorry for a late answer, but we had some connection problems for last few months.
So, your offer has interested us. We would lovely let you to have some trains with our team and see our training facilities.
Unfortunately, we cannot give you a chance to play in the team, but of course if you are very good then we will see ☐.

What do you think?
Stay in touch!

Your sincerely,

Justina Šveikytė, FK Nevėžis

From: Chris Agius [mailto: stgeorgesxxx@xxxx]
To: Ralf Haley
Subject: Requesting a trial

Hi Ralf,

Thank you for your email. You'd be welcome to have some sessions with our club, a first division club, the first football club in Malta founded in 1890.

Regards

Chris Agius
President

Their English language grammar may not be all that great, but who cares. SS Pennarosssa in San Marino, Fk Nevezis in Lithuania, and St Georges FC in Malta were all on board! As it currently stood I now had 2 trials in Malta, one in San Marino and another in Lithuania.

I don't know what prompted these people to get back to me now. I have reasoned that it was the end of the football season in Europe and they had time to write back, but I don't care *why* they got back to me; all that matters is that they *did*. Happy days. I know they weren't encouraging on whether or not I could sign for them, but they were trials. Each one was a chance to wow them, a 1-in-100 shot at achieving the dream, and the more trials I got, the more likely that one of them, just one of them, would let me play a game and pay me. Could it actually be that I was going to be a professional footballer?

This was good news, excellent news. I had continued to work at the university and harass people into giving me trials, so much so that one kind gent in Iceland wrote back to me simply stating 'for the third time… no!'. I admit it was lazy to not delete the clubs who had rejected me from my mammoth mailing list but I couldn't be bothered in all honesty, finding one email address amongst the 1,044 in that spreadsheet takes a bit of time, and by this stage I had actually been rejected by 20 or so clubs from places such as Iceland, Ireland, Portugal, Hungary, Finland and Bulgaria.

With the trip definitely on, I needed to get fit, quickly and with only two months to do it. My first trial was with Santa Venera Lightnings in Malta on September 2nd, just eight weeks away. The ankle still prevented me playing football, which was a major concern, however I could run.

Now if this were a Rocky film, or Karate Kid or another rollickingly great 80s action film, then I would have a midget trainer who could help me in my quest. All films which have a story like my challenge have a midget trainer involved. If you think of Rocky he had little Mick, an old boxer who now as a trainer doesn't take crap from nobody because 'he'd been there'. The Karate Kid had Mr Miyagi, a 3ft 6in Warrior who spoke in philosophical riddles. Even Luke Skywalker and the Teenage Mutant Ninja Turtles had Yoda and Splinter respectively (granted one was an alien creature and the other a giant rat, but they were still trainers). All these trainers employed odd techniques. For example, Mick would make Rocky try and catch a chicken in order to improve his speed; Mr Miyagi would make The Karate Kid paint fences to improve his defences; and Yoda would make Luke Skywalker close his eyes and attempt to move objects with his mind. Unfortunately this isn't an 80s film and I have no midget eccentric trainer, no one who had 'been there done that' to encourage me or give me weird old-school training routines in order to improve my skills. I had tried to contact former footballer Sammy Lee who is 5ft 4in but apparently he was busy.

If this were a film, what would happen next is that a thumping 80s soundtrack would play over shots of the star of the film struggling to do the most mundane of tasks in their sport. For example Rocky would be out of breath punching a side of hanging pork in an abattoir and Daniel in Karate Kid would be finding it hard to kick above his head and keep balance, or paint his fence at lightning speeds. While this is happening on screen the music is getting louder, faster and more furious as you see the star attempt their tasks more and more, and with shorter, sharper cuts each time, until their coach starts to shout encouragement at them, they share a joke and with each failed attempt they get stronger, faster and better, and finally they complete the task with ease, with a smile on their face doing a little jig at the same time. Eventually Rocky can punch a punch bag for a thousand hours on end and catch a chicken with his eyes closed, and Daniel can kick above his head and keep the pose, and after that he can be the fastest painter-decorator in town in case the karate career option falls through.

These types of films have you believe that if you play an uplifting 80s song in the background and have a midget for a trainer then anything is possible and you can get fit in the space of about three minutes.

Having seen Rocky one too many times I foolishly believed that getting fit would be that easy and having watched the box set once more to inspire me I was shocked to find that I was still a fat bastard having even watched the films.

In films it looks like getting fit is fun, that you're getting the eye of the tiger; but after being through it myself let me tell you that every sports film in the 80s where a midget trains people is a lie. It's not that easy. It doesn't take just 180 seconds to go from fat to fit, from weak to strong and slow to quick, and it isn't a laugh. In fact, it's a bloody misery. I wish I could condense my training into a montage for you like films from the 80s because it's boring, mind numbingly dull and painful. Unfortunately montages simply don't work in text format the same way as in film. The same can be said for car chases in books, you don't read about car chases because it doesn't work so I am just going to have to explain to you how painful going to the gym nearly every day for 2 months is like. It sucks, big time. Major big time. Galactic big time. Simple as that. Going to that gym every day after work to run on the same running machine wearing converse trainers and the same sweaty, smelly clothes was not fun, not fun at all. Imagine having to be punched in the stomach excruciatingly hard every day. That's what I was doing to myself, running myself so hard that I felt sick, all the while looking at the screens on the gym equipment, measuring how far I'd run compared to the week previously.

But I did start to get fitter and fitter and fitter. And I was eating a lot more too. One advantage I found of going to the gym is that you can eat as much as you like, because your body needs it. I never thought I'd say this but I became a 'regular'. I'd only ever been a regular at a pub before, one of the proudest moments of my teen drinking career was when the attractive barmaid in my hometown asked if I wanted 'the usual' without even having exchanged words.

That was where the adult version of me belonged, but here I was trying to deliver on a promise that I made to myself when I was 10, that I was going to be a professional footballer. Part of being a regular at the gym is that people start to watch you when you're doing weights, nodding their approval at how far you've come from where you initially started on the granny weights, which admittedly is uncomfortable. I was part of the fraternity. Even Marvin nodded at me every day, and went as far as calling me 'mate'. He didn't use a saccharine 'sir' or 'pal' when he saw me, no. It was a good old-fashioned, solid-to-the-core, salt-of-the-earth 'mate' for me, and although I hated going to the gym, and I hated myself for it, the acceptance of my nerdy nature by the gym lovers donning their far more acceptable trainers and gym attire made the process a little bit easier and I subsequently felt bad for my original prejudice against many of them.

It wasn't easy; the month of July was a nasty one. I contracted a stomach infection that kept me out for a week, and then there was the swine flu pandemic, which, at one stage, threatened to stop anyone from a country that had a confirmed 'case' of swine flu travelling to a country that hadn't yet got one. Thankfully for me, Malta, Lithuania, San Marino and pretty much the rest of Europe had confirmed 'cases' themselves so travelling to these places was going to be okay.

By the end of July, my fitness stats looked like this. My first trial was only in 4 weeks.

Weight: 10.25 stones
Fastest Mile: 5 minutes 46 seconds.
Time spent at the gym: 57 hours.

Jamie had wanted me to be running five miles in 30 minutes for my 'base' before I could start working on anything else. Unfortunately I didn't have time to work on anything else by the time Malta rocked up on my radar, so the 'base' work would have to suffice. I still was some way short of achieving five miles in 30 minutes; I could do it in about 38. I could run a mile in under six minutes but that was me flat out, and afterwards I always felt the need to curl up in a ball and potentially die somewhere. That isn't an option on a football pitch, so I had to continue with the fitness, right up until the last day.

By the end of July I had been offered an incredible 12 trials, all over the world. However, there was a problem with this.

'New Zealand?' Coop said, as he twisted and rotated my bad ankle as much as possible in order to gauge the pain responses.

'Yeah,' I replied, wincing at the remnants of the injury I had acquired months earlier.

'How much money have you got to spend on this?'

'Well I sat down at the start of this whole thing and figured I could save up about £1500, which I am course to do.'

'How does that feel?' Coop said, going off on a tangent.

'Yeah okay, actually, feels okay.' And it did, for the first time in months I had relatively little pain in my right ankle.

'Okay and can you just do some calf stretches for me now please. I want to see how far the right calf has come along; sometimes it shrinks or tenses with a bad ankle injury.' And so I did and it felt okay too. Coop continued: 'You know in New Zealand they're probably quite good you know, all massive Rugby rejects and huge athletes. Going to New Zealand would blow your budget entirely. Which team has offered you a trial?'

'Well there's two, that's why I am considering going, if it was only one then I wouldn't bother, but both Otago United and Wellington FC have said yes, as long as its not going to cost them any money, unless that is I am good enough and they'll end up paying me.'

'So it definitely won't end up costing them money then?'

'It will if I get paid and I am quite the athlete now after going to the gym so much.'

'I wouldn't say you're an athlete, I'd say you've just papered over the cracks of years of neglect. Jamie agrees.'

Coop was never going to buy the fact that I could be a professional footballer.

'Are you two colluding behind my back?' I said.

'A little, just monitoring your progress as it were. It's very interesting. So where else have you got?'

'Well the countries to say yes so far are Malta, Andorra, Lithuania, Latvia, San Marino, Estonia, Sweden, Denmark, the Faroe Islands, New Zealand, Canada and Kenya.'

'Kenya?' Coop recoiled away from my ankle like I was diseased.

'Yes Kenya, they got back to me offering me a trial in November.'

I replied as best I could in dead pan mode.

'But how are you going to get to Kenya? Do they even have football over there? Paid football I mean.'

'I think so.'

'You think so? You can't just go to Kenya on a whim, you need to know if they can pay you or not.'

Coop for the first time was showing a bit of passion about the trip.

'Look, I have a plan, I am going to do the Europe countries over the course of one month, not all have confirmed the trials, some are still hesitant so I have to seal the deal with them but one month to do the trials there as they are easiest to get to and the most concentrated across a certain area.'

'And what happens after that?'

'Well then I will look how much money I have left, and if I have enough then I will identify which clubs in Canada, Africa, Asia and New Zealand I stand the best chance with and make my way there. But I can't do this forever, finances and a committed relationship won't permit it. I keep forgetting that when I leave my job to do this I won't have a job or income to come back to. Once my money runs out I have promised myself to give up because although I am planning to spend £1500 on this I am in effect spending a lot more through loss of income at the end of it.'

The madness of my response had Coop questioning my motives.

'Why are you doing this again? You're not going to make your money back. No football club in the world is going to pay you enough to make it back.' Coop looked worried for the mental well-being of his friend, his eyes opened wider and his head cocked to the side.

'Because I'm sick of my job and sick of never having accomplished anything in my life mate. I can do normal jobs, I know that, I'm good at them, but it doesn't mean I'm happy. I know it sounds silly but a thousand pound gamble to potentially earn 1 Euro back to play a game of football in a completely different country is worth the risk.'

The proximity of the date was getting to me and Coop. I had one month left before my first trial and I could tell he was worried for me; I was worried for myself.

'Well mate it's a beautiful dream.' For the first time in months Coop had shown a hint of sincerity about the project.

'Cheers mate.'

'And luckily for you it looks like you can actually play football again, its still a bit weak, but keep doing the exercises I gave you and you should be alright, but I'd suggest wearing an ankle support and keeping an eye on it.'

Good news just kept on coming.

'All you need to do now is piss a thousand pounds up the wall and humiliate yourself across the world. Oh you also need to quit that well-paid job of yours,' said Coop wiping his hands down with a damp cloth in an echo of my examination with him four months previously.

CHAPTER 7: TRISTAN

My brother Tristan is what can only be described as a lovable idiot who always lands on his feet. Six and a half years my senior and a blond version of me, he is often putting himself at risk of serious injury. Although we have a very similar personality our interests are very different. He doesn't like sport; in fact he loathes football and likes to pretend he knows nothing about it when England play merely to rile me. He's much more into films, cars and mechanical things.

Our parents often like to tell the story of when, as a baby, Tristan enjoyed putting nails in plug sockets and playing with hammers and all things electronic. This sort of reckless behaviour carried through his teens and adult life, notable examples being when he wrote off his car and fell off the back of a motorcycle. Our parents may like to tell stories of him as a child but I like to tell the one of when, as an adult, on a brotherly camping trip on the coast of Wales, he went to relieve himself into the ocean only to literally piss into the wind and subsequently all over his own face. It was no surprise to anyone that he ended up working as a cameraman in the film Industry, or that he had set himself on the way to a small amount of success with the contacts he had made, or the impressive CV he'd managed to put together over five years. He isn't someone who takes being knocked back, or pissed on, as the end of the matter; he'll continually pursue it until something turns out right. What did come as a surprise, however, was his phone call to me.

'Alright slag?' he said ("Slag" is a term of affection between the two of us, it's not an insult).

'Yeah alright mate.' I replied.

'What you up to?'

'I'm just walking home from yet another session at the gym. Today was warm weather training.'

'What do you mean?'

'Well my first trial is in Malta and they have temperatures upwards of 33 degrees so I decided that I needed to get used to running in those conditions. So I went to the gym and did a four-mile run wearing jeans and a hoody on a running machine.'

I had as well, and it was horrible. Never in the entirety of my life, including a trip to Morocco two years previously, had I been so sweaty or so clammy. My hoody had gone from a light blue to a navy blue due to my levels of perspiration. Marvin, who had taken me in as one of his own, looked nonplussed as he watched a nerd in Converse trainers, jeans and a hoody on one of his running machines. I am sure at one stage out of my peripheral vision I saw him do a cartoonesque rubbing of his eyes with his big fists in circular fashion in order to refresh the image, only to find the football geek still there running away in full indie-boy attire.

'That's absurd. Why did you do that?' Tristan obviously couldn't grasp that running fully dressed in heavy clothes makes you warmer than when you're running in just shorts and a t-shirt.

'Because, you idiot, I wanted to be really hot when running to make sure I could handle the temperatures in Malta when I get there, which is now in four weeks! Turns out I can handle the temperature but I'll probably struggle a lot more due to the humidity.'

'You're an odd one,' he replied.

'I know.' I took it as a compliment. 'Anyway why are you ringing?'

'I was wondering if you fancied any company on the trip?'

'What?'

'I was thinking about coming along,' he said.

'What about Kerrie?'

Kerrie, his fiancée, surely would need to sanction any trip like this.

'She's on board. She says I can have a month to do this. It will totally change your experience, that's for sure, but I could help with organising it and buy you a few drinks.'

I was almost speechless. I was happy Tristan wanted to come along, I truly was, it's just that I had the idea in my head that I would be doing this on my own, and it would be my big adventure. But we do get on very well and are always having a laugh, so why shouldn't I say yes? It would make things a lot easier.

'Also,' he continued, 'I was thinking about documenting the whole thing – making it into a film.'

'What?'

Disbelief doesn't come close to what I was feeling.

'Well it's a really good idea mate. I've spoken to loads of people and they all agree. I haven't really done any camera work, I just load films into cameras, so it would be a really good experience for me to film and direct

'I thought you hated football,' I said crossing the road fidgeting with my keys for the flat.

'Yeah I do, it's just a bunch of mindless morons with too much money, and I don't even know the rules.'

Could I really go around Europe – potentially the world – on a football tour with someone who doesn't even know what the offside rule is? Tristan continued:

'Anyway think about it and let me know as soon as.'

I didn't need to think about it.

'Of course you can come, we'll have a great time and you'll definitely help me, with sharing hotel costs, travel arrangements and all that.' I threw my bag to the floor entering the apartment.

'Quality!' he said.

'You do know I haven't done any work in front of camera before? I won't be good at all,' I said, attaching a disclaimer before things got heavy.

'Oh don't worry about that, I'm just using the film thing as a kind of smokescreen so I can go on a month-long piss up with you.'

'No Tristan! I'm taking this seriously and I'll be continuing my fitness lark as we go so that I can get better and better. This can't be a month-long bender. I can't turn up to football trials hung-over!'

'Yeah I know, I know; doesn't stop us having a couple of drinks though does it?'

What had I agreed to?

Following Tristan's call I was a bit at odds with what was going on, the first trial, 2nd September with Santa Venera Lightnings was fast approaching and I wasn't fit enough according to Jamie and Coop but the ankle was better and Tristan was now saying he wanted to come along and film the whole damned thing.

Tristan's proposal, not to mention the alarming rate at which days for training and organising the trip were falling away sent my mind into a tailspin.

The next morning I handed my notice in. No turning back now. I had nearly acquired my £1500 budget, I was getting fit, my ankle was almost mended, and I had a travelling companion who doesn't like football. More importantly, I had at least 12 trials arranged throughout September and October in all manner of places. That's a hit rate of 1.1% when you think of all the clubs I emailed, but aptly that's the same hit rate I have with women.

I pray to god I can be a professional footballer somewhere, otherwise the last five months has been a massive waste of time.

Chapter 8: The Final Countdown

With one month to go and only two trials nailed on with specific dates I have to say I was admirably relaxed about the whole situation. Tristan, however, was not, judging by his panicked phone call.

'Oi Slag, can you send me your travel itinerary, I want to know what we're doing, where we're going and all that. We need to book the flights.' He obviously had his thinking cap on, a very rare occurrence.

'I'll send it through to you, but the only two dates I have confirmed are in Malta, on the 2nd September and the 4th, after that we need to make it up as we go along. But we can blag plenty of trials when we're out there.'

My lack of experience in travelling anywhere was showing.

'Yeah but we need to book flights, it'll be a lot cheaper to do it now rather than later. Just send me the itinerary will you?'

And so I did.

From: Ralf Haley
To: Tristan slag face
Subject: Updated Itinerary – Europe Leg

Alright Punk?

This is the updated Itinerary for the trip as it stands:

Malta 2nd Sept - Trial with St Venera Lightnings.

Malta 4th September - Trial with St Georges FC. They are the oldest club in Malta and are seen as the 'pioneers' of Maltese football.

Andorra 8th or 10th September - FC Lusitanos

San Marino – SS Pennarossa (date unknown, around 9th onwards, waiting for confirmation from the manager) – Stadium size: field in the middle of nowhere up a mountain somewhere. Will only pay me if I am 'incredible'.... Here's hoping.

Lithuania (anytime I like) - FK Nevėžis – Stadium capacity 3,500. Town size 30,000. Located in the centre of Lithuania and also one of the oldest cities in Lithuania. Date unknown.

Latvia – FC Daugava – Riga. Date unknown.

Estonia – FC Levadia – Tallinn. Date unknown.

Denmark FK Glostrup (2-3 days between 20th Sept - and 10th Oct) – Copenhagen .

Norway – Manglerud Star – Oslo. Date unknown.

Faroe Islands – ÍF Fuglafjørður – Erm, the Faroe Islands. Date unknown.

Am trying more Eastern European clubs this week so hopefully will have news then.

Ralf out.

When I composed that email it made me excited but also sad. Of all the football clubs I emailed, all 1,044, only those few had responded with positive news, and most of those were in Europe. Obviously my grovelling email wasn't enough. Or maybe my complete lack of anything to prove to them that I was good at football had been the issue. Either way, being asked to summarise the last six months of my life in one email produced this, and it looked so small, so pathetic.

'Nice one,' Tristan said when he called back. 'I'm definitely on board – we'll get the flights sorted from England to Malta as soon as we can and we'll look into flights from Malta later. Where do you want to go if Malta falls through for you?'

'Well Andorra are really bad at football, and the team there is really keen to see what I can do so I think we should head there.'

'Great we'll book a flight from Malta to Andorra when we can.' Tristan was excited, but obviously his geography knowledge was severely lacking.

'What do you mean flights to Andorra ?' I wanted fish his idiocies out.

'Er, you've got a trial there haven't you slag?'

'Yes,' I replied, waiting for the glory.

'Well we'll need to fly from Malta to Andorra then won't we?'

'Tristan, do you think Andorra has an Airport?'

'Yeah, why wouldn't it?' Tristan obviously hadn't heard of Andorra before today.

'Because it's in between France and Spain, in the middle of nowhere, with a population of about 8 people, 10 if there's a population boom. I doubt they even have trains.'

'Eh, how backwards is this place? How are we going to get there?'

'I've looked into it. We can take a bus from Barcelona to Andorra. It'll take about three hours.'

'Barcelona, awesome! We will be there at a weekend? We can go out and go to a club!'

'No Tristan, I'm taking this seriously remember?'

'Yeah yeah, you'll love Barcelona, it's amazing.'

Tristan still clearly was not listening.

'Tristan I have to go, I am at work. I'll speak to you later.'

I didn't have to go; yes I was at work, not that it made a difference. I just felt a bit of trepidation as to what sort of antics Tristan may bring to the proceedings. I don't think he was grasping that I really wanted to be a professional footballer.

With just three days to go until my first trial and three days until my last day at work I went to the gym one last time. My monthly subscription ran out on that day and I'd be damned if I was going to pay an extra £27.50 for a month that I wasn't going to be there. I was hoping to see Marvin there, but it must have been his day off. We'd probably only exchanged about 10 words after my induction that fateful day nearly three months ago but with an occasional glance and an awkward nod we had built up a mute friendship. He had no idea what all my training was in aid of, but I am sure he appreciated my presence in that gym on a daily basis nonetheless. I haven't changed my stance on most gyms but I couldn't have got to the stage I had without joining one, and I certainly got my money's worth. I left that gym with a personal best of five miles in 35 minutes. It wasn't quite up to the standard that Jamie had set for me, but it was a remarkable improvement on only being able to run 18 yards before a hot sweat, panting and general feeling of wanting to die came over me. That only came around after 35 yards now – almost a 100% improvement.

My final stats were thus:

Weight: 10.25 stones
Fastest Mile: 5.30 minutes.
Press ups done in a row: 100
Sit ups done in a row: 100
Time spent at the gym: Too much.

Physically I was as ready as I was ever going to be and mentally I was getting used to the idea that soon enough I would be playing football with professionals. Infuriatingly my 'before' picture taken prior to joining the gym was exactly the same as my 'after' picture, with no new definition in the muscles and no noticeable change in my stomach. I was hoping to be rippling with muscles, but the only thing that still rippled were my love handles. However, my lung capacity had improved greatly and that's all that mattered to me, kind of. Some things were still lacking, notably a decent pair of shorts, a proper football running top, football socks, shin pads and basically anything you can think of in the equipment department that an aspiring footballer may need. The only thing I did have were a pair of Jamie's old football boots he had given to me.

I had decided to put the equipment off until the very last moment, in order to save what precious money I had, but now given that I was definitely going to do this I figured I had to get some decent gear, and so I went into a sports shop with the aim of actually buying sporting equipment for this first time since I was 15.

The saying goes that you only get chance to make a first impression once and given my tight time frame and budget I'd have to make sure that as soon as I arrived I actually looked the part. Furthermore David Beckham got a ridiculous contract in the US simply because he is David Beckham. If I can market myself as a decent(ish) footballer who is also English in the backwaters of Europe and beyond, then perhaps from a marketing perspective it would be worth their while. It's vital for me to be able to make a decent first impression because my budget doesn't allow me to dilly dally around at a club that's not interested in me or wants to take a 'closer look'. If a club isn't interested after one day, then I would have to try elsewhere immediately. If they were interested then that could warrant me hanging around in whatever country, but it would be a gamble as I would be sacrificing a trial elsewhere. First impressions are vitally important and so I went shopping.

Wearing my plimsoll shoes, baggy jeans and Zippy from Rainbow T-shirt I felt an immediate sense of nostalgia as I stepped into the sports shop and looked at all the footballs, over-priced football shirts, shin pads I already had and screw-in studs that never fitted the boots I actually owned.

There were mountains and mountains of pointless sports accessories. It was beautiful. The older generations and upper classes have art galleries to make their eyes light up with a feeling of wonderment, the rest of us have sports shops. My eyes danced from shirt to shirt, ball to ball, boot to boot, happy that my rekindled dream, rising like a phoenix from the ashes, had brought me to this most holy of places. Even the smell was intoxicating.

'Alreet pal, can I help youz?' I seemed to have been approached by some male gangster wearing a name tag.

'Do you work here?' I replied.

'Aiii.'

I took that to mean yes.

Under normal circumstances I don't actually accept the 'help' from employees in shops, I find them an inconvenience, a nuisance constantly looking over your shoulder thinking 'he can't seriously think that would suit him, it's a waistcoat for Christ's sake.' In this scenario, though, I needed help, as I hadn't bought any sports clothing or accessories in nigh-on 10 years.

'Yes, I wouldn't mind some help actually.'

'Coolio. I is Courteney. What youz looking for?'

'Well, I am trying to be a professional footballer in Europe in a couple of weeks and I need pretty much everything except a pair of football boots in order to play football.'

I had now started to say it like it was normal. Courteney's reaction had brought me back down to earth.

'What? Youza try'na be a professional footballer? Are youz serious?' He scanned my non sporty image incredulously.

'Yes I'm serious.' I said with a twitching face and through gritted teeth.

'No way! Look at youz! That's a joke right?'

Courteney, if you hadn't already gathered, is a massive twat.

'Seriously!'

I was getting involved in a fight with a store clerk. How had this happened?

'Alright, where you've got trials then?'

'My first one is in Malta next week,' I replied, telling myself that the customer is always right.

'Malta? Youza be alright then, they're well shit! Ahee hee hee hee,' he sniggered before flicking his wrist to snap his fingers like a gangster would, in a way to further cement his credentials of being a Grade-A moron.

Although he clearly didn't believe me, he started to do his duty and indulge me in my request, like a tailor humouring a tramp by fitting him for a Saville Row suit, knowing it wouldn't have an end result. At one stage he told me I needed a vest. I had to make it perfectly clear to him that no one ever in the world, past present or future has needed a vest, unless they work in a mine, have a mullet and live in Central America, or have woken up to find they are now called Bruce Willis. No need for a vest whatsoever, none. You can label it a 'training' vest all you like, but no way was I about to wear a vest. I have some dignity, and if my first impression at these clubs was to turn up 'vested' up then I may as well not even bother playing football and leave immediately.

In the end I walked out with a pair of shin pads that were one size too large for me but £5 cheaper than the ones that actually fit, three pairs of football socks, two pairs of shorts, two training tops with short sleeves, an ankle support, and a three-pack of men's briefs that restrict movement downstairs when running, All I had to do now was say goodbye.

My final day at work, just 48 hours before my first trial, was uneventful but pleasant for it. I left my desk for the last time with no pangs of regret. Later that evening Jamie had invited me round to his place for a final goodbye. In hindsight I probably should have given myself a lot more time in between leaving work and flying out in order to perhaps acclimatise to Maltese conditions or simply get my head in order, but evidently I am an idiot, and planning like this doesn't figure in my mind often.

'I can't believe you're going to do this,' said Jamie as his hand delved into the bottom of the gargantuan packet of crisps he was finishing off with much aplomb.

'I know, it seems to have gone so fast. In four days I'll be having my first trial.'

'It's brilliant.' Jamie chuckled.

'Have you played any football recently?' Coop had been invited round too, and couldn't help but bring a sense of logic and reality to the proceedings.

'No.'

'No?' they replied in unison.

'No.' I replied singularly.

'Why?' asked Coop; a valid question.

'When I did my ankle in I couldn't play for months on end, and then when it did feel okay I didn't want to run the risk of injuring it again and missing Europe's pre-season.'

'So you haven't kicked a ball since then?' Jamie asked, licking his fingers clean.

'Again, no.'

Only just then did I realise that not playing football up to this stage created serious problems.

'You haven't played for seven months and you've got a trial in two days?' said Coop.'

'Yup. Now that you mention it, it does seem a bit silly. However, this whole thing has been silly from the off, and if I'm going to make it, with or without a serious amount of training, its going to be by the grace of god or some other higher power than through my own football ability.'

'Ha-ha, so you admit you're rubbish at football?' said Coop, obviously not remembering the last 200 hundred conversations we'd had.

'Of course I'm rubbish at football, we all know that! But the point of this is to see if I can live the dream just once anywhere. No amount of training with a ball is seriously going to increase my chances, that's why I've concentrated on making sure I don't die when playing.'

'You're unbelievable,' said Coop.

'Thank you.'

'It wasn't a compliment.' Coop shook his head with a bemused smile.

'Well I propose a toast,' said Jamie. 'To Ralf and his beautiful football dream. Cheers.'

'Cheers!'

'I've got a surprise for you,' said Jamie struggling out of his armchair.

'What is it?'

'These,' he replied, presenting a shoe-box from under his kitchen table. 'I want you to have them.'

I opened the box and therein gleamed a pair of red Adidas Predator boots, arguably the best boots on the market, bar getting your own professionally fitted.

'They don't fit me and they need to go to a good home,' said Jam with a fatherly hand on my shoulder.

'I don't know what to say. I've already got a pair of your boots I was going to take.'

'Yeah but these are moulded; you can play with them on grass and astroturf... plus those other ones are awful. And with you being awful at football you need something to make you look a little bit good.'

'Aw, that was nice. A bit girly though.'

'I know.'

We then got drunk.

The following morning and hungover I crossed the Pennines along the M62 towards Hebden Bridge – the town that had given birth to the dream all those years ago – and up the steep roads that cut across long green fields towards the family home, where my travelling partner awaited.

Me and Tristan really should have met up before we did, but planning doesn't sit well in our family.

We had only discussed our criteria over the phone, and I had only given him a faint outline. I didn't know too well myself where and when we were going. In the build-up to this trip I had only organised the trials in Malta – one with Santa Venera Lightnings in 36 hours, the other with St Georges FC another 48 hours after that. We had no idea how we were going to get off Malta, as we had only just booked our flights there. It was an apt beginning to what was going to be a poorly planned trip. Granted, clubs had said yes to a trial, but there were no concrete dates, and some of them had taken an age to reply.

'Pardon me, but what the fuck are we doing.' Tristan delivered this line with his trademark smile and buffoon-like shaking of the head that he does whenever he was readying himself for doing something silly, like deciding to film his little brother around Europe despite neither party having any experience in their chosen field.

'I don't know, I really don't. The past six months have gone really quickly. I never actually thought it would get to this stage. It's a good job you're coming because I don't have a clue what to do when we're out there.'

Tristan fortunately is a veteran of 15 months non-stop world travel, and so in situations that we were likely to encounter, he was perfect. He also had an incredible sense of direction, so much so that his nickname amongst friends was 'pigeon'. My sense of direction once got me lost in a shop. In my defence there were two floors.

One thing we were sure of was that we needed to book a flight out of Malta to Barcelona in order to save on costs.

It was a big gamble – if I were offered a contract in Malta then I would sign, play and spend a couple of sunny months out there as a semi-professional or even professional, hoping for a visit from a friend and thus sacrificing the price of the flight to Barcelona; but that would be inconsequential as I would have succeeded, even if I only played for one minute.

However, with the thought that I hadn't actually played football for such a long-time at the forefront of my mind I decided that I should in fact book the flight to Barcelona at least in order to save a bit of money as last-minute flights can be extortionate. It was time to pack.

'So what have you got?' asked Tristan. We were stood in the draughty farmhouse kitchen where we'd spent thousands of hours as youngsters.

'Well I have four pairs of shorts, six t-shirts, ten pairs of boxers, god knows how many socks, 2 football briefs, a jumper, a hoody, a pair of moulded stud football boots for artificial surfaces, a pair of normal football boots and toiletries. You?'

'Pretty much the same as you, minus all the football crap plus a 6 kilogram camera, lights, a tripod, a boom pole, a microphone I can attach to my camera and radio frequency mics I'm going to attach to you during trials and chats to people.'

'I don't think we need so much equipment.'

'Well I think I do, you worry about the football and I'll worry about the film.'

'I'll worry about the football and my back if I have to carry any of your stuff.'

'Shut up,' said Tristan fiddling with his rucksack.

'Great putdown.'

'Shut up slag,' he snapped.

'That's better.'

'What shoes are you taking with you?' he said, trying to change the subject from the fact he had to carry twice the weight of my luggage.

'Just these ones.' I said motioning to the red plimsolls that were already on my feet.

'What them?' Tristan looked disgusted.

'What's wrong with them?'

'Nothing.' Said Tristan resetting his face and stance before attending to his bag straps again. 'Nothing at all if you're aiming to attract the attentions of some gay sailors.'

'Shut up.'

'Great putdown,' he smirked.

'Shut up slag.'

'That's better.'

It was going to be a long month.

I just had one more thing to do before we left: sort out the travel insurance. People say travel insurance is a rip off and if you do end up getting hit by a car they aren't exactly going to leave you there simply because you didn't have the relevant paperwork on your person. I thought I needed it though, given that I planned to play a lot of football, and given my past medical history I didn't exactly want to have no drugs prescribed to me when I tripped over my ankle because I didn't bother paying £20 to some internet-based company. But the options were endless. You could choose Skiing cover, where you are covered for any skiing related accidents, injuries and 'subsequent paralysis of any accidents'. I'm glad I'm not going skiing. You could choose an Extreme Sports package where you are covered for similar scenarios of death and paralysis but to a much greater albeit more expensive extent. Or you could go for Backpackers, where in the event of you being mugged of everything you own, right down to standing naked in the street, you'll still be okay. Annoyingly there wasn't a travelling footballer option though, which I thought was an oversight; I think they lose plenty of business because of that. With no other worthy options available to me I plumbed for the budget option of a customised Backpacker. That's not saying I am customised, but that my policy is. As well as cover for my bag, passport and all manner of smaller things I included the option of insuring my legs for $10,000,000 in the event that if some thug broke both of them in a harsh challenge, thus making me lose guaranteed future income from football, I'd be covered. Sadly $10,000,000 was the limit – if I could have insured them for more, I would have.

As we pulled into Luton Airport Tristan said goodbye to his fiancée and I made my way to check-in. Before we'd even left the country I had already spent £200 pounds of my budget on getting flights to and out of Malta, and I haven't even had my first trial. I was sure that if the last six months were difficult, then the next few weeks could potentially be hell.

CHAPTER 9: MALTA

Touching down in Malta at 9pm my heart couldn't but help skip a beat when the captain informed us that it was a 'not too bad 27 degrees outside'. 27 degrees? It was pitch black and it was still 27 degrees. How hot was it going to be the next day when I had my trial? I was sure that I was going to struggle. Stepping off the plane, it took about four-and-a-half seconds before me and Tristan were covered head-to-toe in a film of sweat – a film of sweat that wouldn't leave us for days. No-one organising their first ever football trial would have picked Malta at this time of year. No-one except me.

I'd decided to stick with Malta as my first destination for three reasons. The first was that, being a former British colony, they speak English and so it would ease us into the trip. Secondly their leagues are currently ranked by UEFA as the 42nd best in Europe out of 43, one spot above San Marino and one below Andorra, so it was likely my best chance. Thirdly they were the first to get back to me and, on a romantic level, I believe they deserved my royal presence first. I just hadn't banked on it being so hot.

On the plane I thought it would be a good idea to do some further research on the country, and it did help. I found out that Malta's population is 400,000 and it is one of the most densely populous countries in the world, with the island measuring just 12 by 12 miles. I also found out that its national stadium holds 80,000. That's a fifth of its population. If you applied that equation to England, then Wembley would hold 10 million people. A stadium for 80,000 people? I couldn't help but think they may have slightly over-estimated their place in the world, especially seeing as they have never advanced to the finals of any major international competition and have only ever won a handful of competitive matches, however I kind of liked this as their optimistic approach to football mirrored my own.

Their most famous footballer is Michael Mifsud, famous for scoring two goals in a Carling Cup win against Manchester United for Coventry City. I also later found out that Manchester United's Gary Neville has a soccer school here, and it did cross my mind that if I failed with either Santa Venera or St George's FC that I could pretend to be a Maltese orphan and get trained by one of England's finest ever right backs. I then had to check myself, realising that would be a ridiculously desperate measure, especially as I haven't even failed yet. Popping off both my parents and gaining Maltese citizenship did seem a bit extreme.

Tristan had arranged for us to be picked up from the airport by Aldo, our hotel manager. When I saw my name on a cardboard placard scribbled in black marker pen, I had truly arrived. Aldo was wearing a vest. In fact most of the locals were. Had Courteney been right about me needing a vest? Only time would tell.

'Yes it is a pleasant temperature at the moment. You should have been here in July, it was 33 in the evenings,' said Aldo who had the frame of Elton John and face and skin of Mahatma Gandhi.

He had a welcoming presence about him, even if his appearance in sandals and boxer shorts (seriously) led us to believe he wasn't making the greatest of efforts, and made me wonder what the hotel would be like. 'Do you like football?' he asked.

'Yeah, I love football.'

'Yes good. You say you now live in Manchester, you a Manchester United fan now yes? I love Manchester United.'

'Actually I don't really support anyone, I'm just a fan of football.' I replied.

'You know I used to play for Valetta?' said Elton Gandhi.

'Valetta?'

'Yes, they are the biggest team in Malta. My son is 16 – he plays for the under 16s.'

Unbelievably Aldo did in fact used to play football in Malta back in the 1970s, and more shockingly it was for only one game, which is exactly my goal. The first person I had met on the journey was someone who achieved a dream I had been longing for all my life. This I should have been taken to be inspiring, as a sign – a sign that somebody upstairs was looking out for me. But I didn't. I was put off at how he was driving a clapped out banger of a car, wearing a vest with more than four questionable stains on and was about 4ft 3in tall and 4ft 2in wide. I hope if I do achieve my dream that Aldo doesn't turn out to be my future.

On the plus side, he looked like he had a similar physique to Tony Drago, so of the three Maltese sports people I knew of, past or present, two of them are overweight. Could I really have touched down in a country where I'm top of the evolutionary pile? It was a slim hope but a start.

'You will be made very welcome here,' said Aldo. 'The Maltese people still have strong connections with the English. They helped us get into Europe and the EU, so you will be liked.'

Aldo drove us from the dusty outskirts and through the narrow streets of the small capital city of Valletta, which would be our base for the next four days. As we swarmed through the nightlife traffic there were signs that an allegiance to the United Kingdom stays strong despite independence from the empire being granted over 40 years ago. British traffic lights, post boxes and advertisement hoardings signalled that this could easily be home were it not for the heat, humidity and sand-coloured buildings. The architecture of the city was amazing and had an old feel with a certain grandeur. Huge churches and palaces were built by order of the Knights, lavish in their size and design. I've always been fascinated by the Middle Ages; I often imagine those in power saying to peasants 'I have nowhere to take my Thursday morning dump. Build me a church so I can do thy deed.' That's the feeling I had as we went past these remarkable structures that had no signs of life in them, apart from Thursdays of course. As the journey went on, the buildings got taller and the streets narrower until we got to the hotel. It was beautiful on the outside, but like so many aesthetically pleasing things, on the inside it was dilapidated to say the least. Tristan described it as being like a Colombian cell block, but I think that's paying it a compliment. The walls were stained with the blood of dead mosquitoes where past residents had waged wars with them, the tap water was brown and the bed sheets smelled like rat dumps. We bedded down for the night as my football quest had truly begun.

'I hope they're not good. Oh god what if they're good? What am I doing?' I said in a panic the next morning over a coffee and panini. My trial was in just five hours – an evening trial to allow the members of the squad who had regular jobs to train with the full-time pros.

'People did and try and warn you mate,' said Tristan. He scanned the bland square in Valletta for anything interesting as we cowered in the shade of a coffee shop umbrella in one of the few open spaces of the city, the sun bouncing back off the concrete around us.

'I know, I know. The worrying thing is I can't even sign for this club, they are merely going to rule their thumb over me to see if I'm good enough to play in a league higher than them, a league which is eligible to sign foreigners.'

'So?'

'So that means I have to be amazing, I've never been amazing, at anything. Ever.'

'I don't know what you were expecting Ralf, a team of midgets rejoicing at your arrival and treating you as a giant?' He chuckled; the idea of me being a giant, despite my small, dumpy frame, amused him.

'I know we're aiming for countries that are obscure, but these are my niche markets. Here in Malta they are the higher-up teams in a rubbish league, same with Andorra, and in Eastern Europe I'm having trials with lower clubs in better-structured leagues, so there's a chance.'

Despite what I was saying, for the first time my eternal optimism had been tempered by nerves and regret over what I was doing, it was like I was going on a blind date with a football club. I also had a headache because my body was in constant need of water due to the temperature of this rock being the same as the surface of the sun. It couldn't have been hotter if I was in a sauna with a fat guy on sat my face. It was boiling, it was clammy, and what little energy I did have was expended on being nervous. I imagine this is how people are before a job interview they really wanted; an experience I hadn't had until now.

We arranged to meet Johann, the Santa Venera Lightnings club secretary by the fountain at the bus terminal in Valletta before the trial. The bus terminal itself is a bit of a tourist attraction with old yellow school-type buses looking like bees swarming in and out at whatever the top speed of that particular run-down bus would allow. Some would come steaming in at 40mph, others a more mild 4mph, but both screeching to a halt. When Johann had mentioned the fountain on the phone I didn't know what he was talking about, but as soon as you turn the corner towards the station you immediately see quite possibly the most ridiculously oversized fountain for its surroundings ever. 'Sire, the fountain is only going to cost £10,000

but we have a budget of thirty thousand. What shall we do?'
'Simple, make it three times bigger than it should be. That'll show the world how Malta does fountains!'

Whilst I waited I looked like a speck against the backdrop of dozens of buses. I wondered in this scenery if Johann would spot me, but then remembered that Tristan and I were the whitest things these islands had seen since the last cruise ship full of British holidaymakers rocked up; we stuck out like sore thumbs. Also the fact that I was in full football kit holding a pair of football boots may have helped. With that thought I was brought out of my train of thoughts by yet another screeching sound, but this time it was no bus, it was a car just metres away from us. From it emerged a handsome man with sunglasses and a tan that belied belief. He looked like a Mediterranean Cary Grant modelling Gucci's latest range.

'Ralf?' said the figure.

'Johann?'

First contact had been made.

Johann was in his early 30s and really was too good-looking to be sat next to me. He wasn't doing my ego any favours. His laidback demeanour, sat in the shade wearing flip flops and shorts could not have been in more contrast to his guest, who was pasty, pacing, sweating and shitting himself. We were waiting at a picnic table for the coach and the rest of the players to arrive.

Johann had driven us to a small government-owned gated astroturf pitch on the outskirts of the outskirts, further afield from the small airport I had touched down in just 18 hours previously.

As Tristan set up his gear to film what could potentially be the most embarrassing two hours of my life, I found out from Johann that Santa Venera is a semi-professional side in the third tier of the league, with little money – only a few of their players actually get paid anything, but he took it from my email that I was desperate and would accept anything and so answered the call. Johann, despite his youthful appearance, informed me he didn't play football. Of course he didn't, he was probably too busy wooing the young ladies of the island. Football for most clubs was a hobby, and most people in football here had proper careers – with the police being Johann's – but some are taking it more seriously now with Valetta, a Premier

Division club leading the way by signing former Barcelona player Jordi Cruyff. That's not Johann Cruyff, by the way, the football visionary of the 70s and the cherry on top of Holland's total football revolution. Jordi Cruyff, his infinitely less talented son, played for Barcelona (possibly on the virtue that his dad pulled a few strings) and Manchester United before Sir Alex Ferguson realised that Johann Cruyff had probably lied to him when he asked if his son was good at football. From there his career took a nosedive as people saw that having Johann Cruyff as a father doesn't necessarily mean you will be amazing at football. If you type in 'Jordi Cruyff' into Google on the internet you will get hits saying 'Whatever happened to Jordi Cruyff?' Well now I know. He is busy being seen as good at football by the people of Malta, further evidence to my mind that I could potentially make something of myself here. That is if I hadn't lost 7 pounds in weight due to sweat in a matter of hours. Jordi Cruyff's story made me wish that my father had contacts in the game to tell people how great I was in order for me to achieve my dream. I could have won the Champions League by now if my dad himself had had an illustrious playing career with Barcelona in the 70s. Unfortunately the only contacts my dad has are in the antiques trade and I own few, if any antiques.

After what felt like an eternity the players started to filter through to the pitch side to begin their daily pre-training banter, except this time there was a foreign element in the mix, and that foreign element was me. I was greeted with warm handshakes and questions of what I wanted to achieve. They had been informed that I would be arriving, however I'm sure they envisaged a far more impressive specimen than the short-arse stood before them. What was encouraging was that on first glance they all seemed to be of an average build, nothing like the hulks that now play for teams in England. The ages ranged from what looked like a youth team player at 16 all the way up to the late 30s. They all spoke English to me, which was kind, and I was introduced to a range of names that were brilliantly English such as Dave, or foreign such as Nenad. Conversations were then exchanged to gauge where my level lay, with them asking where I'd had trials before (which I dodged magnificently) and where I was planning to go if I failed here. After five minutes of a positively warm welcome, he arrived – the man who would be passing judgement on me, the coach Patrick Zammit.

He was wearing a football kit, holding a clipboard and had calves the size of tree trunks. He looked muscular, strong, greying at the temples before his time. But thankfully, and most importantly, he looked kind.

Patrick introduced himself, crushing my hand in a handshake that proper men do.

'Are you English?' I replied. His accent wasn't the same as I had encountered elsewhere on the island. But my question brought a smirk.

'No. I'm from Malta. Let me just do the register and we'll talk.'

Did he just say register?

He did!

Patrick sat down to do a register to see which of his players had turned up for training that night, even in Junior Football in England there is no register, and it was a sign of how, because they are semi-professional, some players may not turn up and hope to get away with it like naughty schoolchildren. The results of the register were that a couple indeed had not shown up due to work commitments.

'Sorry about that Ralf.' I was still struggling to place his accent. 'Now Johann has informed me of your situation and luckily for you today will be a light training session.'

Ah yes, my 'situation'. Before going out to Malta I had told an ever so slightly small fib to Johann that I wasn't exactly in the best shape despite being in the best shape I had ever been in my entire life. This was simply because I wanted them to go easy on me with it being my first trial, and secondly if I played well whilst apparently being 'not fit' , then they may recommend me to a contact at Valetta and I could be playing alongside Jordi Cruyff. With 10 minutes until training was due to start I got a chance to speak to Patrick

'What do you look for a in a player? How is it that I'm going to impress you today?'

'If players don't have good character then I have no problem in removing them from my team, I have done it before in the past and I will do it again.'

Crikey that was quite an abrupt answer, I didn't want to test what he meant by having done it before but I took it to mean that I needed to keep my head down during the training session and try my hardest.

'In England we are moving towards more and more physical types of player, 6-feet tall, strong, fast, athletic as well as technical, are you the same?' I said.

'In Malta we can't do that because of the numbers of people who play football as well as the finances so we need to identify certain skills and work with what we have got.'

This was music to my ears. I just hoped Patrick would see something in me to give me hope. He rounded up the players and informed them that the warm-up should commence and on his command they obeyed by filtering through the gates to the artificial pitch. Warm-ups were the bane of my football playing career. They always knackered me out so much that by the time I got to play I was exhausted and couldn't do anything. Doing laps of a pitch at 20% pace seemed pointless to me but I needed to show good character.

When the players started to move towards the pitch I noticed something, something worrying and highly alarming.

Trainers!

Let me explain.

When the players turned up they were all wearing snazzy Adidas football trainers or what have you, but trainers none the less. I was expecting them to change into moulded studded boots, the type that I had brought with me; the type that every single person who plays on artificial pitches in England wears. I was told before arriving we were playing on an artificial pitch by Johann and that looked the case, the ground was green but evidently not grass. However on closer inspection it wasn't the type of astroturf I was expecting. In England artificial pitches have a bit of 'give' in them, a bit of bounce to replicate playing on grass allowing a player to wear moulded studs, however this pitch didn't seem to be like that at all, it seemed harder, shallower, more like the old astroturf pitches in England, pretty much concrete painted green with some sand thrown on. One by one the Santa Venera players filtered past me through the gates wearing trainers, trainers and more bloody trainers.

I had my moulded studded boots in my hand and was panicking. Fuck, I'd brought the wrong shoes, the moulded studs wouldn't work on this type of surface. I grabbed the arm of the last player to walk past me in the hope that he could offer an opinion.

'Do you think I could play in these?'

I asked desperately, thrusting my boots I had acquired from Jamie months previously into his hands.

'No. You need trainers. Playing in those on this could give you a serious injury, you'll have no grip. You need trainers, a flatter surface to the shoe.'

Bollocks.

Bollocks.

Bollocks.

Bollocks.

Quadruple Bollocks.

I ran over to Tristan panicking. What was I going to do? I was like Cinderella at the ball, I'd come all this way to have a trial and I'd brought the wrong sort of shoes.

'There's only one thing for it mate,' said Tristan with a grin the size of a Cheshire cat motioning towards what was already on my feet.

'You've got to be fucking kidding!'

Tristan cackled with laughter.

Doing laps of the pitch with the rest of the players during the warm up I felt good. The sun had gone in and although it was humid the temperature wasn't as baking as it had been during the day, and I certainly wasn't standing out. That was until you looked down at my feet and the plimsoll shoes I was wearing. These were designed to make an indie boy look trendy or a homosexual look camp. They were destined for the costume department for Peter Pan stage productions, they were not designed to play football in. They were also flame red; just to nail on the fact that I looked like a giant twat. If it wasn't for Jamie and his gift of his Adidas moulded boots I would have taken proper football trainers and avoided this sorry debacle. I blame everything on him.

'Are you going to be okay in those? They look a bit unusual,' asked one concerned player jogging alongside me.

'These?' I motioned and he nodded. 'Oh yeah I'll be fine, these are new in England, they're all the rage, they fit like a glove. Everyone's wearing them for football now.' I lied, big time, I didn't want my first impression to be a bad one. I'd travelled over a thousand miles to a football trial and had taken the wrong shoes.

That's like going to a job interview at a charity organisation wearing a T-shirt that says 'Gandhi was a dick' on the front.

Once several laps of the half-sized football pitch had been completed the agility sessions started. Immediately I began to wish that I had taken Jamie's advice on me doing agility work. Only now did I fully realise what agility work actually was. Running in zig zags, hopping, skipping, star jumps with movement and sprinting all in the space of 15 minutes had the result of me feeling the need to cough up a lung. This was the warm-up; a football hadn't even been kicked. If we were to run six miles I'm sure I would have been fine, but the agility aspect and the stop-start-sprint nature made me feel like I was breathing fire through a thick filter of phlegm. I looked longingly at my bottle of water 50 metres away, knowing I couldn't go get it if I was to make this my first, and only, chance with this club count.

Patrick started to speak in Maltese and the instructions of what exercise we were doing next were lost me and so I just copied everyone else. Some of the exercises I had never encountered whilst playing football in England before, the ones we see the stars of the Football league do before every game, but I'm sure at one stage we were doing something that had been adopted from Morris Dancing, minus the props or costumes. Lunges in the air and arms being thrown around made me look even more stupid, especially as I wasn't as efficient as the others at it. Luckily this was the last of the agility work before footballs were introduced, unfortunately for me after just 15 minutes of what Patrick had called a 'light warm-up' I looked like a pregnant woman who was in the middle of a 44 hour labour. If my options were death or carrying on I would have chosen death, unfortunately my heart is in a lot better condition than I thought, so my only choice was to carry on and not risk the humiliation of having to walk off the pitch. I did, however, have more than a few tactical shoe-lace breaks because those pesky plimsoll shoes do tend to come undone easily. That was my excuse for sitting on the ground anyway. In those moments I thought of Marvin at the gym a thousand miles away, and how disappointed he would have been with me.

Thankfully Patrick allowed us to break and drink some water. I caned my 1.5-litre bottle faster than you can say I-think-I'm-going-to-throw-up, whereas everyone else, who I had now discovered were quite fit, drank a small measure of their thimbles of water and wiped their tanned brows before returning to the pitch. I gave a quick glance to Tristan which said 'What have I done?' to which he mouthed 'Slag' behind his camera, and I went back to training.

Patrick explained that what we then had to do, simple passing and moving between two players, controlling with the right foot, passing with the left, controlling with the left foot and then passing with the right. As I stepped up to do my passes with my newly acquired team-mate I looked down at my right ankle that under the disguise my light blue sock and flame red shoes was a bandage supporting it from any silly twists or turns. I hadn't kicked a ball for months and now it was my time. I planted my left foot next to the ball exerting all my weight upon it and then swung my right boot down in a casual fashion to side foot the ball to my team-mate. No pain, no twang and no yelp from my ankle, the quest, six months of planning had brought me to this, my first kick of a football with a semi-professional team in Malta. It was beautiful. Back and forth the ball went between me and my colleague, back and forth, right foot left foot right foot left foot right foot left foot, continuously for ten minutes, sometimes running around cones, other times moving sideways but always having to pass the ball to the same man. Not a difficult task, even for the worst footballers in the world, and so I passed with flying colours. But I still felt shaky from the horrific warm-up.

Following the passing, a session of attack-versus-defence began. This seemed simple enough, unfortunately the overriding feeling of wanting to sleep or die, whichever came first, would have a severe effect my performance.

The defence team stayed the same all the time, with three men defending a goal, and a goalkeeper. The attack teams were made up of three men rotated in turn, so that in effect a ball was always in play. As soon as the previous team of three attackers had either scored or missed, the next set of three would start with a ball from the halfway line and head towards the brutes of defenders. Although I wanted to impress at playing at right back, this is what Patrick wanted me to do and so this is what he would see, with me part of the attacking trios.

More than a dozen assaults on the opposition goal later and all I had succeeded in was falling on my arse, retching at feeling so unfit and missing a half-chance opportunity when I failed to meet a cross flying through the air to me at speed due to the flimsy plimsoll shoes not connecting with the ball properly. However, none of the attack teams scored, not once in about 100 attempts. The standard I was seeing was similar to my own, but I hadn't wowed them, I hadn't stood out, and so I wouldn't be recommended to anyone higher up the league pyramid who could sign a foreigner. I cursed my English heritage under my breath and continued to the bitter end, all the while knowing that if I were Maltese I could probably play for this club.

With the two-hour training session over I hobbled over Patrick to talk about how he felt I got on. I had a hole in my foot the size of a mint imperial due to the plimsolls, which I won't be endorsing for football purposes.

'I think you did well. You managed to just about keep up with the rest of the players even though you say you haven't done any fitness work for three months so I was impressed with that. Technically you are lacking a bit, but mentally you are good. When we had the attack versus defence scenario you understood people's runs and they understood yours, so I think with hard work and dedication you could potentially make it, but with hard work and dedication anything is possible in life. But you need work.'

If all the facts were true, and that I hadn't done any fitness work for three months, then I would have taken this as an encouragement, but instead I took it as a damning verdict on where my fitness was. He also seemed to be playing safe on not hurting my feelings, but I tried to stay optimistic. I questioned if I had it in me to train harder or could get any fitter given that my modest budget was already being eaten away, and I'd promised myself that once it had run out, I would be done. My window of opportunity was now, and it seemed I was a little out of touch.

At the end I got talking to one individual Nenad, who as it happened is a former Maltese international, and he informed me that he was being paid a very small amount to play for Santa Venera, even though he is now 38 and edging towards retirement after an illustrious few years at Malta's highest levels. He had even played against England once upon a time in a 2-1 loss for Malta. He did have better technical ability than me, but not by much, not in training anyway, but this was the problem. I felt like I was trying at 100% but

I had no idea if they too were at 100% or just 20%. Luckily for me they had a game the next day, which I would be attending to measure my standard against them, Nenad in particular, to see if I could make it and be paid in Malta.

After the trial I felt more positive that achieving the dream was possible and the chances of me impressing at St George's FC in two days time were strong – as long as my fitness kept me on the coat tails of everyone else and then they could potentially sign me and play me, or sign me and loan me out. Patrick was neither damning nor celebratory of my skills, and for the sake of my sanity and the rest of the trip, I decided that this was good news even if I wasn't going to be recommended to the higher powers in Maltese football. Trial one over and I wasn't too disconcerted, even if they weren't moving heaven and earth to get me signed. Patrick kindly gave us a lift back to our Hotel, where I learnt that he too was a police officer, and that he dealt with plenty of English tourists. I could see it now, him having to deal with drunken holidaymakers over how they think it's acceptable to piss in a giant fountain at the bus station, I realised then why his English accent was so good.

Myself and Tristan spent the next day moving our overloaded bags to a new hostel, deciding that the hole we were festering in wasn't doing our mood or sleep patterns any favours.

'We need to get out of here. These mosquitoes are doing my head in; I've never had so many bites on me in all my life,' said a half naked Tristan, scanning his body for fresh bites.

'Agreed. Lets find somewhere nice to stay.'

Moving downstairs, we were interrupted by Aldo who had gotten wind of my football exploits and asked how I had got on with Santa Venera. I informed him that it went well and I wasn't too downhearted for St Georges or the rest of the trip. He again informed me that his son played for the Valletta under 16s side, but this time changed his age from what he had said previously, 16, to 15. Was this kid Benjamin Button or was Aldo not entirely with it upstairs?

I decided on the latter and, because of this, even though we were taking our business away from him, I dropped a few hints that we could do with a lift to our next hotel, hoping Aldo would be daft enough to offer.

'God these bags are so heavy. Do you know of any taxi companies around that could help… or anyone that might give us a lift?' I said, fully knowing Aldo had nothing to do but sit around all day. I raised my eyebrows and looked at him doe-eyed. Unfortunately he wasn't swayed by my charms.

'Taxi is 20 Euros,' he said abruptly.

'We'll take the bus.' We exited the hole – sorry, hotel – as quick as we could (so with the bags it took about quarter of an hour, 14 minutes longer than it should).

We had booked our next accommodation for two nights to take us up to the end of our trip in Malta, if I wasn't offered something concrete with St George's, that is. It was a little out of Valletta so we had to catch the bus from the bus station, which I now used as a landmark in case we got lost. This was really the first time I got to see Malta despite being there for two nights already. Parts of it were beautiful, the architecture really was something to behold and it had a great medieval feel about it with huge amounts of fortifications overlooking the harbour highlighting its strategic importance over the centuries. But the fact that it was so hot, with little rain throughout the year made the place feel a little dirty, and I was yet to see a blade of grass. I was longing for the Yorkshire countryside of my youth. Even London has parks, but Malta just seemed to be one concrete street after another.

We struggled onto the bus with our bags. The fare was a mere 40p – a refreshing change in a place where everything seemed expensive. I was hoping to find Malta to be a cheap country, but with the pound doing so poorly against the euro, and Malta being a popular tourist resort, especially for the English, prices seemed to be inflated. My budget was being eaten away, and the thoughts of potentially going to New Zealand or Kenya as a last throw of the dice were already looking slim. If this dream was going to come true, it was to be in Europe.

'Stop the bus!' Shouted Tristan as the sign for our stop slowly rolled past.

As we disembarked, bashing everyone on the head with our clumsy baggage as we went, our companions tutted and grumbled at our meek apologies. So much for the love of the English that Aldo had vaunted.

Off the bus I was lost. It used to be that travellers, when looking for their lodgings, would be forced to stand on street corners, heavy bags weighing them down peering into a street map that was clearly out of date before asking a local where to go. I had never done any travelling but I have been reliably informed that is the normal thing to do, and had readied myself for such tribulations. However, my walking production company and brother Tristan had other ideas. With his iPhone at the ready, a street map downloaded off the internet and a built-in compass we found the Ramplas Hostel with relative ease and although relieved, I felt a little romance of the experience had been taken away. A plus point, though, was that it was so easy my clothes were only mildly moist by the time we got there rather than sodden to the extreme like the previous day. It occurred to me at that point that I perhaps should have packed more underwear, as I had already rifled through 6 pairs in 2 days.

We were welcomed to the hotel by an elderly lady and a much younger woman in her mid-to-late 30s. After hurling our bags to the floor and breathing two manly grunts of relief at the shedding of the weight we were given the tour of the house and then shown to our room. We would have to share with two other English people but that was fine with us – it was far cleaner and far cheaper than staying in town, at least compared to the last place, and the fact that you could drink the tap water meant I could restore my body's saturation levels to something nearing normal after days of dehydration. It wasn't so much a hotel or hostel, but more of a spacious house, and it was a welcome change.

'You will be sharing with Colm and his young friend who arrives today,' Said the younger of the two women.

'Colm?'

'Yes Colm. They are from England like you.'

'Okay cool.'

'Yes, he has been out here a month trying to be a footballer and his friend is visiting. If you need anything I will be next door.'

And with that she left.

Did I hear her right?

He's English and out here playing football? That can't be, she must have got confused with the fact that in our booking we'd said we were out here playing football, making a short film about me attempting to achieve my childhood ambition. Yes that was it, a simple mistake to make.

15 minutes later we found out from the horse's mouth.

A young, shirtless, shaven headed, toned Adonis of a man entered our shared lodgings with a football under his arm, and introduced himself.

'Hi I'm Ralf. Random question but are you out here to try and be a professional footballer?'

'Yeah, why?' he asked, furrowing his brow at what he thought must have been a psychic ability.

Unbelievably, I had a nemesis.

Colm Hastings had come out to Malta a month before me and had been training with the reserve/youth squad of Valletta Minors for a month. He had got the trial after his Dad had set him up with it, in the Jordi Cruyff Barcelona/Manchester United kind of way. His father knew somebody from Malta who had contacts with the club after he played for them and so that's how he got in. I, by contrast, had spent two weeks compiling what is the most beautiful spreadsheet in the world in order to pester clubs into submission over the course of three months only for over a thousand clubs not to reply. To say I felt aggrieved at this would be a slight understatement. Valetta were one of the clubs I wrote to but never got a response from, and here I was faced by a man who got in on the virtue of his father's mate.

Colm, still shirtless whilst chatting to us (and actually shirtless for our entire stay), was taller than me, slimmer than me, younger than me and after four seconds of conversation I realised he was also better at football than me.

'Yeah I had trials with Leicester, my home town club, when I was 10 but never got signed and that was it, no more big clubs showed an interest. I did represent the county though for a few years in defence and midfield and I spent the last few years playing for Rugby Town FC.'

Rugby Town play in the 7th tier of football in England. My standard equates to about the 212th tier, one lower than the over-75s league.

His semi-naked body didn't have an ounce of fat on it. He was a good 6ft and had perfect teeth. He was the complete opposite to me but had the same goals. He started before me, with a better club, is better at football than me and is being asked to hang around. I should have hated him. However, no matter how hard I tried I couldn't, he was too nice. Bastard.

'I haven't actually played a game yet.' He said straining his teabag against the side of his cup in the lodging's communal kitchen. 'I haven't been signed and I haven't been paid. The problem is in the Premier League here, which what Valetta are in, you are allowed to sign 5 foreign players. If the club sign someone who is outside the EU though they then take up two of the spots. Annoyingly Valletta have a Cameroon player on their books meaning I can't sign yet so I'm just hanging around. Anyway they're now thinking about signing me and loaning me out to another club. In the first division their allowed one foreign player and in the second division none.

'Yeah I know, I trained with a team that couldn't sign me yesterday.'

'Its unbelievable isn't it. Did they tell you before you came out here?'

'Well yeah, but I was hoping for them maybe to pass me onto someone else if they were impressed.'

'And were they?'

'No.'

'Right.' Colm looked confused before continuing his story. 'Anyway I looked at the Malta FA website before coming out here to see what the rules were for signing people but couldn't find anything. You'd think they'd make it more apparent.'

He seemed a tad annoyed but also remarkably laid back, a sign of someone who was just 18 years old. If that were me hanging around for a month I would have been livid. I thought what I was doing was incredible, but then to think he was several years younger than me and on his own was something I give him praise for.

I wanted to ask him how he could afford to stay out here but thought that would be prying, so kept it light. It was nice to talk to someone who understood exactly what I was trying to achieve, and who shared the same goals. Tristan, after all, had shown no interest in football whatsoever.

'I don't know why people in England give up,' Colm said, slurping his tea. 'Like you say it's pretty competitive in England with a lot of foreigners, so why shouldn't we try elsewhere? I think, and I don't know why, people in England love England, if you see what I mean? If they can't make it with a club there or are released then the majority just give up and get a normal job and forget about football. I know of one other English guy out here who was released by Coventry and now he's playing for Sliema, but that's it.'

'Have you thought about any other countries you might try?' I asked, hoping to see if he had targeted countries such as Andorra, San Marino and the Baltic states, like myself.

'Well I was going to do this in France or Italy initially because I just liked the idea of going out there, but I haven't had chance yet because this opportunity came up. Anyway enough about me, what about you? Did you have any trials with anyone growing up?'

'Not exactly,' I said, unfolding my arms and rubbing the back of my neck awkwardly. I proceeded to tell him all about the last 24 hours, the last seven months and, as a consequence, the last 24 years. He found it amusing but uplifting, and for that I liked him even more.

That evening, fully settled into our new and improved lodgings, me and Tristan caught another bus out to where Santa Venera were to have their friendly and where I would be able to see if their players were any better than me. If I felt I could match up to Nenad in particular in a match scenario, then Malta may be the place for me, regardless of whether the next trial at St George's was a success. The bus journey was a long, painful process, exacerbated by rush-hour traffic, the heat, and the moronic English businessman on his mobile phone sat next to me talking 'figures' and 'downturns'. He obviously thought a lot of himself with the volume he was speaking at and the watch he was jangling in the sun, however I took great pleasure in the fact that I'm smart enough to wear shorts and flip flops when it's warm, unlike him in his full garish tie and suit attire. It seems money can't buy common sense.

We had arranged to meet Patrick outside two petrol stations. Why there were two identical petrol stations next to each other I don't know and I didn't bother questioning it after seeing the fountain in the bus terminal – I just accepted it as a Maltese thing. When Patrick picked us up there was a far more relaxed atmosphere between us than the night before, and he told us how one day in a couple of years he would like to retire and move to Australia and potentially coach out there in semi-retirement.

The pitch that the game was to be played on was another artificial affair but this time it was one that my moulded studs would be at home on – what football aficionados call '3G'. The ground overlooked the Mediterranean and I was sure this would probably be one of the more random games of football I would see in my life (though I would find out later in the trip that I was wrong about that).

They were playing Mellita, a completely amateur outfit who were promoted out of Santa Venera's league the year before. I learned that their approach was towards developing their own youth team, hence the amateur nature of the club. I was glad I hadn't arranged a trial with Mellita as there would have been no chance of them paying me due to their amateur status. The ground and pitch was unusual to say the least. It was housed in a net environment to stop the ball from flying off into the wilderness or even the sea, and the spectators had a choice of sitting at either the bar/café that overlooked the pitch or the more traditional seats next to it, of which there were about 20 with nothing but open space on the other three sides of the pitch. Seeing that no one was sat in the spectator seats I went with the former option and against my better judgement ordered a beer. I felt like I had earned one.

Sat there drinking, watching the Santa Venera players warm up with balls and sprint sessions, I was enjoying myself. I felt like the expensive new signing sat in the stands, unable to play until the paperwork was sorted out. Tristan was out and about the pitch filming with his gargantuan camera and it was the first time that we, or at least I, could relax and just appreciate football. Just before kick-off, a man approached me. He was obviously a Mellitta representative, and was unhappy about the camera being there. I knew this before he had even opened his mouth, as there was no reason for him to approach other than that, and already despite only being in Malta for two days I had developed a sixth sense for people eyeing Tristan's camera equipment while my brother launched himself into silly positions on the floor, climbed trees or, in this instance, sat on a football pitch to get the best shots.

'Excuse me what are you doing?'

I explained it to him at length, but the man didn't seem to have a sense of humour and just stood there staring into my eyes. I explained it again in a different way but again he remained silent, staring into my eyes harder, his eyes narrowing, as if it were a Jedi mind trick to extract the truth from me.

'Seriously we're just making a film about football. We have release forms we were going to ask the club representatives to sign so we could use this location in any film we make.'

He obviously wasn't having any of it, and soon Tristan's own sixth sense kicked in and he stopped filming and came over.

'You're not scouts are you? Because I have a lot of people come here to scout my players, and I won't have it! You're scouts from England aren't you?' He wasn't a scary looking man or even a scary sounding man, and I really wanted to watch the game and didn't want to be ejected.

'We're not scouts, we're just making a football film. Ask any of the Santa Venera Players, or the coach, or the secretary.'

I wanted to point out that if we were scouts, then we might try to be a bit more inconspicuous than having a camera the size of a baby rhino being operated by a man who was crouching down at the feet of the players to get footage. Scouting happens the world over, but in extreme circumstances when a club abroad don't want a Premier League club to poach their star player, many well-known scouts are not allowed into certain grounds, black-listed as it were, so they have to employ extreme measures to the see the diamond in the rough, scaling walls to avoid turnstiles or sending people in their stead with hidden cameras.

I took it an insult to our intelligence that he thought we would actually film the players from pitch-side for scouting purposes. How confident would you have to be to do that? We might as well walk right up and say 'Excuse me mate I'm a scout from England using this Camera to record everything, can you do some kick-ups for me please, and maybe say your name and age, medical history and preferred position to the camera?'

Finally after telling him everything he finally accepted that we weren't scouts and were making a film. However, he proceeded to sit next to us for the entire game, just to make sure we weren't paying too much attention to one particular player. It was slightly uncomfortable.

However the game was an enjoyable one, and when Santa Venera took an early lead it looked like my team were going to march to victory, however Melitta came back to seal an entertaining 3-2 win. The game was good and the standard okay; certain things I saw I thought to myself I could do better and other things I thought if I attempted would probably result in a hernia. Annoyingly for me and the club, Nenad had to be taken off, injured with a pulled hamstring after only 15 minutes, and not impressing. If he kept up that standard for 90 minutes then I would have harboured some hope of making it here, however because of his early withdrawal there was no way to tell how we compared. Against the rest of the players, I think I could have played and not made an idiot of myself, but none of them other than Nenad were paid professionals. Another issue was that every muscle in my body was now as tight as a drum due to the 'light training session' I'd endured the day before. Although the game finished 3-2 and I'd had a couple of drinks, the most entertaining part of the evening was Tristan missing all five goals because he was too busy filming blades of grass or me scratching myself. He also looked tired and bored, which prompted him to come out with the line 'Why can't you have aspired to open a strip club or something? That would have been way better than this.' Sadly I couldn't indulge Tristan's desire for any night out on the town, because tomorrow would be trial number two, and I needed to be ready. I was confident after seeing that Santa Venera game. I could impress if I played well enough, and I could get signed by the next club.

The next day I was awoken by a combination of cramp all over my body and Colm speaking ridiculously loudly to his friend on the phone in our room at 8:30am. I'd forgotten how young Colm was yesterday due to his openness and intelligence; however I was given a swift reminder when he was talking to his friend about things that really could have waited until later. Obviously social etiquette in shared accommodation isn't something you acquire until you're older – that or Colm really couldn't wait to tell his mate about how hot it was here.

Me and Tristan had decided that before the day's trial, neither of us could really be arsed to do anything. We were both getting sick of the heat, the insects, the dustiness and endless amounts of concrete without a non-artificial blade of grass in sight. If I were to make it as a professional footballer in Malta, I wasn't going to hang around like Colm to make a career out of it. Because of our laziness and my incapacity to fully extend my legs due to cramps and fatigue – which I wholly admit is a worrying sign if you are aiming to be a professional footballer and have an imminent trial – we headed for the beaches of Sliema to sit around, drink lots of water and admire the sea. At least that was the plan.

On arrival we noticed that there was no soft sand to lie upon, just jagged rocks; nor was there a nice man wandering these jagged rocks with a cooler selling ice-cold bottles of water and Magnums. In fact, the beach's only redeeming feature was that it had swarms of beautiful women lying worshipping the sun with next to no clothes on. This would normally be enough to keep any young male British tourists happy, were it not for the fact that me and Tristan had forgotten our sun cream and had to spend the majority of our beach trip banished to a thin sliver of shade beneath the sea wall. I dread to think what people thought of us on that day, but on seeing two pasty men cowering in the shade nodding their approval at the beautiful women who walked past, their first impressions of us couldn't have been good. We resembled Gollum out of Lord of the Rings.

Following this no doubt great advert for British tourists, I desperately tried to stretch my muscles in order to bring back some elasticity into my legs before my big trial. Unfortunately for me though, every time I attempted this I felt either the onslaught of cramp in my hamstrings, or the much more alarming feeling that they were going to snap. I have never had any problems with my muscles before, and put this down as a by-product of being so dehydrated from three days of constant sweating, football-playing and bag carrying. Soon enough after accomplishing no relaxation time or improving my fragile physical state, it was time to return to the bus terminal. The saying goes that all roads lead to Rome. That may be true, but in the case of Malta they all go to the hazardous bus terminal first.

The town of Cospicua looks pretty much the same as any other in Malta, slightly dusty, plenty of concrete, overlooking the harbour. I was finding it hard to distinguish between two towns anywhere in Malta; people told me to get the bus to a certain place but it all looked the same, no fields in between towns or signs to signal your arrival, and few landmarks. It was a concrete metropolis, and I was confused, struggling with the heat, sore and had a trial in just 45 minutes.

Waiting there in the shade once more I didn't know what to expect from the Club President Chris Agius. In our conversations over email and phone it didn't seem like he was too excited by my arrival and perhaps saw me as an inconvenience. The conversations lacked any small-talk and pointless dialogue, and ended rather abruptly. I'm big fan of pointless dialogue, like 'What's your favourite type of tea?' or 'What recurring nightmare did you have as a child?' Knowing this type of information about a person reminds you that everyone is human and has their quirks, but unfortunately Chris didn't seem to want to divulge this information to me.

I was far more nervous than when I was at Santa Venera. That was a dress rehearsal, this was the real deal and I was doing my best to pace around to banish such nerves but my muscles wouldn't allow such a fluid movement so I ended up just jiggling on the spot. A red Toyota zoomed to within three feet of my body in what looked like a well-executed handbrake turn. The slim, middle-aged driver leant over to shout through the open passenger window.

'Ralf?'

'Chris?'

Second contact had been made.

Why had I been nervous about Chris? What a true gent, another man with an olive-skin glow and a welcoming nature. As soon as we were inside his car, Tristan wedged in the back seat, he offered us bottled water as he raced through the narrow streets of Cospicua to show us the club offices, while discussing my aims. I had my heart in my mouth as the vehicle shaved many a kerb and parked car as we made our way to the offices, and on arrival, when Chris opened the office's shutter doors that looked like they belonged in a shanty town and led us down a seemingly never ending dark corridor that had little plaster on the walls and had no sign of it being used for football matters, I was beginning to wonder if my organs were about to be sold on the black market. But then it happened, something wondrous; something that reminded me why I loved football so much. Chris opened a set of doors revealing quite possibly the most compact but fit-to-bursting trophy room you can imagine. Each trophy glistened with the sunlight that shone through the window and Chris began to unlock the cabinets one by one, to give me a description of each trophy, how it was won and what it signified.

There were too many to mention, but as Tristan struggled with his camera to film the whole thing, Chris spoke at a thousand miles an hour about the club and its history. Established in 1890 by British Army representatives stationed there, hence the 'St George' name, it's the oldest club in Malta. Currently in the second tier it's by no means the most successful club in Malta and has little money, but it has a mountain of history that Chris was evidently proud of. They won the league title in 1917 and I was privileged enough to hold the very trophy. This, I was certain, was the closest I was going to come to the Maltese league title, and so I savoured the moment. There seemed to be some English names on the team-sheets and the trophies presented to them from years gone by, but unfortunately I learned little of these world football pioneers.

Chris himself got involved in the club as a player for a number of years before joining on the committee and eventually president. His reasoning for becoming president was modest, in that nobody else really went forward for the job, but I think he was a popular choice and was asked to be president, rather than simply winning by default. His ambitions for the club were romantic and he seemed to simply love football and the club.

'For me personally the biggest prize is the FA cup and always will be. That's what I want for this club: a better cup run history,' he said.

'You're a man after my own heart Chris.' We both gave a wry smile; I wasn't flirting with him, you understand, just admiring his love of the game. I love football because it has a magnificent sense of theatre, the game is beautiful itself and it's also a universal language that brings people together and that's what was happening here. Over a thousand miles from home, I was in the offices of a club in a run-down building with a bloke who loved football, what's not to like?

Things did take a turn for the sombre when Chris informed us that the Maltese football season had been suspended under match-fixing charges against two of his players, who were duly sacked – one a goalkeeper and another a midfielder, who were paid off by bookmakers in order to attempt to throw a game. It seems the wide-reaching arm of the bookies and those who manipulate the markets is a worldwide problem. Chris tried to find out who it was who had been paid off but it took a team-mate of the two to ring out the confession.

'It was a very sad time for me,' said Chris, 'and because of it still going on we are still waiting for the season to start.' Chris seemed very sad at this juncture and so I tried to change the subject to more light-hearted matters. I asked what he thought of what I was doing, whilst casually laying down a disclaimer that I wasn't feeling too well in every muscle on my body.

'Unfortunately you're too late I think for this season. Many teams have already got their full squads sorted now and have their full allocation of foreign players.'

Bugger.

'But you are welcome to try out. There is still a chance.'

One thing I could bring to this football club is someone who never would throw a game of football. Not intentionally, anyway.

Towards the end of our interview with Chris he was interrupted by a small child, probably his son, though no introductions were made. It was during this moment of tranquillity amongst the madness of the previous half an hour that Tristan removed the weight of a camera from his shoulder to exclaim:

'Ahh! I've never sweated so much in my life. That went on for ages but I couldn't stop filming, you have to film everything! Sweat was pouring into my eyes and there was no way to stop it.'

As Tristan peeled his drenched shirt from his body and mouthed profanities, highlighting his disgust at the heat and at the situation, I ignored him and instead took a look at some of the photographs on the walls. They were truly incredible. Team photos going back over a hundred years, featuring Englishmen and Maltese players side by side in big baggy shorts with traditional stuck-down hair made me gasp at the appeal of football worldwide, it was truly awe inspiring. As my eyes wandered I was caught by something else more intriguing. A photo of the St Georges youth team from a couple of years ago appeared to have the spitting image – no, the clone – of former England International John Salako. They looked exactly the same. Round face, chubby cheeks, small afro, definitely a Salako. Could it be that John Salako had an illicit affair with a Maltese woman and the results of that night of passion was a child who'd inherited John's football skills?

'Okay are we ready to go?' Chris had interrupted my train of thought and I didn't want to ask. It was now 4.50pm and my second trial was just ten minutes away.

On the way to training we picked up Tony. Tony plays for St Georges FC, and as a Nigerian is their registered foreigner, stopping me from being their registered foreigner, unless they see something spectacular in me and decide to fake Maltese citizenship for me by marrying me off with one of the locals or simply sign me and loan me out to another club who doesn't yet have a foreigner in their ranks. Tony, on paper, should have been another nemesis standing in the way of my goal, but annoyingly he was just another nice guy.

'I love football! That's what I'm doing here,' said Tony as we got out of the car after the short journey to the top of the hill overlooking the rundown streets of Cospicua.

Tony's muscular torso made me think that I really should have packed and worn a girdle at all times on the trip. Measuring up to my nemeses Tony and Colm there was no contest physically.

'But what brought you here?' I said, wanting to know if he too, like me, had sent out a thousand emails, or like Colm had nepotism to thank.

'Well every boy in Nigeria wants to be a professional footballer. They see it as a way out, and so all we do is play football all the time. I was 16 playing on the streets and an agent saw me and things moved along and I have now been in Malta seven, maybe eight years.'

Eight years? I couldn't even last eight days here.

'Is there anywhere else you'd like to play?'

'Well football is the dream. I love it, like you obviously love it. I am only paid a little here, and if the dream takes me to Europe or Asia where I can earn more money then I will take my family there.'

Tony was exactly like me, and would go anywhere to be paid to play football. Unlike me though, he looked like a warrior and had achieved his dream in part and settled on the island, with a wife and child. Although he was approaching his thirties, he was still hopeful of bigger things than St Georges FC, and for that I admired him. I decided to call him Nigerian Ralf behind his back because that sounded infinitely better than a name like Tony ever could. He deserved a better name.

It was interesting to hear him say how he was spotted by an agent. More and more often, in Africa in particular, youngsters are told by 'agents' that they have a talent, and that the agent could make it happen for them because they have contacts with big name clubs like Manchester United and Barcelona. More and more African players are flooding the player markets in Europe and they are usually associated with being strong and athletic, something that the game in England is gravitating toward. Most Premier League clubs have at least one player of African descent and some have several. Players such as Michael Essien, Kolo Toure, Didier Drogba, Emmanuel Eboue and many more show what can be achieved, so it's easy to see why a youngster from Nigeria or Ghana or wherever would believe that they could too make it in the promised land of the Premier League when an 'agent' approaches them. However, there are expensive 'processing fees' that the player's family needs to pay in order to get in contact with the clubs, and before you know it the agent has their money and no word is heard from them ever again. In the worst-case scenarios, these 'agents' sometimes even use the money to fly the youngster to the country they are supposed to be having a trial in, where they report to the club only to find they've never agreed to a trial with the youngster, who is then marooned in Europe, selling goods on the street or simply begging. It's become a new kind of people trafficking, and is a growing industry. There is even a charity, Culture Foot Solidaire, which tries to stop it continuing but with football the industry it is today it seems it may be a long-standing problem for African families.

As Tony reeled away to talk to his assembling team-mates I did a quick change of tops and shorts in order to save the other people embarrassment about how exceptionally toned my physique was, and was beyond relieved to find that the training pitches would accept my moulded studs. An embarrassing repeat of plimsoll-gate was not on the cards.

The training pitch was bigger than Santa Venera's, and also seemed newer. With floodlights towering over us, it was evident this club had more money than my previous hosts, and to me that could only be a good thing.

I was introduced to Joey, the team coach who looked like he was some sort of America B-movie actor, with a dazzling white smile and well-built appearance. After informing me that his English wasn't so good, he then proceeded to introduce me to the rest of the team in Her Majesty's tongue fluently before doing a bit in Maltese, probably saying 'This English bastard here thinks he's better than you. Make sure you kick the crap out of him.' I noticed whilst he was doing this that the John Salako lookalike was there! He must have graduated to the first team ranks, which wasn't surprising given his father's genes.

'Ralf,' said Joey, motioning me over. 'We are now going to do a short warm-up, and today's session will be quite light as we went for a six-mile run in the forests yesterday.'

I didn't know whether to laugh or cry. To laugh at the fact that Malta had forests stowed away somewhere away from tourists, or cry in relief at the fact that today would be 'light'. However, if that was the same translation as Santa Venera's definition of a 'light training session' then I would need Tristan brush up on his CPR skills, as I would be keeling over in the next 15 minutes.

'I have spoken to Chris,' Joey continued, 'and he has informed me of your situation so if you feel you need to, don't press too much. I will watch you and give you feedback at the end.'

Thank you Chris, and my 'situation'. All those hours spent at the gym evidently came down to bog-all, because I was still quite a way short of fitness compared to these guys.

Fifteen minutes in and things were going well. Granted, it was only the warm-up, but as far as warm-ups go that one was okay. There were cones involved and zigzag movements required and running backwards and forwards through all manner of things, and I had little idea what was going on, so I just decided to copy everyone, and that worked out a treat. The biggest plus was that my hamstrings didn't snap. In fact, they were feeling surprisingly limber following a light stretching exercise, and fortunately for me it looked as if this really was going to be a light session – nothing like the marathon pain-fest at Santa Venera. Then, just as we were about to begin some ball work, something highly amusing happened. The sight of the club treasurer jogging alongside players asking them if they were going to turn up or not to the friendly they organised the next day was reminiscent of witnessing Patrick do the register at the previous club. If the players said no because they had family commitments or what-have-you, the treasurer would remind them that they are being paid (or at least registered with the club) and had responsibilities. I doubt very much you'd ever see Liverpool's team of accountants jogging alongside Steven Gerrard asking why he thinks a dentist appointment is more important than an away Champions League fixture against Inter Milan.

I was happy that the drills we had planned involved the ball rather than an endless cycle of sprints and drills. Excellent news for me, the longer I spent on the ball, and not actually having to show people I can run 100 metres flat-out without suffering a collapsed lung, the better. The ball work was to be five versus two, 'piggy in the middle'. Five players form a circle in a restricted area and try to keep the ball between them using only one touch, whereas the two try and get the ball back or play the ball off the pitch. Lose possession and you go in the middle until you can win it back, and if you do you then swap with whoever lost it and so on. It's a game used universally across football pitches in England and, as it seems now to me, the world.

The squad was broken up into four different groups and I was to play with Tony (or Nigerian Ralf) and five others. I had been given the nickname 'Manchester', simply because I revealed that's where I lived, and of course they all assumed I was a Manchester United fan. Those who believed they were my kin in supporting the red devils made themselves known to me, and I immediately made my excuses and moved away from them in order to concentrate on the trial.

Starting as one of the five in the outer circle I was confident that my technique, undoubtedly the second-strongest part of my game behind 'reading it', would hold up in a game like this.

I was wrong.

It started well, with me expressing my full repertoire of skills, and after a couple of nice touches, shimmies and flicks to keep possession I was feeling good. However, someone must have flipped the 'off' switch in my head and suddenly all knowledge of how a ball behaves deserted me, and I was in the middle for about 90% of the game time, unable to get the ball back, and when I was lucky enough to have it ricochet of my shin off the field to thus earn my place amongst the ball-keeping five, I lacked the skill to stay there and immediately gave the ball back, resulting in me returning to the middle, running around like a fat dad trying to keep up with the ball as it pinged over, under and around my body. Joey was giving me an occasional glance, and he didn't seem too enamoured with the potential English signing.

More Maltese came from Joey's mouth, which for all I knew could have been 'This English boy is really shit. Look at him, look at him struggle. Ten Euros says he dies in the next hour. Who wants a piece of the action.'

Thankfully no one seemed to take the bet; that, or no one had their wallet on them.

The final task was two separate games of seven on seven, and if I didn't shine here I could kiss the dream in Malta goodbye. It was simple, it was a game which had no Goalkeepers, and you could only score if you either hit the post or bar, or scored with a header. No formations, no tactics, just free-flowing football and I was determined to succeed in a game that suited my attributes, bar the heading bit. Pass and move, pass and move, do that well for an hour and a half and I would have a chance of impressing Joey sufficiently for him to get the wheels into motion of me eventually being a professional footballer.

Five minutes in and things were going well for me; I was evidently taking it a lot more seriously than the others, and my aggressive sprints and sharp passes to my team-mates' feet helped raise the tempo from a very buddy-like start to something of a proper game. As the match progressed and a large red sun set over my shoulder, there were no signs of the deadlock being broken, and I was desperate that the person breaking that deadlock would be me. I just hoped Joey would be watching when I fizzed a 30-yard screamer against the bar, scoring our team a point. It seemed his attention was mainly on the other pitch, where the players seemed more alert, more talented and much bigger. It was at that point I realised I was playing with the reserves, the dregs, but that didn't bother me. I felt I was as good as, if not better than, the players I was with, so this was the area I was going to shine in.

One player on the opposition caught my attention, because he was rubbish. Seriously rubbish. To summarise how bad he was, he was noticeably worse than me. Seriously awful. Take the player you've always berated, either from the stands or from the sofa, and then make them lose all functions in their limbs and you'll get this guy's skills on a football pitch. He was known to his team-mates as Dimitar, and I reasoned this was because of his familiarity to Dimitar Berbatov, although it could just have been his name. They did look similar, but that's where the similarities ended. Every time he got the ball he dawdled, did some poor attempt at a trick and then lost the ball. There was no urgency about him, no drive and no skill. At first, when he was attempting these outlandish tricks, I was thinking that he was taking the mick, having a laugh with his team-mates about doing some silly skill during a training session which to them was no more than a mess-about. But it wasn't a joke, at least it didn't seem to be because no one was laughing and the intense concentration on his face every time he got the ball suggested that he was serious, but he was rubbish! Furthermore, his team-mates, who were definitely taking it seriously, continued to indulge him, giving him the ball and looking for the return pass that never came. They actually thought he was contributing something, but they would have been better off without him. Slower, shorter and less skilful than me, I was elated that if Dimitar set the standard at St Georges FC then I would have a chance here. Muttering into my microphone that Tristan had attached to me I let it be known to him and the camera that I was going target him. Hell, I thought, I need to show I am great at football, I need to be a ball winner, a play maker and a dangerous finisher all in one over the next hour if I'm going to be offered any glimmer of hope here. Even if Nigerian Ralf prevents me playing for this particular club, they could sign me and loan me out, then ditch Nigerian Ralf and have me back the next season. I was going to be a king in Malta through football.

With my curly hair stuck to my face from the buckets of sweat I was creating, I spent an hour targeting Dimitar, taking the ball of him, sprinting past him, taking him on and beating him. Every time he got the ball, BANG, I tackled him; every time he was on a mazy, slow run, BANG, I shoulder barged him and won the ball. Every time he went for a header, BANG, I shoved him out of the way and made the ball my own. Every time I got the ball I ran to him and skinned him with ease making me look like Cristiano Ronaldo. I looked incredible at football simply by virtue of being in a five-metre radius of this man. My confidence was sky high, every time: BANG, BANG, BANG. No one else in our team had picked up on my tactic of challenging him to make myself look good to the on-looking manager, and I didn't care. Every time I got the ball I manoeuvred myself close to him so I could then beat him with a basic skill such as knocking it past him and running, that's as far as my repertoire goes. I even timed some of my challenges so that I had to slide tackle him rather than just nicking it off his feet, thus showing my commitment. CRUNCH, CRUNCH, CRUNCH; BANG, BANG, BANG. He seemed like a nice guy and didn't take my bullying to heart, and why should he? He's a footballer after all, he's used to it. BANG, BANG, BANG; CRUNCH, CRUNCH, CRUNCH, every time he was anywhere near the ball. Brilliant.

At half-time Tristan, still dripping in sweat from the trophy room filming, came over with a litre water bottle in hand.

'How do you think you're going?' he asked, handing me the water and thus a lifeline.

'Good. That guy's crap isn't he?'

'I don't know much about football but I do know he's terrible. Maybe you should leave off him a bit, you're not being too kind.'

'Tristan this is football, and this is my dream, if he can't handle it he shouldn't play.'

I returned to my team-mates for the second half, confident my tactic would work. The only thing that was bothering me was that I hadn't scored yet, and unfortunately no matter how hard I tried in the second half I couldn't get my head to a cross or smash either the post or bar. I was getting annoyed, but at least trusty Dimitar was there to make me look good. I did manage to get an assist. I beat my man, Dimitar of course, and crossed for one of our players to nod in an equaliser to make it 2-2.

During the course of the game Joey swapped players from the other pitch with some from our own. Nigerian Ralf even came over to our team and he did seem better than me, by how much it was impossible to say, but one thing for certain was that I wasn't the worst player out there, and I was way better than one in particular.

As I sensed there were only a few minutes remaining I had one last opportunity to impress. With Dimitar wobbling down the left wing slowly moving the ball from right foot to left foot and left foot to right, I immediately made my way to him to crunch him once more before the full time whistle. I lunged two footed into his shins and sent him spiralling into the air, took the ball *a la* Bobby Moore calmly and laid it off to a team mate, my prey just coming round from the brutality of my challenge. Take that Dimitar, I'm going to take your place in this squad.

At full-time I was beaming, I had enjoyed myself and made a good impression. For the first time in a decade I could say I had played a decent game of football all thanks to Dimitar, the beautiful man. As I ran over to Joey to get his opinion I was sky high in confidence. I was sure even if it was a 'no' now because of legislature against foreigners, I could come back and sign for whatever team I liked.

'So Joey, what did you think?' I said with a slow blink of my eyes and slow nod of the head to suggest to him I knew and he knew I was amazing at football. I was the knees of a bee.

'Well, sorry Ralf, I don't think you are good enough to make it here in the first division.'

'What?'

I was stunned.

'Yes, you lack physical strength, pace and the mental sharpness of which pass to play, and that's the difference between the first division and the second division here.'

I couldn't believe; it I thought I'd played a brilliant game. I was genuinely upset.

'But... but... but...'

With this I made a slight gesture towards Dimitar. He was 20 metres away drinking from a bottle of water after the battering I had given him. I was signalling to Joey that I had noticed him, and hopefully Joey would read between the lines and know what I'm talking about in that everyone knows he's rubbish.

'Him? Oh don't compare yourself to him. He is only 17 and he is erm... Special Olympics.'

Oh.

My.

God.

'Sorry?'

'Yes he is erm, Special Olympics... mentally handicapped. We let him train sometimes with us. He is the son of a friend.'

Oh.

My.

God.

I wanted to be sick.

I'm a horrible person.

A horrible, horrible person.

I had just spent the last hour in a job interview physically and verbally assaulting a mentally handicapped boy. I could have cried. When Joey mentioned this, it made sense; Dimitar was clearly much worse than everyone else, I just chose not to think about why, assuming that he started on the left wing for them and was on £250 a week. But obviously not. The other players, when they did really try, were much better than me, but I'd just denied it. I've never hated myself so much.

I thanked Joey and Chris and made my way to the hostel knowing I wouldn't make it in Malta, wanting to hang my head in shame.

'Being a professional footballer is going to be a lot harder than I thought,' I said to Tristan as we trudged off the pitch.

'Yup, if the first two are anything to go by you'll be a jammy bastard if you make it anywhere.'

Malta's Santa Venera Lightnings and St George's FC had shown us incredible hospitality and gave me a decent chance, and I thank them for that, I just don't thank them for being so much better at football than I had anticipated.

I learnt a few things in Malta, but the two most prominent lessons were that plimsolls don't make good football boots, and you should always get a full medical history of people you are going to play football against before physically assaulting them during a match.

CHAPTER 10: HEY IT'S ME...

Saying goodbye to Colm was relatively easy. I had only known him 48 hours, and in that short space of time he had made the grave error of waking me up due to his lack of volume control, and last night had taken the mick out of the 'Special Olympics' saga, which Tristan had taken great delight in relating. However, I wished Colm luck and was then on my way again. I really want Colm to succeed. We are both football mad, and not very good (one much worse than the other), but haven't given up hope. Our paths were now parting but I would continue to think of his quest.

Boarding the plane out of Malta I was a mixture of sadness, trepidation, excitement and generally all-over aching from spending too long lugging heavy bags around and playing football. I vowed to myself that I would never have two different football trials in the space of three days again, it's too much hard work and hell on my body. From now on any trials I am rejected from would be followed by a nice saunter to wherever next is left willing to have me if the budget allows.

Andorra is to be the next stop. Situated in the Pyrenees Mountains sandwiched in between France and Spain, it's one of the smallest principalities in the world and easily reached by bus from northern Spain. Simple. Unfortunately, due to the bus schedule to Andorra, I was to be stranded in Barcelona for three days. After Andorra, if I failed, the plan was to move on to San Marino. Now sat down in a 4-star hotel in Barcelona (cheaper than any hostel we could find thanks to a last-minute internet deal) we discussed our next moves.

'Where is San Marino?' asked Tristan, flicking through his iPhone.

'It's a mountainous country landlocked by Italy, a bit like Andorra .'

'And how are we going to get there?'

'Well there's a tourist resort called Rimini at the bottom of the mountain we could fly to, and then we'll get a taxi up there. Or we can get a boat from Barcelona to Genoa on the west coast, and then make our way through Italy's cities on the train network.'

'Sounds like a plan.'

Indeed and it was a decent plan. However, looking at the cost of flights to Rimini from Barcelona, and the length of time it would take to get to Genoa on a boat, both of those options were immediately ruled out. Me and Tristan hadn't so much as moved from our breakfast table outside the hotel and immediately the San Marino leg of the trip was in jeopardy.

'When is the trial in San Marino ?' asked Tristan, looking agitated.

'Well that's the thing, they said they wouldn't know the training schedule until the 8th or 9th, so we don't actually know yet which day they'd be willing to accommodate me.'

'And what's the date today?' asked Tristan, polishing off another coffee.

'The 5th.'

'I think you should call him try and get it arranged sooner, otherwise we're going to be stuck in Andorra not knowing what we're doing next.' Tristan was donning his big brother hat.

'Well that's the other thing, he doesn't speak English. Whenever I've emailed him it's taken ages for him to reply because he has to translate it, then translate his own message into bad English, so calling him isn't going to work.'

'Okay,' said Tristan through gritted teeth. 'When's your trial in Andorra?'

'Don't know.'

My lack of research into these trials was really beginning to tell.

'What do you mean you don't know?'

'Well it's either the 8th or 10th. Just don't know for sure because their contact hasn't got back to me yet.'

'So, as it stands you don't actually have any more confirmed trials, as in dates?' Tristan was losing his patience a bit.

'I've got one in Lithuania .'

'Where's Lithuania?'

'Don't know really. I want to say somewhere near Poland but I wouldn't bet on it.'

Normally I don't act so stupid, but watching Tristan get more and more infuriated with my complete lack of organisation was making me smile inwardly a great deal.

'So what are we going to do then?' asked Tristan, almost smashing his fist into the table.

'Well the San Marino trial is definitely on, so in a worst-case scenario we can just turn up and have the trial there and then. But then I don't know how we'd get there; the cost of the flight is ridiculous.'

'We could take a boat!' Tristan's eyes turned from rage to roaring excitement.

'We've just seen the ferry takes almost two days and it's too expensive, plus I am not spending a night on some sort of Italian booze cruise.'

'We don't have to get a ferry.'

Tristan wasn't making any sense…

When people mention Barcelona you think of beauty, passion, Gaudi's architecture, an incredible football team and incredible nightlife. It is one of the most beautiful cities in the world, apparently. When I think of Barcelona, however, I think of boats, boats and more boats. Lots and lots of boats. Thousands of boats in fact, some big, some small and some of the most expensive the world has ever seen.

In our meeting of minds over breakfast Tristan thought it would be a good idea to get a boat from Barcelona across the Mediterranean to Genoa and then get a train from there up to San Marino, assuming the unexpected happened and I didn't make it in Andorra. Pretty much exactly the same plan as my own, except he thought it would be a good idea if we could try and blag a lift. On a yacht. With an eccentric millionaire. He thought this was a good idea. His case was: 'Football brings loads of people together, we've seen that. If we just tell people what you're doing then maybe they'll give us a lift.' I was immediately and foolishly won over by the romance of it all. He and I both believed this was a good idea.

What Morons.

Armed with flyers printed off from the most expensive internet café in Spain we walked the boardwalks of many marinas on Barcelona 's seafront, pestering Captains and deck-hands to try and get a lift to Genoa. The flyer simply said:

Young aspiring footballer and a Cameraman are looking to see if they can get a lift from Barcelona to Genoa or anywhere on the South Coast of France. If you or anyone else are heading that way then please contact me on xxxxxxxxxxx@yahoo.co.uk or on 004479XXXXXXXXX. You will be thanked greatly in the film.

Muchos Gracias,

Ralf Haley.

Two days we spent doing this. Two days. That's not right. In hindsight I would have quite liked to go and do something else in Barcelona, I'm sure we could have found something to do amongst all the bars, markets and museums. Hell, I could have even visited the Nou Camp, home of the greatest football team in the world, Barcelona FC, with its incredible history. But did I? Nope. I decided I would be a posh tramp, trying to get a lift on a yacht. Idiot.

At the time though, this seemed like the best option, and if I could get a lift then it would save hundreds of pounds on my budget, thus enabling me to continue to have trials until the dream is realised.

At one stage I was drinking beer whilst sat on Barcelona's vast promenade watching the city and its many beautiful women go by me. That itself sounds romantic (or lecherous). However, when you factor into the equation that I was making dozens of paper aeroplanes out of our fliers in order to launch them over the posh marina fences, and hopefully onto the deck of one of the more expensive-looking boats, you begin to question my sanity, which I now know I lost in that office job of mine sometime the year before. As for my brother's sanity, I think Tristan lost his mind when it dawned on him this was a football trip, which he should have realised beforehand really.

Dozens upon dozens of paper aeroplanes made their merry way through the air and onto the decks of those incredible-looking ships. It was quite a sight, and suffice to say me and Tristan got a few funny looks from tourists, boat owners and locals alike.

'Ralf look we've got to flyer that one!' said Tristan, pointing towards a boat the size of Buckingham Palace.

'No way, that's massive. We'd never get a lift on that.'

And we wouldn't, it would cost a million pounds in petrol to move that ship out of the harbour.

'The Al-Mirqab,' said Tristan, gazing up at the name of the boat. 'Sounds like it's owned by a Qatari oil sultan or something. Oh come on if you don't try you don't succeed.'

'There's no chance, I'm not wasting the flyers on that.'

I think the flyers were already a waste come to think of it.

'But it'd be so good wouldn't it? Oh, hang on,' Tristan paused. Maybe the penny had dropped that we could not get a lift on a boat this size. 'They're Muslims aren't they? They won't have any alcohol on board.'

Unbelievable.

'I think that would be the least of our worries if the Sultan of Qatar or wherever it is was willing to give us a lift to Italy in his floating palace. If his fridge didn't have beer on board I really wouldn't care. Look, that boat over there only looks like it has 12 bedrooms, lets try that one.'

'There's no need to be so harsh. Not everyone is like you, being horrible to Special Olympics.'

'You know it's a tradition in this country for stupid blonde curly haired idiots trying to hitch-hike on a boat to shut up!'

'Slag.'

'Slag.'

Two days! At this juncture I decided to hold off on emailing my San Marino contact, simply out of embarrassment that my trial with them hinged on whether or not I could get a lift on a yacht. All we could do was wait.

Having spent two thirds of our stay in Barcelona attempting to hitch-hike in luxury we demanded that we deserved a night out. My next trial still had no definite date, nor did San Marino.

Having never been to Barcelona before I followed Tristan's lead, as he had been to the city three times previously, and was now a tourist veteran. After catching the underground which is infinitely nicer, cleaner, more spacious and better run than London's Tube we emerged through the exit of the Catalunya stop, there we saw a kaleidoscope of people in the town's flagship square, which was abuzz with vitality. It amazed me how, despite it being 10pm in the evening, kids were still in the street playing. Under no circumstances would kids as young as six be able to run around London's main attractions at night without attracting attention or raising a few eyebrows but here it was simply accepted. We decided to eat at a delightful small restaurant called McDonalds. The food may have been horrible but the price was far more acceptable to my palate than any of the other restaurants in the area. I even managed to exhibit my patronising slow English voice to the person serving us, only for them to reply in an American accent that had more than a touch of annoyance in its tone. I so wanted to eat Tapas and dine on wine but the reality was that I had a tight budget and I needed to eat on the cheap if I was to string out this trip and have as many trials as possible.

As Tristan and myself made our way through the bars of Barcelona drinking beer and cocktails I was beginning to wonder whether or not I should just hit the whole football thing on the head and accept I was not going to be a professional footballer. Most people at some point in their lives go travelling; my trip is with an aim though but its occupied 99% of thoughts and activities since leaving England. I was hoping it would be more of a 50/50 balance of football and leisure, but it seems to have turned out to be far more hard work than I anticipated. If I couldn't make it in Malta how on earth would I make it in a country that is bigger and better at football? I wasn't drinking because of that though – I still wanted to be a professional footballer – the drinks were simply a reward after an intense week; even the world's greatest athletes are allowed to blow off steam. The clubs in Andorra weren't answering my calls or emails, no yacht was willing to give us a lift and Lithuania was thousands of miles away (probably) so I think I warranted a night off.

More drinks flowed, and here is where my memory gets sketchy. I remember having a Mojito that cost Tristan £16, and from there Tristan somehow convinced me that going to a casino was a good idea. As we entered we were asked for ID. I had mine and was glad that Tristan did not have his, as the policy of the casino is 'no ID, no entry', regardless of how old you look.

As we drunkenly exited I heard a familiar voice that I couldn't quite place. I turned round to find out who it was with this voice that rang a thousand bells in my mind.

Hiccupping and stumbling round, I squinted at the owner of this unique voice that I had known all of my life. My drunken eyes aligned themselves and there he was.

Boris Becker.

The former Tennis world number one and winner of three Wimbledons, Boris Becker.

One more time for clarity: *Boris Becker*.

I couldn't believe my eyes.

This man is a legend. In total he won six grand slam titles and over £10million in prize money. He retired at the age of 31 and has since led an incredible lifestyle, illustrated by him casually hanging out in Barcelona casinos on Saturday nights. I needed to meet him; I needed to document this moment in my History.

'Do you know who that is?' I asked Tristan, gazing at Boris Becker.

'No.' Tristan's knowledge of sport was shining through again.

'That's Boris Becker. *The* Boris Becker. You need to get a photo of me with him.'

Approaching Boris Becker, I couldn't help but be in awe of the man.

'Excuse me Boris, I'm a big fan. Would it be okay to have my picture taken with you?' I asked tremulously, interrupting his conversation.

'Ya sure,' he replied, like only Boris can.

Tristan prepared to take the photo, when something quite surreal happened. Me and Boris Becker were posing for a photo together and, as Tristan readied his small hand-held camera, a wave of staff from the casino started running in our direction, waving arms and screaming 'No pictures, no pictures! No pictures allowed in the casino'. Security and croupiers were running towards us and the receptionist was launching herself over the desk to reach the camera. What were we going to do? I needed this picture with Boris Becker.

Had Tristan already got the picture, were we going to jail?

What was Boris thinking?

A thousand-and-one thoughts raced through my mind. I was frozen. *Bugger*, I thought, *I want my photo with Boris Becker*, So I held my pose, as did Boris, the consummate professional. Then in a moment of greatness that only legends can muster, Boris Becker broke free from his statuesque pose, threw his arms wide, cocked his head to the side and exclaimed 'Hey it's me!' effectively saying 'I'm Boris Becker, I can do whatever the fuck I want.'

As Boris was castigated by the staff and pushed against the wall to be searched I shared a glance with Tristan and mouthed 'Did you get it?' With two thumbs up coming from my brother we both made a break for it, leaving Boris to face the music. That is making the top ten 'Great things to happen to Ralf' list for sure.

The next morning I had a hangover that was awe-inspiring both in its painfulness and its duration.

Memories of a nightclub that smelt like vomit and people drinking and dancing in the streets were buried under a headache and the need to throw up. But that didn't matter, for Andorra had gotten back to me.

'Tristan?'

'Ughhhhh.' said Tristan, clearly not wanting to have any sort of conversation for another eight hours.

'I've got a text message from Andorra; we can train with them tomorrow night. We need to get the bus now.'

'Ugghhhhhhh.'

Chapter 11: Taxi

Stood at Barcelona's central bus station, nursing hangovers, Tristan and I launched our bags into the belly of the vehicle and made our way to our allocated seats where we had agreed that more sleep was in order after eating overpriced sandwiches that disagreed with our tender stomachs. Obviously Andorra isn't a huge tourist trap in the summer, as there were only 12 people on the gargantuan coach. We decided not to sit next to each other so we could sprawl out to achieve slumber.

Unfortunately, I couldn't sleep. I was too preoccupied thinking about the previous seven days. I'd failed in two football trials and had only managed to arrange one further one in Andorra, still having no concrete dates from the rest of the European clubs I'd spoken to. I'd already spent £400 of my £1500 budget, and so any hopes of doing this until I succeeded were dwindling. Counting the pennies was now as prevalent in my mind as was becoming a professional footballer. Because of this I decided we would camp in Andorra rather than stay in another 4-star hotel and so, using bad French on the phone, I'd managed to book us a spot where we would stay and hopefully curtail the money leaking from my pockets.

The coach crawled through the suburbs of Barcelona towards the highway, passing by the largest football training complex I'd ever seen. Dozens of pitches, small and large, with high-rise floodlights and the flag of Barcelona Football Club draped all around it. I still can't believe I went to Barcelona and didn't visit the Nou Camp and I am angry at myself for this. Would I have visited if Tristan hadn't come along? Most definitely. This was the only time I regretted my brother joining me on this trip.

The journey itself took a little under three hours. It was scheduled to take four, but the driver didn't seem to know where his brake pedal was, and when it came to tight hairpin corners that overlooked severe drops down into a valley he obviously thought attack was the best form of defence by accelerating into them. I'm a nervous flyer, but strangely okay with overweight Spanish men driving at ridiculous speeds on mountainous roads on a rickety bus with no seatbelts. Rising higher and higher, civilisation eventually gave way to the odd small house or farm, which dotted the landscape.

Situated in between two very green mountains, Andorra's capital city is aptly called Andorra La Vella, and is built around the very clean-looking Valira river. The city is about the same size as my thumb, but it would be home for a while. I expected Andorra to be all dirt tracks, small sheds and snow-capped mountains, but what we found as we pulled into the modestly sized bus terminal was yet another concrete paradise, with 5-star hotels everywhere, shops selling expensive jewellery, and more car showrooms than anyone's eyes could handle. Having now read up on it, it was a bit naïve to think of it as purely a farm country.

Andorra itself has a population of about 80,000 with Andorra Le Vella accommodating 30,000 of those. Andorra natives, of which there are 27,000, make up less than half the population, with Spanish (30,000) Portuguese (17,000) and French (5,000) making up the majority. There are no famous sports people from Andorra that I know of, which I suppose can only be a good thing, and the highest level of football teams they have are semi-professional, with their internationals making a living as bakers or bankers. Obviously other professions are allowed but I'm not going to list them all. It is also a tax haven, much the same way as Switzerland, with little or no tax existing on products, hence the jewellery shops and car showrooms. It is obviously a good area to visit if you want an expensive purchase at a knock-down price. Its biggest industry by far is winter tourism for the ski season, however I am here to play football, and how many tourists in Andorra can say that? Coming here in summer is obviously a bad idea, as it doesn't seem to be the most exciting place. It's also the only country in the world whose official language is Catalan, followed by Spanish, Portuguese and French. This was going to prove problematic for us, and I was about to find out just how problematic.

We needed to get to the campsite and, annoyingly, Tristan's phone wouldn't give us directions, probably because it had never heard of Andorra, so we would have to do it the old-fashioned way. Getting into the Tourist Information office was no easy feat. In fact the Tourist Information office was so small that only I could fit in there, and only after shedding the bags, leaving Tristan outside to watch all our worldly possessions.

'Hello, do you speak English?' I asked.

'Pardon?' The receptionist said with a Spanish/French accent.

'Parlez vous anglais si vouz plait?' I repeated in broken French.

'No. Catalan, Espania, Portuguese, Francais.'

Bugger. In Malta they spoke English, in Barcelona they spoke English, but here, it appeared they did not. The arrogance of the British for centuries has known no bounds, as we just go anywhere in the world to a restaurant and ask for a full English without even reading the menu. I have inherited the belief that everyone in the world should speak English, and this means that my language skills are pretty much non-existent, but there was no choice – it was time for my sub-standard GCSE French to shine. All I needed was directions to our campsite.

'Vouz parlez francais? [You speak French?]' I asked, doing the only sentence I know fluently.

'Oui. Un petite-peu. (Yes, a little.)'

I froze; I didn't know what to say next.

'Je Voudrais directions to Campsite Vella,' (I would like directions for Campsite Vella) I ventured, fervently pointing at the name of the campsite in our guidebook. Always a good way round things when language is a problem, lot and lots of pointing.

'Campsite Vella?'

'Yes, I mean *Oui,* Campsite Vella.' I said stumbling.

'Okay.'

Excellent, we were getting somewhere, I was better at this than I remembered. He continued :

'Ce que vous devez faire est de marcher hors d'ici, de nouveau à la route principale qui est ici sur la carte, la droite de tour et ses environ un et demi kilomètres en bas de la route sur votre gauche.'

Oh dear.

'I'm sorry you wouldn't mind repeating that please?' I said with a furrowed brow deeper than the Grand Canyon.

'Pardon?' He said, matching me in the furrowed brow stakes.

'Erm, *répéter les directions. Je écouter si vous plait.* (Repeat directions. I listen please.)'

'Eh? (Eh?)'

We were both struggling with this.

'Je voudrais Je veux des directions pour Campsite Vella. Où habite-t-il? (I want directions for Campsite Vella. Where does it live?)'

'Okay. ce que vous devez faire est de marcher hors d'ici, de nouveau à la route principale qui est ici sur la carte, la droite de tour et ses environ un et demi kilomètres en bas de la route sur votre gauche.'

Arrrggghhhh!

What was I going to do? I didn't understand anything coming out of his mouth, not at that speed anyway.

But then I had it – we'd get a taxi. That's all I needed, a taxi, and it'd take us there.

'Merci Beaucoup. (Thanks a lot).' Pretending I had understood every word. *'Je Voudrais une taxi si vous plait.* (I would like a taxi please).'

'Taxi?' he queried, as if I'd asked him if he would like to sit on my face.

'Oui, une taxi,' I replied, deadpan.

'Non Taxis dans Andorra. (no taxis in Andorra.)'

'No taxis in Andorra?' I said, furrowed brow returning.

Everywhere has taxis, no matter how small a place.

'Non, Andorra tres petite (Andorra very small),' he said.

'Okay.' I said, struggling what to do now. There were no taxis and this man didn't speak English and I didn't speak any of his four languages. I know, I thought, I'll ask again.

'Je voudrais Je veux des directions pour Campsite Vella. Où habite-t-il? (I want directions for Campsite Vella. Where does it live?)'

He rolled his eyes; we were back to square one.

I can't say how long I spent attempting to get directions to the campsite but finally, using a complex numbering system, I managed to work out how far I needed walk and which streets to take. Exiting the office armed with a map of Andorra which was almost as big as Andorra itself, I was ready to hit the road.

'You took your time,' said Tristan standing up from our assortment of bags.

'He didn't speak English and I only speak tremendously bad French when English isn't an option.'

'So where is it then?'

'That way,' I said, pointing in several directions at once, my eyes fixed on the map.

'And how far is it?'

'We'll find out.'

We picked up our bags and made our way using blind luck as our navigation system. Just as we reached the main road, a Taxi sped past into the distance.

Finding the campsite was as easy as the man made it out to be, even though we hadn't understood each other. It was surprisingly close to the city centre and we reached our destination after just 15 minutes.

Situated on the side of a leafy hill at the foot of a mountain, the campsite was picturesque and peaceful; they even had wifi and a pool. As campsites go it was pretty snazzy, although the distinct lack of grass did seem to be a major oversight. Pitching a tent on concrete is never a good idea, and sleeping on it isn't much fun. This campsite had no grass whatsoever. Camping on grass was obviously a concept that hadn't reached Andorra yet. We had little choice but to pitch our tent on solid rock.

As I watched Tristan do the manly task of putting up the tent using a small rock as a hammer to drive pegs into yet more rock, I got a bit bored and decided to have a wander. As I walked the perimeter of the site I noticed that the area overlooked a very small football stadium with just one stand. Funny, I thought, this trip seems to have had plenty of coincidences, being picked up by a former footballer as soon as we touched down in Malta , meeting Colm and Nigerian Ralf, and now having a view of someone's stadium, it all was a tad weird. I then thought how random it was for Andorra to even have a football stadium, there's only 80,000 people who live here. How many football stadiums does it have? I set out to find out and after speaking to some of the other residents in caravans who seemed to live there and whose English was way better than my French it turns out the answer is just one. It happens to be the stadium for every club, as well as the national stadium. By sheer chance I was staying at a campsite that overlooked Andorra 's national stadium.

My train of thought was interrupted by Tristan who had successfully put up the tent despite the lack of soft ground to insert the pegs into. The tent itself was a fair two-man size. However, our bags were the size of three men, meaning that space within would be at a premium.

Tristan wanted me to ring Diogo Festa – my contact at the football club FC Lusitanos who had set up the trial – to ensure it was still on the next day. I'm consistently reluctant to call anyone when overseas because of the charges incurred, but this time I admitted it was a necessity.

The phone rang for an age, until a rustle and slow groan drifted down through.

'Hello Diogo?'

'Yes?'

I had never spoken to Diogo verbally, only via email or text. It took him about seven seconds to come out with his 'Yes'; he seemed a bit slow.

'It's Ralf Haley, the English footballer.'

'Oh, hello Ralf,' said Diogo, far too slowly for my phone bill's liking.

'I was just calling to make sure that my trial was still on for tomorrow and I could come and train with you?'

'What? There are no trains in Andorra.'

'No, sorry not train, play football with you in a trial.'

'Yes, yes it should be okay. It's a national holiday tomorrow, though, it's Saints day, so we may not be training.'

'What?'

Looking at my tent and the environs of Andorra, the thought of having to hang about for my trial was not something that appealed.

'Yes, everything will be closed, and we practise on Tuesdays, but I'm not sure if we will be playing tomorrow because of the holiday. I will ask tomorrow and let you know. Bye.'

That was it. I looked at my phone and calculated that short conversation, had cost me £3. I looked around. We were in a country where the only things to do were skiing and walking. Me and Tristan are neither fans of skiing nor walking, and given it was summer there was a distinct lack of snow anyway. Staying in a tent with no form of entertainment and potentially no trial for three long days my heart sank. Barcelona is famous for so many things that the tourist can do; Andorra is famous for naff all. Only I could plan something that that would give us three days in Barcelona, spending the majority of the time begging for a lift on a yacht, followed by god-knows-how-long in Andorra with nothing to do. I decided to go to bed early that night. In fact I went to bed at 9:30pm, on a mattress that was literally a bed of rock in a country that was about to shut down for 24 hours, with not enough space in the tent to roll over. Peachy.

The next morning I was begging my phone to ring. Everywhere in Andorra was closed. I attempted to go to an internet café as soon as I awoke, but nothing was open. Literally nothing. No one was around in the small town. It was like a scene from a post apocalyptic film – the streets were empty and my footsteps echoed through the valley.

The national holiday is called Lady of Merixtell (*Mare de Merixtell*). In the late 12th century a wild rose in bloom was found by villagers from Merixtell going to mass in a neighbouring town called Canillo. It was out of season and at its base was found a statue of Mary and Jesus, a statue no one knew about. The statue was placed in the Canillo church. However, the statue was found under the same wild rose the next day. The statue was then taken to the church of Encamp. However, as before, the statue was found under the same wild rose the next day. The villagers of Meritxell took this as a sign and decided to build a new chapel in their town after they found an open space miraculously untouched by the winter snows. I've heard better reasons to have a national holiday, but each to their own. The original statue was destroyed in a fire on 8th September 1972 and a replica was built, which is now housed in the Chapel. I tried to see it, but of course the bugger was closed.

Where was everyone? If this was England and everyone was on a national holiday, the streets would be lined with drunken idiots, even if it was still only 10am. Returning to the campsite to see Tristan manufacture the first of what would prove to be many ham and cheese sandwiches, I was tetchy. and not just because he is lactose intolerant and the cheese would have serious repercussions on his digestive system in our small tent. Did I or did I not have a football trial in the next few hours? Thankfully, my phone finally buzzed.

'Hello?' I said. I waited for an answer but there seemed to be no one there one there 'Hello?' I repeated.

'Hello Ralf, its Diogo,' he droned, in a voice about four octaves deeper than yesterday, and at an even slower pace. It had obviously been a heavy night for Diogo. 'You can train today, we train at 8 tonight but I can meet you at 5 in town so we can talk, and you can meet the President of the club.'

Diogo was still speaking very slowly; I was glad that this conversation was going on his phone bill.

'That's sounds excellent,' I said 'I know the tourist information office, I can meet you there?'

'Okay, I will meet you then.'

Thank god. I had been in Andorra less than 12 hours and I was already starting to lose my mind but at least I had a trial. For the first time since leaving the UK I didn't feel sore, or tired or seriously dehydrated. I was back to thinking I may have a chance.

The time was approaching 5:20pm and Diogo still hadn't turned up. Sat outside that tourist information office in a town that seemed to be mourning the passing of its revered leader, I was not in the best of moods. Why was he so late? Where was everyone? What was I doing in Andorra? Tristan had his camera pointed at my face as I looked severely annoyed at our predicament. I hate lateness, it's my second biggest pet hate behind people who cause queues at train station ticket offices. If you want the information about a train, look at the boards or go to the information stand, not the ticket booth. It's a similar thing with lateness. Why say 5pm when you are clearly going to rock up at 5:30pm? And that's exactly what he did. Another tanned young man wearing a baggy chequered shirt and the darkest shades I have ever seen strolled up to me at 5.30pm on the button, whilst giving a casual army salute.

'Hello Ralf,' said Diogo, removing his shades to reveal bags under his eyes that suggested he hadn't slept in four days. 'Sorry I'm late. I had to go to the bank and I have some Swedish girls staying with me. I needed to make sure they were okay before I left.'

All was forgiven.

My lack of research into the clubs and countries we were visiting had caused a few problems, such as not having trials nailed down or even knowing restrictions on signing foreigners, but it also had its plus points. I was enjoying the mentality of going to the clubs who had said yes to my initial email and letting fate do the rest. Whenever I first met the contact at the club, that was the first time I learnt anything about them and I liked this element of surprise.

Diogo was the director of communications of FC Lusitanos and informed us that the team was set up in 1999 by Portuguese residents of Andorra. Diogo said that they only have Portuguese players on their books. At this moment my heart stopped, thinking that I would have to become a Portuguese national to play for this team, but he allayed any fears when he said 'We welcome all nationalities though and we are always looking to improve.' Could I potentially improve this team?

Diogo led us to the club headquarters, which were a short walk away, even by Andorra's standards. Normally the 'headquarters' would be an office or stadium, but instead he took us to a Portuguese bar that the players and fans frequent together and that is owned by the club President, who of course is Portuguese. Walking through the smoke emanating from cigarettes it was like something out of the Sopranos. The walls were decorated with FC Lusitanos memorabilia, with a white, red and green theme. Card games were being played at most tables. We were then taken round the back and introduced to some board members and from the crowd emerged the President. He was 5ft 3in tall and evidently hadn't smiled in about 10 years. He looked like a mob boss. At that point I honestly thought I was having a trial with a Mafia-financed football club. He led us next door to the club's offices.

'Diogo, what does the president think about what I'm doing?'

After a brief exchange between the two, during which the President's face became even sourer, Diogo provided the broken translation.

'He thinks it's brilliant and he thinks it is sad that you didn't have the opportunity in England, but he admires that you are willing to go anywhere to achieve your dream.'

Now for the question that I was most interested in.

'And what sort of finances does the club have? Do they have any money to pay players?'

'No.'

Shit.

He continued: 'The only money the players get is bonuses if they win a trophy or cup competition.'

'Oh okay. Are you a successful club?'

'Not really, but we have more fans than anyone else in Andorra. However, we don't have as much money, and so our best players are often offered money to switch clubs, and we can't stand in their way.'

'So this club is like a shop window?' I asked, seeing a spark of potential in playing for this club.

'Shop window?'

'Yes, they play for you and if they do well a bigger club will sign them.'

'Yes, that is the case. But we aren't the worst team in Andorra. Last season we finished 4th out of 8 and were runners up in the cup. We lost 6-1 in the final but our fans still made the most noise; we have the best fans and they love the club and we love them.'

Diogo loved the football team and showed a passion for it despite clearly being hung-over. The club at times got attendances of up to 1,800 people, which for a population like Andorra's is an impressive feat.

The President then left to attend to more urgent business. I dread to think what it was – probably to order a hit on me and Tristan. Diogo was then free to show us around properly. He was also in charge of the press side of things and keeping the books and registration of the players. The office was adorned with pictures of the President meeting famous people from world football. One picture in particular that caught the eye was of him meeting Luis Figo. Figo, with his hair gelled up and then back in the Portuguese fashion, stood there beaming his Hollywood smile to camera, next to the stony faced president of FC Lusitanos. He had just met arguably one of the greatest players of all time, one that his country Portugal had produced, and yet he stood there looking as if Figo had just insulted his mother before the flash went off. The President was the man with the money who could pay me – if Figo couldn't make him smile then I certainly couldn't, thus reducing any chances of getting either a game or payment.

I didn't like the laid back way Diogo had arranged my trial, or his timekeeping, but he was a very friendly, easy going man – even if the language barrier reared its ugly head on a few occasions.

From what had been said it didn't seem there was an issue with me playing in Andorra, but for me to be paid I would either have to win a cup competition with FC Lusitanos and subsequently be paid a bonus, or sign with them and then, over the course of six months, impress the clubs with the money who would then sign me and pay me. Living in a tent for six months seemed like a big sacrifice to make, but just like what happened at St Georges, once I was amongst the club's history, speaking to members of the club and the passion they had for it, I was enamoured by the sport once more and wanted to achieve my dream no matter what. I just wanted to make sure I could sign.

'Are there any barriers to you signing a foreign player?' I asked.

'No, none at all. Of course, to be registered with a football club in Andorra you need to have a job, and to have a job you need to be able to speak either Spanish, Catalan or French, but the ski resorts would accept English.'

Hmm. Working in a Ski resort in order to become a professional footballer isn't a path the game's greats would have had to walk I imagined, but I have little choice… so why not? Oh yeah, there's sod all to do in Andorra and I didn't want to live in a tent, that's why.

'We go back to the bar now,' Diogo said. 'Maybe have something to eat and we will drive you to training. You have your passports don't you?'

'Sorry?'

'Passports. You need your passport to cross the border into Spain.'

'You train in Spain?'

'There are trains in Spain, yes.'

'No, sorry, you practise, training in Spain?' I asked, miming playing football using my fingers in the air in a scissor like motion.

'Oh yes, of course we practise in Spain .'

I thought things couldn't get weirder.

Apparently, because land in Andorra is so expensive, it's not unusual for people to buy land in Spain or France and live there, and then commute to work in Andorra, or as in the case of FC Lusitanos and other clubs, buy the land with the help of UEFA and then train on it. Of course we didn't have our passports, and so we had to walk back to the campsite to get our documentation, thankfully minus the bags this time.

We were picked up by Tony, one of the players, who had a very nice car. Unfortunately, I can't comment further on that because my knowledge of cars and what questions to ask when someone buys a new one ranges from 'What colour is it?' to 'How many gears?' The latter question I stole from my limited childhood knowledge of mountain bikes.

Tristan on the other hand was in his element, sat in the front seat speaking to Tony (who was fluent in English) about all the features. As Tony showed off the speed of his toy to Tristan, I was wedged in the back seat, with no seatbelt, between Diogo and a club director who only spoke Portuguese, Spanish, Catalan and Italian. I took this opportunity to speak to Diogo, seeing as he was the only one who could speak English who wasn't talking about 'brake horse power' or what-have-you. It turned out his throwaway comment about the Swedish girls was true, and they were couch surfing for a few days. He only accepts women onto his couch because, as he says, 'they are more fun', and who can blame him? He seemed to be a man of the world, laid back and football-loving..

Couch surfing, if you don't know, is a very cheap way to travel. By using a sort of dating website, but for couches, people who are willing to let travellers sleep on their couch for a particular period put their details online, and then those travellers search to see if there is a couch available to match up with their travel times. It's free and is built on trust and a vouching system to ensure the safety of the hosts and visitors, and the idea is that once you have finished your travelling experience you then put your details online, thus passing on the favour to the next set of travellers. I had considered doing this myself, but once Tristan was on board the chances of getting someone to put us up dwindled immediately. Added to that, Tristan wasn't so keen leaving so much expensive equipment lying around the apartments of people we didn't know, and I fully understood that. It would have been a great way to save money, but I was grateful for having Tristan there, especially at times like this, speeding through the Pyrenees Mountains with no seatbelt.

When we reached the Andorra-Spain border I wasn't required to present any documentation, thus rendering our mad dash back to camp pointless. However, Tony was asked to open his boot by border control in order to show that he didn't have several thousand packets of tax-free cigarettes stowed away. I thought this was a bit silly – he was having to prove that his passengers, who comprised a man with an oversized camera, a clearly hung-over man, a young man in football kit and older man in a football tracksuit weren't just there as one of the most random and worst cover-ups for a smuggling operation known to man. Thankfully, Tony hadn't resorted to smuggling, at least not that night anyway, and we were allowed into Spain for my trial to take place.

The training pitch was situated further down the river that ran through Andorra Le Vella, and was about a ten minute drive into Spain. Lit up by floodlights and quite clearly another modern astroturf pitch similar to the one at St Georges FC, it seemed that the Andorran league was quite professional. From the car I could even see the windows of changing rooms – this was certainly a step up for me.

Upon exiting the car, though, the training facilities went down severely in my estimation. The humidity was about 90% for reasons unbeknown to me, and I was immediately drenched because of it. We were on a mountain, a thousand metres up, the air should be fresh. Furthermore, there was a strong smell of dead meat on the air, and the vast quantity of mosquitoes and flies that hovered continuously over my head weren't exactly welcoming. Due to the darkness it took me a while to realise that this training facility was bought on a swampland – the constant soundtrack of crickets and insects combined with the humidity being a dead giveaway. I hadn't kicked a football or done any warm-ups but I immediately felt that a shower was in order.

Diogo introduced me to the coach, Francois, who, like the rest of the team, was Portuguese, and spoke just the three languages of Portuguese, Spanish and Catalan, so Diogo had to translate. A rotund man, he was the type of coach I was expecting to encounter at all the clubs I visited. He looked like an England Sunday League coach. He was wearing shorts that showed off legs that were in far better shape than the rest of him, and a T-shirt that, if it could speak, would have been screaming under the pressure of staying intact around his ample figure. He seemed happy for me to be there and led me to the dressing room where I was introduced to 15 or so different people, five of whom were called Hugo and where I was relieved to see that none of the players were in matching kit, or even Lusitanos colours, confirming that they were as amateur as could be. I then was sat down on a bench and told to await further instructions. Those instructions would be a while coming, as Francois was giving his team a talk about what he thought of their previous performance.

Sat in a changing room in Spain with 16 Portuguese people for a trial with a football club based in Andorra, my mind began to wander as I finally realised why so many foreign players in England struggle to 'settle'. For years as a football fan I would get excited by a big name foreign player coming to England, only to see so many of them struggle. Sebastian Veron and Andriy Shevchenko were signed for £28million with Manchester United and £31million with Chelsea respectively, but both failed in the Premier League despite being world class players in Italy, and went on a downward spiral in their careers after leaving those clubs. It's understandable why people would struggle, but it was only being made so startlingly apparent to me now I was living it and without the talent of Veron or Shevchenko. The language difference, lifestyle shift and complete change in style of football that they are used to makes many foreign players suffer. Some take to it like a duck to water but many drown, and sat in this changing room with everything that had gone on in the last 24 hours, not understanding a word that was being uttered, I felt like I couldn't breathe.

Once the team talk was over we exited towards the pitch to do our warm up. Another tame warm up I'm glad to say, similar to St Georges, with a couple of laps of the pitch and some minor sprint work, and not a cone in sight – that was all well and good for me.

As always, the camera was raising a great deal of interest from the players as we ran round the pitch at a steady pace, although one player didn't seem too bothered. On closer inspection this man looked like the spitting image of American actor Matt Dillon, right down to the square jaw and piercing eyes. If it wasn't for the pony tail I imagine it definitely would have been him. At this point one of the other players approached me.

'So where have you been so far?' asked Roy (pronounced Rlrlrlrloy, basically roll the 'R' at the start, something I was unable to do).

'Just Malta, but I didn't make it there because I was a bit unfit and also there are loads of problems with registering foreign players over there,' I said jogging along side him.

Roy was small and greasy, in the hair department at least, but he was very approachable, and seemed remarkably muscular and youthful-looking for a man who said he was in his mid-30s. His biceps were struggling not to rip his shirt – not grossly muscle-bound, but enough to make me think I wouldn't be going for any 50-50 challenges against him. I was struggling to place his accent, because although it had the Portuguese element to it, it as wasn't as strong as the others and his English was the best we had encountered in Andorra to date.

'You know I used to play in England?'

That's why.

'Really?'

'Yes with Oxford United. We were looking to get promoted to the Premier League but our form tailed off and we had to sell players, then we got injuries. Yeah it was in the mid-to-late 90s; I was playing left midfield for them and I did okay, but then I moved to Germany. The club went into freefall after that.'

'So you've lived the dream then?' I said jealously.

'Yes, but now I'm too old. Anyway, I think what you are doing is great, the human spirit is incredibly powerful and you keep striving for your dream okay? When I was in Germany my career finished when I crashed my Porsche 911 and wrote it off. I was in a coma for three months and the Doctors said I would never play again.' He said this in a remarkably laid back way for something that must have been incredibly harsh.

'Really?' I didn't know what else to say.

'Yeah, but I didn't believe them and wanted to prove them wrong so then I put everything into my recovery and managed to walk again and get back on my feet and then eventually run and be okay. I wasn't the same player but I can still play to a degree.'

Roy's story was amazing; a further reminder of how great football can be.

'Football is great isn't it?' I said, confirming what he already knew.

'Yes, and it's the same the world over. You go anywhere and you'll find it's all the same, except in China where they've all got smaller dicks.' He then did a masturbating motion with his hand, jigged on the spot and laughed with the team-mates who overheard and understood the comment before sprinting off to be the head of the jogging pack. What an odd end to our discussion. Perhaps he hadn't fully recovered from that coma?

After our light jog came the stretching exercises. We stood in a circle in the centre of the pitch, and the coach led the way. With my muscles fully recovered from Malta, I was hoping to show some sort of limberness, only for Francois to completely outdo me and stretch every muscle you can think of beyond what looked natural for a man of his stature. As he stood upright keeping his legs kept straight and lunging down to place both his palms onto the floor to stretch his hamstrings I was aghast, and it seemed his t-shirt screamed a little bit more. I couldn't get anywhere near that level of flexibility, and so with a tactical slight bending of the knees I managed to impressively 'fake stretch' my hamstrings. My fingertips would have barely passed my knees if I'd attempted it properly.

More so than in the other trials so far, there seemed to be real interest in me. Francois was keeping a keen eye on me during the warm-up and stretching, and he obviously wanted to know if I could play.

After the stretches came some long-range passing. Separated into two lines on each side of the pitch we each took it in turn to strike a ball cross-field 30 or 40 yards to a team-mate, who then returned the favour to the next person in the line. I hung back to wait for my turn and assess the competition, and it was varied. Some passes went straight to the other person's feet or chest; others were hacked at, were sliced or bobbled their way to the other side. My first effort was okay, low and drilled, the ball fizzed across the surface into the other player's shins. My second effort was sliced, and my third was dragged about 10 yards wide of the man I was aiming for. With Francois keeping a keen eye, this was not the best start. Roy, on the other hand, was excellent; with a cultured left foot he casually stroked the ball to the intended target perfectly each time and was certainly one of the better players there, technically at least.

More passing followed, but this time it was with both feet over shorter distances and something even the worst football player in the world can accomplish, so luckily I just about got by with that one. When the session ended, and I'd demonstrated I could use both my feet, the coach gathered us round.

What followed was a lengthy string of Portuguese but I soon figured out that we were to play a game of seven-on-seven by virtue of the bibs being handed out. *Excellent*, I thought, as I swatted a mosquito from my sweaty cheek. What wasn't so excellent was when Francois grabbed a player in a friendly gesture and pretended to knee him in the ribs followed by two thumbs up to his players and then to me. Doing this or being on the receiving end of something like this isn't exactly my cup of tea. I looked round lost on the pitch, not fully understanding what was going on. Thankfully Diogo approached me to say over my shoulder: 'It's going to be a game of handball, and the coach wants as much body contact as possible; it's important you show aggression.' What! Handball? I've never played handball in my life, and I made this known to Diogo.

'Don't worry, its exactly like football,' he assured me.

No it's not! The clue is in the name: *foot*ball, *hand*ball.

I like to use my feet for sport and my hands for more laid back things like cooking, drinking and cuddling. All of a sudden the game had started, with the ball being launched by people who have a skill that I don't have – being able to throw something more than 10 yards and at speed. I was stood there with the game going on around me, with tackles flying in left, right, and centre, the ball flying in all sorts of directions. The tackles looked quick, aggressive and above all, very painful.

'Please don't come to me, ball, please don't come to me,' I muttered under my breath. I looked like a child in an open shopping area who had lost his parents. I was stationary and my bottom lip was quivering, flinching at anything that went by me. All of a sudden these guys seemed about three times bigger than when I first was introduced to them, including Roy who was in the thick of everything. The ball continued to fly at great velocity from player to player with late challenges flying in on those who had just released the ball and early challenges on those who were about to receive it. I wanted no part in this; this was rugby, not football. You can compensate for your physical shortcomings in football with skill and speed of thought, in rugby all you need is to be a big bastard. What I found puzzling is that they were all enjoying it; it was like I was in a parallel universe where pain seemed to be an enjoyable evening out. I glanced over at Francois, only 30 minutes of a two-hour training session had elapsed and I was not doing well. I had to do well, I had to. I started to watch the game more keenly, and decided it was up to me to make the most of my opportunities. I had to get involved and I began to psyche myself up, the way geeks do. I thought of bullies from the past, injustice in the world and the feeling I used to get when my weetabix went soggy too quickly. I began to get furious, raging even; I was like the Hulk.

My eyes were wide open now and my nostrils were flaring, I could feel adrenalin coursing through my veins; I've never felt stronger. I was going to show FC Lusitanos who was the boss, unleashing years of pent up aggression that I'd never used on anything.

I clenched my fists so tight my palms began to scream out in pain and began running towards the opposition player in possession at full tilt, head down, arms pumping and legs smashing me across the ground. Inwardly screaming and with gritted teeth I launched myself at the man in a full on rugby tackle attempt around his waist, and without hesitation my body bounced off his and onto the ground. I was eating dirt and hadn't got anywhere near the ball. I imagine it looked like a poodle attempting to start a fight with a hippo.

I got up, dusted myself down, and felt the most incredible pain in my neck.

I had whiplash.

The shockwave from running into a Portuguese man-mountain had gone through my core and into my neck and stayed there. I couldn't move it right to left or up and down. Marvellous, just marvellous. Up a mountain playing a game of rugby in a football trial and I have an injury.

After limping over to Tristan, whose continued sterling skills on the camera meant that he missed the incident, I got him to give me a neck massage. My brother the cameraman was now my physiotherapist. I was able to once again move my neck but not without a great sense of pain or feeling the rattling of loose cartilage in the top of my spine I decided to continue in the game of handball but in a half-arsed-look-at-my-face-don't-actually-pass-me-the-ball kind of way. The game went on.

And on.

And on… and on.

Four thousand and twenty-three years later, the game finished but the lingering neck injury remained. Playing handball and openly encouraging beating the shit out of each other probably isn't the best way to prepare your team for a match, especially seeing as they said a few people were absent because of injuries. At one stage there was an old-school 'pile-on' where I counted seven people involved in a scrum where limbs could have easily snapped. I attempted to shake my head in disbelief but it hurt too much, so I just tutted like a true English gent. Half the trial had gone and I had no opportunity to impress. I was expecting Francois to gather us round where they would take it all in turn to kick me in the nuts, but that obviously only happened on Wednesdays.

Back to proper football matters, Francois then said we would start to play a normal game of football, which would have been perfect had it not been for my incapacity to travel at more than 1mph without sharp shooting pains down my neck and spine. But opportunities like this don't come around often and so I persevered.

The game started and I did brilliantly. Again like St George's there were no set positions so I decided to sit in the middle of the pitch and direct proceedings from there spraying balls over the park to their required destinations to set our team up for another attack, while putting in a few a timely interceptions; all this and I wasn't really moving much, which given my predicament was perfect. I could feel Francois' eyes burning a hole in the side of my head but didn't know if it was approval or not. Was I playing well or was I delirious from the pain?

I ploughed on, making more passes, reading the game intelligently and getting a foot in when possible. I decided I wasn't delirious, I was actually playing well, and I ensured this time that I wasn't targeting any one specific player unfairly – I didn't want a repeat of the disastrous St Georges trial.

15 minutes in and our side winning comfortably with me actually making a difference, Diogo began to walk through the crowd of running players in the manner of someone crossing traffic not really caring if he was killed or not. Was he really that hung-over? I moved to the side of the pitch with him.

'Ralf. The coach says it is difficult to assess your level of skill in this environment, so we are going to go to the other side of pitch with him and he is going to do some tasks with you and another player to see your skill.'

Get in, a one-on-one chance to shine. We moved to the other side of the pitch, and although I was in agony from my neck the adrenalin was helping me stay light on my feet.

What followed was certainly something that wouldn't happen in a top-tier environment anywhere across Europe. There was me, a young player called Tomas who wasn't taking full part in training because he was slightly unwell, Francois, Tristan and Diogo, with several footballs and all eyes on me. Francois would say something in an animated fashion waving his large hands to help emphasise his point. Diogo would then look lost as he rattled his brain for a translation, then he'd relay the instructions to me in broken English. Sometimes the instructions were spot on, and the skills tests were what I have done in England before, and at other times I was lost, and made sure I let Diogo know. I didn't want to do any of the tasks incorrectly due to a lack of understanding.

Because of this, Diogo illustrated what the coach wanted me to do, such as running with the ball in a tight figure of 8 using only his left foot going one way, and then using only my right the other, or having a ball thrown high in the air that I had to meet with my head mid-jump and nod back to the coach. Diogo illustrated these tasks for me while wearing his loafers, jeans and a baggy shirt, holding a fag in one hand and his shades in the other, and he seemed better at it than me.

Francois and his protégé Tomas began to pass to me in turn, with us stood in a triangle formation. I was barraged by passes on the ground that I had to return to the source with either foot. Although the passes were coming to me at great speed from both of them, one at a time, they only had to go six yards and I did well. Back and forth, back and forth, it was soon like clockwork.

Then came the heading. I'm not averse to heading, I'd just rather not do it, especially not with whiplash. That's not to say I'm no good at it, however, and with Francois throwing the balls in high in the air 6 yards from me I showed a decent level of competency in the jump stakes and headed it back well, and with power to highlight my skill in the air even if I don't enjoy that aspect of the game. Just ten headers were required; I didn't excel, but gathered from Francois' body language and facial expressions, as well as the thumbs up he gave me, that he was happy enough. Maybe he sensed that I wasn't the type of player who would need to be going up in the air for balls like that anyway.

With my neck throbbing and clicking with every rotation away from a stationary position I squinted and continued, this time running figures of 8 between a set of cones with the ball at my feet, speed was key. Unfortunately for me I fell over the first cone, leaving the ball behind me.

'Again!' The coach yelled at me. 'Again!' He seemed to know some broken English when angry.

I dribbled the ball as fast as I could but tackled again by the nemesis cone. I quickly retrieved the ball.

'Again!'

I zig-zagged my way through the cones set before me, the ball barely under control, tackled.

'Again!' The Portuguese seem to have little patience.

I tried once more only to be felled by the cones.

'No! Again!'

Lying there face down in the middle of the Pyrenees Mountains, I slowly pushed myself off the floor, and went again.

Finally I nailed it, and again and again and again, until the coach even had time to take a call and leave me running around for 5 minutes in perpetual motion, his eyes never wavered from me though and my confidence began to soar. I was doing well but needed something to really show off my ability, a blockbuster moment – and my chance was coming.

We made our way to the edge of the penalty area with an empty goal. Francois was to be the goalkeeper and I would stand 30 yards out, pass a ball to the feet of Tomas who had positioned himself on the edge of the penalty area 20 yards out. I would run to the right of him as he returned my pass square and complete the one-two, and I would then shoot 20 yards from goal. It's a technique I have most certainly come across in England to judge a player's ability to strike a ball. With a few short, sharp breaths and a jiggle of my limbs followed by a bit of jumping on the spot, I was ready.

With a crisp fizzing pass to the feet of Tomas I started bombing forward to my position where he brilliantly returned the pass to me so I didn't have to break my stride for the strike at Francois in nets.

20 years of being obsessed with football came down to this moment.

All those hours in the garden, pretending to win the World Cup for England with the last kick of the game, those daydreams in school and work and days on the treadmill at the gym was for this chance, this strike.

With every sinew of my body I lifted my right leg and struck that football with the laces of my boot, with the fury and power of an atomic bomb.

The ball shot through the air, continuously rising and not rotating on its axis.

I had never hit a football so sweet.

It felt like an age but in reality it only took a moment to get to its intended target, such was the ferocity I hit that ball.

The ball went into the top corner of the goal, the net rippled and no goalkeeper from the Pyrenees to the Moon would have stood a chance with that strike.

Francois nodded his approval, as did Tomas.

I didn't celebrate the goal, I needed to look cool and composed as if I scored goals like that every day, but inside I was beaming with pride. Bobby Charlton, Bobby Moore, Gary Lineker, Paul Gascoigne and David Beckham, sit up and take note, there's a new English football legend on the horizon, and that man is me.

Could it happen with FC Lusitanos in Andorra? After such an incredible hit that almost belied the laws of physics – and certainly wasn't an accurate representation of my skills on a football pitch – I felt anything was possible.

If Francois needed to make an immediate decision I'm sure the contract would have been drawn up there and then. Everything clicked into place, quite literally as my neck was even feeling better.

Unfortunately for me, Francois still had me for 15 minutes under the floodlights of the swamp pitch and as so often was the case in my life, with football and indeed with women, it appeared I'd peaked far too early.

Francois asked for the task to be repeated except this time the pass would be returned on the other side, I would have to run to my left and strike it with my left – and considerably weaker – foot. I spoke to myself in those moments, waiting for Diogo to return the ball to me: 'Come on Ralf, Come on!'

I passed to the feet of Tomas, ran, had the pass returned to me, swung my left leg down with all the power I could summon and launched the ball wide and high into the stratosphere helping the team return the ball over the Andorra border. It could not have contrasted with my first shot any more if I had tried. Francois shook his head and I buried mine in my hands.

One more chance to redeem myself was open to me: free kicks. I have never taken free kicks before, ever. There was always a more talented team-mate who would do the duty. Taking free kicks and penalties is seen as a privilege and a reward for the best players as there is a certain amount of prestige associated with them, and so naturally why would I need to practise them? I can kick a ball 30 yards, sometimes 60 with a strong wind and the grace of god behind me, I just wedge my foot under it like a golfer would with his club out of a bunker. But to kick a ball 30 yards with pace, dip, swerve and accuracy as was requested by Francois was not something I could do. Francois, the young player Tomas and Diogo made up the wall to block part of the goal. I had three balls to hit in the style of David Beckham that had to rise over them and then into the net. In my strides up to the first ball I demanded from myself that under no circumstance was this allowed to bounce before it went into the goal. Free kicks that bounce before they go in look terrible.

'Don't bounce, don't bounce don't bounce'.

I hit it; I hit it as hard as I could, attempting to put swerve on the ball.

The ball didn't bounce once… it bounced three times.

By the time the ball got to the net it didn't even shimmer with impact such was the softness I had hit it with. A blind snail using only the sense of smell could have saved that first attempt.

My second wasn't much better, this time again clearing the wall but bouncing twice and going wide, and the third attempt… well, the less said about that the better. Let's just say even a punch-drunk Womble would have been disappointed with it.

Trial over, it was time to see what Francois thought, but I had an inkling it wasn't good news.

'The coach says that you are not good enough to play for our first team,' said Diogo. My inkling was correct. 'Your left foot wasn't good, you lacked any physical aggression and he says you need to be stronger because Andorra is a physical league.'

I kind of expected that feedback but it still didn't stop me feeling upset.

'He also says…' oh good, there's more '…that he thinks what you're doing is great and you are welcome to play with our second team who are of a lower standard, but they play more for fun.'

Hang around in Andorra for purposes of fun? That sounds like a bit of a contradiction.

'Thanks but we'll go to a different country now and see if I can make it there instead. Thanks for your time,' I said.

We shook hands, Francois smiled and made his way over to the other players, probably to talk about the weak, rubbish English kid. Tony, our driver for the evening approached me with a look that said 'Too bad.' He then offered me a cigarette on our way back to the car. I can't even make it in a team where the players smoke. Brilliant.

Back at the bar-headquarters I was offered a free commiseration meal by the President, and a beer that helped numb the emotional and physical pain. He then presented us with shirts from FC Lusitanos, as well as small badges, and with this kind gesture he actually broke into a smile. He doesn't smile for Luis Figo but he sure as hell smiles for me.

Again we had been shown incredible hospitality by our hosts and we were unable to reciprocate the gesture by giving them a decent footballer. We drank our beers, ate our food and made our goodbyes to the players and Diogo before making our way through the permanently sleeping city of Andorra Le Vella. Opportunity number three had come and gone.

Sleeping on a bed of rock in a cramped tent with a brother emitting noxious gases into the small, contained atmosphere of the tent probably wasn't the best thing for someone with whiplash and a bad mood. My neck, I was sure, would be fine in a couple of days. but I wasn't so sure about my mood. With the sun rising over the mountains I stumbled out of the tent for fresh air to clear my head. With no other clubs in the area (or, indeed, all of Western Europe) willing to give me a trial, I needed to think fast. I wasn't the only one panicking. Tristan had been panicking too, as he had no way of viewing the footage he had recorded, so he didn't even know if what he was getting was any good or not, or if it was even in focus. The next morning I sent him to the shops to get me some deep heat for my neck so I could gather a plan together and so that we both could get our heads clear.

A lack of itinerary is often seen as a romantic ideal when travelling, but it didn't help my ambitions. Nobody had got back to me about giving us a lift to Italy on their multi-million pound yacht, which me and Tristan were distraught about. We had rather got used to the idea of sailing across the Mediterranean for a week. With no lift to Italy on the cards, I had to make an executive decision as to 'Where the smeg are we going next?' I immediately sacked off San Marino. The fact that the contact struggled to speak English, and San Marino pretty much being Italy, I decided that they would probably be too good for me. Besides, they are an amateur league so for me to be paid I'd have to be the greatest footballer ever, the fact that I wasn't was something I was now coming to terms with. From there I struggled on that mountain to come up with a plan. We were up shit creek without a boat, never mind a paddle.

I admit I thought about quitting, and voiced the idea of returning back to England. Tristan then literally slapped me round the face.

'You've been waiting all your life for an opportunity like this to be a professional footballer. So what if you've got whiplash? It'll be fine in a couple of days.'

'Did you just slap me?' I said, startled.

'And as for you being shit at football, well we knew that, but now is not the time to give up.'

'Did you just slap me?'

'Come on, this is your dream, and annoyingly it's starting to be mine, to see yours happen – and yes I did slap you.'

'I can't believe you just slapped me!'

'Get over it, you deserved it you pansy. Where are we going next?'

I felt inspired, at last I had a Mr Miyagi, my little Mick from Rocky.

'I'll tell you where we're not going… home.'

'That's it, Betty.'

'Did you just call me Betty?'

'Yup,' said Tristan, happy that he had literally knocked me to my senses.

'The slap was warranted, but don't call me Betty.'

'Fair do's. Come on; plan, Batman.'

I still had provisional yeses from Lithuania, Denmark, Norway, Sweden, Latvia, Estonia, the Faroe Islands, New Zealand, Canada and Kenya, and I still had £1,000 of my budget remaining. Me and Tristan looked at our map of Europe and discovered that Lithuania, Latvia and Estonia are all next to each other and make up the Baltic states, sandwiched between Poland and Russia. For the first time I was learning about European geography without watching the Eurovision song contest. It was decided we would go to Lithuania, then Latvia, and then Estonia, west to east in order.

After a quick phone call, my contact in Lithuania seemed happy with this arrangement and even offered us accommodation with a club representative, which we welcomed as a nice change of pace from camping and hotels. We would arrange Latvia and Estonia en route, because I didn't want to arrange a trial when Lithuania may or may not sign me. There was only one problem with this plan, and it wasn't my neck. I was sure that would be okay in a few days' times given a few more doses of homoerotic rubbing from my brother and several coats of deep heat. The problem was that the distance from Lithuania to Andorra was over 2,000 miles.

The cost of flying from Barcelona to Lithuania with one day's notice? £250.

No thank you.

The cost with two days notice? £180.

The cost to my sanity of staying in Andorra for another 3 days? Not worth it.

We went with the two-day option. Two more days in Andorra, capital of sod-all to do, before a trial in Lithuania, which, after reading the guidebook, didn't seem much better.

It's tough to convey how little there is to do in Andorra if you don't have a bike to go downhill biking on or skis and snow in order to go skiing. You could go for a walk, but if your only walking boots are plimsolls and you have delicate ankles it's probably not advisable, so I didn't bother. Imagine watching paint dry or grass grow and then take away the paint or grass and that closely approximates to Andorra during the summer. Lots of concrete, tarmac and traffic. I'm sure in winter it's a wonderland, with snow-capped mountains and thumping nightlife, but in summer it's far from it. Also because of the strong Euro, the restaurants are over-priced so me and Tristan were living off sandwiches we were making from goods bought at the campsite shop.

In my desperation for some sort of entertainment I texted a lot of people hoping they would call me, and luckily Jack Rodgers, responded.

Speaking to Jack was great, and although I had only been away 10 days I felt like I had so much to tell him, and it was nice to hear enthusiasm about my quest from someone else, because me and Tristan were a bit jaded by the Andorra situation. Conversations about work and football flowed until I mentioned that our campsite overlooked the national stadium.

'Wow that's ace. Are you going to watch the game tonight then?' he asked.

'You what?'

'The game. Andorra vs. Kazakhstan. World Cup qualifier. It's in Andorra isn't it? They're in England's group. We're playing Croatia tonight. Coops' going.'

Of course!

Before I left on this trip, Coop had offered me a ticket to go and see England play Croatia at Wembley in a game that, if we won, would secure our passage to the 2010 World Cup in South Africa. I'd completely forgotten.

'I'm pretty sure its in Andorra,' said Jack. 'Let me have a look.'

Sure enough the game was in Andorra and it was that evening. Brilliant. I went to the tourist information office in haste to try and find out how to get tickets for a game between two of football's international powerhouses. Thankfully I encountered a clerk who could speak English, although I didn't take kindly to them almost laughing at my request. Apparently they don't charge people to see games – people just turn up. It was like football should be, like it was the 19th century.

If the tent had walls I would have been bouncing off them in excitement. Tristan, on the other hand, was far more relaxed, but welcomed the idea of buying a few beers and watching it from our perch on our campsite, because we couldn't be bothered to walk down to the proper seats, plus the beer would be much cheaper from our shop.

Up to this point, Andorra had scored just two goals in their previous 10 games. They were by far the underdogs even though they were at home and against Kazakhstan.

Regular updates from friends filtered through to me that England had scored, again and again, eventually romping to 5-1 win to secure their place in South Africa. Normally I'm the most ardent England supporter, but stood there watching Andorra play Kazakhstan, drinking a beer with the stadium set to a backdrop of the sun setting between two colossal mountains, I was genuinely happy that I was there. Andorra went down 3-0 quite quickly in a rather tame manner, defensive errors and a penalty costing them dear. But when they pulled a goal back to make the final score line 3-1, their home fans went absolutely wild, me included. It was a victory to them that they managed to even score a goal.

Kazakhstan had three fans that didn't stop singing from start to finish. I thought I was committed to what I was doing but flying from Kazakhstan to go all the way to watch a football game against Andorra takes a special kind of commitment, unless there are some Kazakhstanny tax dodgers living in Andorra, then it would have just been a nice evening out for them. I got drunk merely to numb the pain in my neck and loved how I was watching a game of such poor quality, and yet I knew now after recent events that I couldn't play for either of them. I always used to wish I had an Andorran grandparent so I could play international football, but as it turns out even if my family history was that interesting it wouldn't have made a blind bit of difference because I'm not good enough anyway.

The next day myself and Tristan went to a neighbouring town, La Massana, in order to take a ski lift up to the top of one of the mountains in a desperate hope to fill the day. There we had an incredible 360-degree view of the Pyrenees mountain range, and below us the few towns that make up Andorra. From that height, and with the football still fresh in my mind, I understood it a little better, but was still glad to be leaving the next day. I'd never go back to Andorra, and I wouldn't recommend it outside of winter. Our European guidebook covered Andorra for 12 pages out of 700 and that was being generous. However, the people involved with the football club FC Lusitanos, like those in Malta, were good to us. If you're good at football, end up working in Andorra and are Portuguese, then I couldn't recommend them highly enough.

CHAPTER 12: NO TERRORISTS...

To get to Lithuania we had to change flights at Riga in Latvia, ironically a place I hoped to have a trial with in the coming days if it fell through in Lithuania.

Touching down in Latvia there was a noticeable difference in climate and culture to what we had been experiencing. The temperature was cooler and the buildings greyer. The last thing we wanted to do was board another plane, but we had no choice. However, if we thought that Riga's airport couldn't be matched in minute stature, we were mistaken.

We had already been travelling 10 hours in total from Andorra to Barcelona by bus, and then Barcelona to Riga by plane. In Barcelona airport, during some repacking in order to get the weight distribution right between us, disaster had struck. Fishing into my bag to arrange space for more of Tristan's gear such as microphones and clips, my hand delved beneath clothing and football kit and ran into something moist and sticky, and it was everywhere. I retracted my hand with a look of disgust on my face and saw the white tipex like substance on my hands I knew from the pungent smell that it could only be one thing. Deep Heat. It had exploded and leaked all over my clothes, over everything. I was going to be smelling of Deep Heat all across Europe until my dream ultimately came true or ended in defeat. If you don't know what Deep Heat smells like, the only way to describe it is yak's urine if you set it on fire.

Before this whole thing, I knew little of Lithuania. I didn't know its language, its currency, its history or geographic location, and me and Tristan had arranged to spend a minimum of four days there. One day to watch a match, two days of tourism and one day at the end to do the trial. We had arranged to meet Justina and Solus from the club at the airport, and they would drive us to our lodgings.

Justina was the club's press officer and Solus was a club director. The club in question is FK Nevezis, a second-tier team in the semi-professional league of Lithuania. Although much larger than Malta and Andorra, with 3 million people living there, I was hoping that a league structure that was more professional with more teams may lead to a thinning out of talent amongst those teams, rather than the dense concentration of players I'd encountered in Malta and

Andorra. In Andorra there were no more than 16 teams, in Malta 47. In Lithuania, players went from professional to semi-professional, all the way down to amateur and Sunday League. I was hoping gaps in talent needed to be filled.

We were to stay in Kėdainiai, slap bang in the middle of Lithuania. We couldn't work out how to pronounce it, but finally the language school of Ralf and Tristan settled on *Keh-die-nye*. Unfortunately our guide book had no information on the city despite its ample population of 30,000. Andorra had a population of 70,000 but still got 12 pages – surely Kėdainiai should get at least six?

Our news gives us the impression that everything is East Europe is grim and cold and that they are still coming to terms with freedom from the Soviet Regime after they gained independence in the early 90s and the film Borat did little to detract from prejudice views of Eastern Europe and on touchdown our expectations were met when the Airport in Kaunas, Lithuania, was no more than a concrete box on a runway with the giant steal letters KAUNAS atop it looking frighteningly, well, eastern.

Disembarking the plane, walking across the runway at nightfall, shivering from the cold and huddling inside to the baggage carousel, I noticed out of the corner of my eye two very smiley and two very distinctive people in the arrivals lounge. They stuck out like sore thumbs simply because they didn't match. One was a girl with long hair, no older than me, and the other a slim, balding man in perhaps his early 40s wearing an open leather jacket with a blue football shirt beneath. This was them, I knew it, but I didn't dare make eye contact. I just stared down at the floor waiting for my cumbersome companion to catch up. Tristan noticed I was nervous and asked why. I didn't have a concrete answer for him, but in hindsight I think it was because I had realised I was probably going to disappoint these happy, smiley people with my lack of football skills.

Once our bags arrived, and with no passport control to speak of, we went to meet the strangers.

'Hello Ralf,' said the girl. Her face lit up with happiness and enthusiasm.

Sat in the back seat of Solus' car with my brother driving to god-knows-where, it's fair to say we felt nervous about the whole thing.

It didn't help when Justina, sat in the passenger seat, turned and asked in fluent English some very worrying questions.

'Can I ask you, why do you think it is safe to get in a car with two strangers in a country you have never visited before to a town that even people in Lithuania have not even heard of?'

I gulped. I was expecting a soundtrack from a horror movie to start playing as Justina drew out a knife. Luckily, Tristan was there to interject.

'Why do you think it's safe to pick up two English people you've never met before who may have ulterior motives?'

I was hoping he may have said something a little less challenging than that, something that didn't have the potential to quicken our departure from this world.

'I don't know,' shrugged Justina. 'We just liked the idea of Ralf's project, and Solus likes English football people so we thought we'd say yes.'

'Same here. Just want to see the world,' said Tristan, and smiles were shared between everyone.

Justina's English was excellent. She was only 19 but was fulfilling her job as translator very well. She showed her age though; her enthusiasm at bringing two English people to her hometown of Kėdainiai (pronounced Keh-dye-knee apparently).

Solus' English was not so good, and he only knew key words, and certainly no pronouns such as 'me', 'he', 'they', etc. So he would simply say 'Solus. Pleased meeting.' Despite this it was impossible to dislike a man who had driven 40 miles out of his way to pick us up, take our heavy bags off us and who shook our hands on our first meeting with so much enthusiasm and strength that I began to feel I could do anything. He had an infectious charm and smile that broke through any language barriers and I eventually, despite the odd situation, felt at ease in his and Justina's company.

I never thought it would be possible, but on meeting Solus and travelling in his car I actually had managed to meet someone who could drive slower than my Mum. All the roads in Lithuania seem regimented and as straight as an arrow across a landscape that is as flat as a pancake, but despite this and with obviously no sign of danger ahead, he seemed to insist on going at a leisurely pace. Perhaps he just wanted to protect his valuable commodity in the back seat – my football-playing legs.

As the journey continued so did the enthusiastic questions from Justina.

'Did you know you have chosen to visit the number one polluted city in Lithuania?'

We didn't know how to react to this because she seemed proud of the fact.

'Really?' we said in unison, eyebrows raised.

'Yes. We also have something very special: a giant mountain of chemical waste.'

'Really?' Unison again.

These people were proud of some weird things.

'Yes, you can't go there though because it is dangerous.' Sadness crept into her voice. 'But when we get home I will show you pictures.'

The journey went on and on.

And on and on.

And on.

I was sleepy. Our journey time was pushing 12 hours in total from Andorra, and although Justina calls herself a Kėdainiai resident she was actually raised on a farm in the middle of nowhere. When Solus took the turn onto the gravel track to cut across miles of fields, the suspicion that we would be forced into some sort of slave labour returned to my mind. The car rumbled along contently for miles and miles with the bumps of the track rippling through the suspension. No wonder Justina was so happy to see some other people's faces; we were potentially the first outsiders ever to visit this village.

The journey continued, with Justina firing more and more questions at us about ourselves and England and my dream to be a professional footballer, and where it had taken us so far. She would then relay these back to Solus who would chuckle and think of another question to send our way. We were obviously a novelty to them.

After what seemed like forever we arrived at Justina's house in total darkness, with biting cold temperatures to greet us. My teeth chattered on the short walk from the car to the house, which stood tall and detached in a pretty village surrounded by farmland. Solus agreed to come in and meet Justina's parents for the first time, and help us with our bags.

As we entered the house I clocked the welcoming sight of freshly chopped logs, and the more peculiar one of jarred cucumbers. I made my way through to the hallway, heavy bag in tow, to see a smiley middle-aged couple, Johann and Onna. They were both over 50 – I deduced this from the novelty clock I spied over their shoulders, which had the gold number 50 on it against a background photo of them arm in arm. In kitsch value it was priceless, and I presumed it was there to celebrate their 50th birthdays together, rather than 50 years of marriage – if it were for marriage they certainly looked great for their age (or that they simply marry young in Lithuania). Stood before us in a pose not too dissimilar to the birthday picture clock behind them, we immediately felt at ease. Johann's small stature, smile and workman-like hands told a story of a happy, hard-working man. Onna smiled and welcomed us into her home as best she could, without being able to speak a word of English, but that didn't stop them. With grand pointing gestures and waving of their arms they invited us with a smile into the lounge. Immediately I noticed there was no television in there, which I've always found odd. Where does the furniture point? In this case it was at each other, but of course they did have some forms of entertainment, as the room was adorned with a piano, two keyboards and a guitar. Within 30 seconds of stepping through the door, me, Solus and Tristan had food and cups of tea presented to us – exactly what the weary traveller needs after a long day.

A meal of cucumbers and dumplings isn't something I have encountered before, but it was delicious. My only criticism could be the amount that I felt compelled to eat, with Justina saying 'If you don't want to sleep outside, eat it all.' She delivered this with a smile, but I still wasn't entirely sure if she meant it. To save embarrassment I continued to eat until I was fit to burst, so much so that my belly button almost went from an 'inny' to an 'outey'.

Feeling parched and not liking tea with no milk in I was desperately thirsty. I hesitantly asked Justina if I could have milk my tea hoping not to sound rude and she took immediate action. However, when she took the cup through the back door into the yard outside and returned with my drink replenished with milk I was slightly taken aback. Where she had got it from? I feared a cow in the garden may have just been rudely awoken from its slumber in order for me to have a drop of milk in my tea. Sometimes ignorance is bliss, and I didn't want to be appear rude, so I just drank my milky tea and thought of England .

Mercifully, the meal ended, but then the alcohol commenced. And not just any type of alcohol – Lithuanian vodka, and Lithuanian wheat vodka, the latter of which was 60% proof. The shot glasses were put on the oak table in front of us and next to the shot glasses were slices of ham. I was tired, so I rubbed my eyes hoping to see the ham transform into a nice glass of beer, but without success. Slices of ham were to act as the chaser. Everyone was smiling, including us, although by now it was more of a frightened grin rather than the natural ones of our hosts. Down a 60% shot of Vodka and then chew on a bit of ham. Simple.

'A toast.' Said Solus venturing into using English on his own. 'Safe flight. No terrorists!'

'Esveikata!' They said in unison.

Me and Tristan looked at each and shrugged. Fair enough.

'No terrorists!' We proclaimed.

It was definitely one of the more random toasts I'll drink, but one I'd be saying again very shortly. I should be more thankful that my life hasn't yet been affected by terrorists. I drank the shot and chewed the ham, my nostrils burning and ham flaming in my mouth.

Tristan, Solus, Johann, and I drank again and again.

'No terrorists!'

Boy was it strong stuff. I have never gone from ready for bed to drunk so quickly in my life. It took about five minutes for that first shot to hit me and when it did I wasn't just tipsy, I was fully gone. My eyes couldn't focus, my face was numb and I felt the constant need to burp or hiccup. More followed and I was wary that I may become a bit of a wreck, and asked for a glass of water. Thankfully this came from a tap and not an unknown source outside.

Solus was limiting his intake due to him driving, but I couldn't believe he was smiling and laughing away. If a club director in England went to pick up a potential signing from the airport and then watched him get pissed, I imagine he wouldn't be best pleased, but Solus was loving it. This was my kind of football club.

As the evening couldn't get more surreal, it did. Johann leant over and put his keyboard on his lap, Onna stood up, and they began to play Lithuanian folk music. It was everything I expected from Eastern Europe, but in a great way.

As they were playing and singing, Justina explained to me they are famous in the local village for their music, and that they are even releasing a CD. I asked if this was a special treat that they had put on for us, and she simply replied 'No. They do it whenever they have guests.'

So much laughter was had at me and Tristan struggling to eat ham after shots and us being drunk as well. It was incredibly hospitable and warming. We were forced to drink more, Tristan doing so whilst operating a camera which was most certainly a first for him. I suppose you could argue we should have feared that, in the middle of nowhere, these drinks could have been used as an anaesthetic to do dastardly deeds to us, but there wasn't an air or awkwardness or cynicism – it was just brilliant.

Johann and Onna played three songs, the highlight of which was no doubt being the Lithuanian version of that classic Boney M track 'By the Rivers of Babylon'. Roars of applause from me and Tristan had them smiling with pride, but unfortunately it was time to wind down for the night as Johann had to get up at 5am to do some work. It was now midnight. If I had drunk as much as him and had to work the next day at 5am then it simply wouldn't happen.

Solus said his goodbyes and agreed to meet us at midday to show us the club and take us to the match that his team were playing.

Me and Tristan had the honour of sharing Justina's bedroom – with each other – whilst she slept in the lounge. As I clambered into bed, Justina entered the room.

'Can I have my man?' she asked excitedly.

In a panic, me and Tristan looked at each other, hoping wires hadn't been inexplicably crossed in the most heinous of fashions.

'Erm...' I said.

'Errmm....' Tristan said.

This wasn't good; our dithering hadn't deterred her and she made her way toward the bed. My heart rate, already high from the vodka, touched new levels. She peeled the bed sheets back, reached in, and retrieved a pink stuffed pig. She held it aloft.

'My man!' she said proudly.

She had just gone from potentially the least innocent to the most innocent person in the world. She left the room saying goodnight and we both breathed again.

'Jesus, were you thinking of what I was thinking?' asked Tristan.

'I think so, although it's not a thought I like.'

'Me neither mate.'

'Lets go to sleep, and no touching.'

'Agreed.'

Although it was a small double bed and we had to share, I was confident given my drunken state that I could easily fall asleep. I was wrong. I know it's unlikely to ever happen for you, but in the event don't ever try and share a bed with Tristan. His noxious gases and flailing legs make it an uncomfortable experience, and so for the fifth night running I ended up sleeping on a hard floor.

The next morning I felt rough, terribly so. To get a true aspect of how I felt I have outlined some of the definitions of what the Oxford Dictionary has for the word 'rough'.

Rough
- (of persons or behaviour) lacking refinement or finesse;
- approximate: not quite exact or correct;
- rocky: full of hardship or trials; 'the rocky road to success';
- grating: unpleasantly harsh or grating in sound;
- causing or characterized by jolts and irregular movements; 'a rough ride';
- crude: not carefully or expertly made;
- harsh: unpleasantly stern.

I was certainly all of the above. But I was facing a three-day job interview, so I had no time to complain, especially as the reason I had awoke was the sound of Solus speaking to Tristan in the kitchen.

'This is, er, good cheese!'

I went downstairs to see Solus waving cheese in my brother's clearly hung-over face.

'Morning,' I offered, in my best attempt to sound cheerful.

'Hello, good cheese!' said Solus again, before exiting the room with Justina.

'Onna makes homemade cheese. Solus seems to be a big fan.' Said Tristan, with a suicidal look in his eyes.

'I see.'

We stumbled into the kitchen and sat down to save our aching legs, but before I knew it I was helping Onna with the breakfast of fried chicken with a side of fried chicken followed by yet more fried chicken. I also saw the leftovers from the night before and there were still a dozen or so giant dumplings in the pan, we hadn't even made a dent. Now, feeling rude for not eating all of her food last night, I made an assault on the fried chicken, not a great idea when a hangover is still lingering. How I longed for some fruit; unfortunately that wasn't an option.

Tristan, too, made an admirable job of eating the fried chicken. We were both squeezed onto a small bench in the kitchen. This was fine in itself, but the piercing glare of the toothless 100-and-something-year-old opposite us was a little too much to handle.

'Can you see the old person?' asked Tristan, maintaining a huge smile so as to not raise suspicion in Onna or the elderly lady, whilst Justina and Solus loaded up the car and discussed our itinerary.

'Yes,' I replied with a smile and nod to Onna who was paying half attention to us.

'That's good. I thought I was suffering from the world's strangest hangover. Who is she?'

'I don't know. I'm guessing the grandma, but no one's said anything to me.'

'Me neither.'

'Poor love is a bit confused, she must be senile. They've probably reasoned it's not worth introducing us to save confusing her,' I said out of the corner of my mouth.

'Thus keeping us as figments of her imagination as opposed to actually introducing us?'

'Now you mention it, she must be really confused,' I said, looking back at the old woman sat directly before me.

'Unless we're both having the same hallucination?'

'I think we were both on the money with senile grandma, let's not introduce psychedelic elements into this equation, it's too early and I'm feeling too rough.'

Solus and Justina entered the kitchen and ushered us out to the car. We waved goodbye to Johann and Onna – we didn't want to impose on them any further, and I needed to get as far away from vodka as possible, so we decided that we would look for a cheap hotel and figure the rest out later.

Passing over the same dirt track as the night before, except this time in daylight, we realised that we really were in the middle of nowhere. Acres of empty fields reminiscent of East Anglia stretched for miles. They were all we could see, with the only thing breaking the monotonous view being the small grey blob of Kėdainiai on the horizon. Travelling along the dirt-track we saw a glum-faced man ploughing a field the size of Cornwall using only a horse and a piece of rusty equipment. That was more like the Eastern Europe we'd envisioned.

Kėdainiai is a small town about the same size as Andorra Le Vella. A sleepy town built around the river Nevezis, which the football club I am having my trial with is named after. It is essentially an old and new town welded together. The old town comprises no more than four streets, with the new town now dwarfing it, but despite this it was peaceful. I saw no signs of a mountain of chemical waste, and no clouds of pollution that Justina had hinted at as remnants of a brutal Soviet regime that had no regard for the environment or its workers.

Solus took us to his office where he works both full-time in an advertising career and part-time as a director of FK Nevezis. In his office, through Justina's translations, he regaled us with tales of how the glory years of the club were in the late 60s and 70s, when they won three league titles, and how he wanted them to slowly return to that level. Solus himself, when he was younger, was going to be a player and was sent to a football academy in the capital city of Vilnius in order to study football under the Soviet Regime. Horrifyingly for him, however, he developed a knee injury and heart condition towards the end of his three-year course in his early 20s that meant he could no longer be a professional. I didn't know what to say.

'It was tough for me,' said Solus, via Justina, 'but I prefer to look forward and not back.' The mood in the office turned from jovial to something resembling a wake. I felt sorry for Solus. To have the dream taken away like that before it even starts because of an injury is not an uncommon story, but I had never met anyone first-hand who'd had to come to terms with it.

Solus had two boys who he often spoke about and so I asked him if he wanted to push his lost football dream onto his children, as is the case with many British parents (and also what I'll do if I ever have any kids).

'No, no, no, no,' said Solus. 'Erm Justina...' Solus spoke enthusiastically at his translator.

'He says he wants them to be happy first and if they then want to play football that's okay, but of course he would prefer it if they played football.'

Solus told us that the national sport in Lithuania and Latvia is Basketball and in Estonia is Ice Hockey, with football a distant second. 'Basketball religion,' Solus said. This might not be excellent for Solus or anyone else involved in football in this region but for me it was exceptional news. If all the young players were choosing basketball over football then that means there is less talent getting to football, meaning the rubbish talent like me can swoop in and play.

'Are there any restrictions on signing foreigners here?' This was now my staple question after the problems I ran into in Malta, as well as my lack of talent.

'No, no restrictions, although there are not many foreigners any more,' said Justina, translating.

'Why?'

After a lengthy exchange in Lithuanian I had my answer.

'Because it costs 3,000 Euro to register a foreign player in top league and about 2,000 Euro to register player in our league.'

Bugger.

Bugger.

Bugger.

The romance of just going to these places without doing research on the countries' regulations was starting to wear a bit thin. I had a feeling that this club's budget was obviously not going to allow them to sign me on current form, given that the club director works part-time out of his actual professional office.

'But if I play like Cristiano Ronaldo can I play?'

Solus laughed. Hard. Very hard. Then cried with laughter.
He then said something to Justina and mimed zig-zagging with his hands.

'Solus says if you play like Ronaldo you can stay here forever.' Solus laughed again. I think he had sixth sense and knew I was crap at football.

Tristan then approached me under the guise of having to fix my microphone and began to whisper in a discreet manner so that Justina, who was still talking to Solus, could not hear. I hoped Justina was explaining to Solus what Tristan was doing with his hand up my shirt and not simply saying 'These brothers are very close aren't they? They even had a lover's tiff last night that caused the smaller one to sleep on the floor.'

'2,000 Euros to register a foreigner mate,' said Tristan under his breath.

'I know it's a massive ball-ache, but I can still give it a go can't I? I'll never know how good they are until I actually play against them and I see this match.' I tried not to look at him as he was unnaturally close to my face, fiddling with the small microphone attached to my shirt.

'Fair point. By the way do you have any chewing gum?'

I knew exactly why he wanted some.

'Fried chicken?' I asked sympathetically.

'Yeah, it's been repeating on me all day. My throat is burning and my breath stinks. I can't stop burping.'

'Me too mate. Me too.'

Disguising a hangover, horribly bad breathe and my shock at the 2,000-Euro registration fee, I decided to change the subject and moved towards his football tactics board with coloured disc-shaped magnets signifying each player, to try and gauge what positions Solus felt he thought his club was lacking.

I begun to fiddle with the board, making formations out of the 11 magnets to show Solus the position I like to play as well as what type of player I was. After a few moments of brief dialogue Solus looked surprised at me when I said I like to play right back, something I was hoping to train in at the start of this journey but was hampered by injury so I had to merely concentrate on fitness. Solus seemed to be questioning my height and physical stature in order to play a defensive position, which he was right to do. This led us onto physical stats, and I immediately regretted playing with those magnets.

'Solus would like to know how high you can jump.' Said Justina.

'Eh? I don't know.'

'How fast you can you do a 30-metre sprint?'

'Don't know.'

'50 metres?'

'Don't know.'

Justina explained to Solus.

'Solus says testing is a big part here, and when he played under the Soviet Union regime it was test, test, test.' Solus then interjected. 'He asks how fast can you run 100m?'

Although the atmosphere was still more than friendly I felt bad not knowing any of my results. The only one I did know was the 100m, and that's only 15.87, and that was measured when I was 11.

I hate to say it but I decided to lie to make myself sound better than I was.

'11.70 seconds' I said without hesitation before rapidly blinking my eyes in horror at what I had just done. I had just taken four seconds off my personal best. Clocking this, I adopted a certain swagger, believing that to be an incredibly fast time, only for Solus to stick his bottom lip out, open his eyes wide and wobble his head from side to side as if to say: 'that's okay, I've heard better.'

How does 11.70 seconds not impress the man? I'd just taken four seconds off my personal best in a heartbeat. If I were to take another four seconds off then I'd be the fastest man alive.

It was time to visit the ground and watch the match. The 2,000 Euro registration fee had shaken me. Flying all that way to have a trial with a semi-professional club who clearly would be reluctant to pay such an amount, unless I was Ronaldo, was a bit silly, and my budget had gone down to £700 because of it. I'd had problems in Malta and Andorra convincing them to pay me 1 Euro; here I was hoping for them to pay 2,000 Euros just to register me, and then extra for my wages. But if I was learning anything from this trip it was that stranger shit can and has happened, and so I would have the trial anyway.

The lush green landscape rolled past us as we passed over a rare hill towards what Solus described as 'Lithuanian Old Trafford'. Kėdainiai really was gorgeous and not what I was expecting from my prejudiced western upbringing. Perhaps I had caught it on an upward curve, as I was finding Lithuania far more welcoming and prosperous than I had initially anticipated.

With my hangover still in full effect and fried chicken repeating on me, we pulled up by Nevezis's new stadium at the edge of town.

Again my expectations were smashed – the ground was far superior to what I had expected. Four uncovered stands built into a natural amphitheatre overlooked the pitch. It was impressive considering the level they were at – suddenly that 2,000-Euro fee didn't look out of the question. Unfortunately it wasn't quite a finished project, highlighted by the fact that the playing area was still concrete and was the subject of years of work for Solus, who on arrival barked some abuse at a builder who was sat on his arse. They're the same the world over. Solus simply turned to me to say: 'Work Saturdays. Quicker finish.' If this guy could make a builder work on a Saturday, perhaps he could pull a few strings for me.

The game would take place on the reserve pitch next to the ground, which for all the world looked like a standard park pitch you would find in the UK or anywhere else in Europe, were it not for the fact that that temporary seating at one side of the pitch increased the capacity from 0 to 40. With no turnstiles or indeed tickets for sale, people could filter through whenever they liked to watch. The club, I was told, made the bulk of its money through advertising and merchandising, and although they were reluctant to tell me how much their turnover was it can't have been much, which confused me given the decent stadium under construction.

Solus led us to the club offices where he showed us more photos of Nevezis's and Lithuanian football's former glory. The building was a horrible brown cube overlooking the two-pitch complex, and was falling apart. This was more what I was expecting from Lithuania. Solus apologised for the state of the place as we walked through the office doors, but I really couldn't care less.

Walking into this building it was like going back in time into my own childhood. The 'museum' of the club had one wall adorned with pictures from Lithuanian football all through the 20th Century. Of course, it wasn't the men in black-and-white pictures wearing baggy shorts that made me nostalgic; it was the wall opposite this that held the key to my childhood memories. Don't ask me why, but it was plastered with posters of footballers from England in the mid-90s, cut out of the popular 'Match' Magazine. The faces of Alan Shearer, Eric Cantona, Gary Pallister, Tony Yeboah, Matt Le Tissier, Stan Collymore and plenty more filled the room. Just as I thought it couldn't get any better I saw a picture of Ruel Fox from his Norwich City glory days from the 93-94 season. With a name so satisfying you have to say both names together, he was a tricky right winger, small and fast and very agile. Growing up he was one of the players I would imagine myself as when I dummied molehills and fired shots into the empty goal in our garden. Seeing him there was like seeing an old friend. The faded photos brought back memories I had thought lost years ago, they were probably only there to stop the building falling down by acting as some sort of wall support, but I saw it as a sign.

Solus talked us through the historical pictures. I wanted to talk to him about Ruel Fox's career but I held back. It was only when Solus started talking about the pictures did I realise what a scarred history Lithuania has had over the 20th Century.

Starting in 1940, Lithuania was occupied first by the Soviet Union on 'tactical grounds' against Nazi Germany. However, Nazi Germany then occupied the nation as the Soviets retreated. As World War II neared its end in 1944 with the Nazis falling back to Germany, the Soviet Union reoccupied Lithuania and held onto it as its own until 1990 when Lithuania became the first Soviet republic to declare its renewed independence at the collapse of the USSR. The black-and-white pictures from the occupation were of people who were oppressed, without freedom of speech or the freedom to go where they wanted or do what they wanted due to the restrictions of the regime they lived under. If they were told they were going to be an electrician, plumber or builder, they had no choice. But playing football let them express themselves in a manner that normal life wouldn't allow.

Kick-off time was fast approaching, but Solus didn't seem to care if we were late for the game; he seemed happy to hang around in the crumbling club offices and the dilapidated 'V.I.P' area which he pronounced literally in one word as 'VIPS'. I then remembered he was a club director, and club directors are famous for turning up to games late as they eat their prawn sandwiches in the hospitality area, chatting to officials and their opposition counterparts. No matter how run-down the offices are it seems all club directors around the world like to rock up to games ten minutes after kick-off. Solus was the same, as he sipped on his coffee from a plastic cup and munched on buttered biscuits in the dark grey room.

I loathed being late for the game, but luckily we didn't miss any goals, and as I took my seat in the smallest stand I have ever sat in,

Solus left to talk to the coach and other very serious-looking men. It was only 30 seconds into watching the game when I saw something that made me realise that my chances with Nevezis were slim. As a long ball punted up-field fell over the shoulder of an FK Nevezis defender, he calmly lunged his leg in the air, controlled the ball first time, flicked it over his own head and the oncoming opponent's, before calmly passing it off. The pace, strength and technique on show was far higher than what I was expecting from a country that of Lithuania's size, where apparently many don't play football. Way better than Andorra and Malta. From past experience of watching football in England it was a standard similar to England's sixth tier – low professional to high amateur levels. Way out of my league.

But stranger things have happened. I would still do the trial, but as the game fizzed along at an alarming pace with few errors and with moments of magic involved, I thought about how going all the way to the Baltic region to realise my dream probably wasn't the greatest decision I have ever made. Sat there watching this game of football, I was reminded of countless Sunday afternoons I had as a teenager where I would be the substitute for our team, waiting for my ten-minute run-out once all chance of me affecting the result negatively had gone, either by us having a 2 or 3-goal lead or a 2 or 3-goal deficit. The only difference this time was that I was here by invitation.

Justina kept me company during the game and continued to ask questions and I finally got sick of it turned the tables on her and she seemed uncomfortable to have to talk about herself. Wanting to grow up to be a translator, she had recently started a university degree in Vilnius, where she was now living, and had only travelled the two-and-a-half-hour bus journey home for our arrival and would be returning to Vilnius that evening, so she wouldn't be around for my trial. I also found out, despite being the press officer for the club on a part-time basis, she didn't even know the offside rule, or any of the other rules for that matter. My faith in rubbish football teams was restored briefly and my hopes that Nevezis weren't as good as I thought on first inspection returned, on the basis that the press officer didn't know anything about the game. She did tell me that the referees are only paid 20 Euros a game, about £18. However the Lithuanian ref's paltry wage didn't stop him getting a severe amount of abuse though from the 27-strong crowd. It must be a horrible job being a referee, but more so at that level where there is no stadium noise or other fans to drown out the insults being launched at him. Of course I couldn't understand the volley of abuse, but I imagine his mother's sexual history was called into question, and his preference of gender would also have been queried. The only other time I saw such a specifically focused wave of abuse towards an official in such a small stadium was when I was covering a game for a local paper on work experience. One very drunk man with three plastic pints that he couldn't hold level launched wave after of wave of chants and insults at a linesman stood just inches away for no reason whatsoever. However, when the fan was off his guard the linesman accidentally-on-purpose caught the man full blood in the face when raising his flag to signal an imaginary offside. I've had a higher respect for officials since then, which only increased during this match.

More importantly, however, Justina told me how much the players were paid, and some of the top earners were on 250 Euros a months, which is a very middle-of-the road semi-pro wage of about £60 a week. The money is more than enough for me to achieve my ambition of one game one Euro, I just needed to get round that blasted registration fee.

Nevezis lost the game 4-1 and afterwards Solus seemed inconsolable. He was the embodiment of enthusiasm and happiness in our time with him thus far, and it was clear that he loved his team. Me and Tristan decided we should buy Solus a drink in a local bar to drown his (and my) sorrows. Solus would commiserate about how poor Nevezis were that day, and I would commiserate about how good they were. Crossing the pitch to meet Solus we were interrupted by a woman and man who carried a tiny video camera and tripod, and a microphone. After they'd spouted some Lithuanian at us, Justina translated that they were part of the local news website and wanted to interview me about my quest to be a professional footballer. Solus had tipped the press before the game, seeing it as a good marketing opportunity. Obviously an Englishman in Lithuania is big news. Naturally, I couldn't turn her down, I was going to be a star in Lithuania!

It was a good interview as far as I could tell. I pretty much said everything I needed to about what I wanted for FK Nevezis and myself. Justina did a sterling job as a translator again, and halfway through my answers the reporter did a great job by nodding along despite not knowing a word of what I was saying. But I didn't care, I was marketing myself, and if Nevezis didn't want a rubbish footballer, then maybe someone else watching would.

Interview 'in the can', we made for the pub with Solus and Justina, where after one pint I was feeling remarkably merry, probably because I was merely topping up the alcohol levels from the night before.

When Justina had told us she was a student, and was going to back to Vilnius in a matter of hours, we made a ridiculous decision that would affect the rest of the Lithuania leg of the trip.

Me and Tristan looked around and locked eyes. We both knew what the other was thinking; Kėdainiai is beautiful, but not somewhere two young men would want to spend a Saturday night, or all day Sunday in preparation for a trial on the Monday. Wordlessly, it was agreed we would accompany Justina on the train back to Vilnius. We booked a hotel with the help of Solus, who was all too happy to help. It was clear he was a young man at heart and you could see he wanted to come with us, but family commitments meant he couldn't. Sadly Justina had other arrangements, so once we reached Vilnius it would be me and Tristan in a city we hadn't heard of 36 hours prior to arriving in Lithuania.

Sat in the cabin of the train on a Saturday night, Tristan and I had brought some classy Englishness to a rickety old train boarding the form of several beers for the 100km journey to the capital. Sharing a cabin with an elderly lady and Justina we tried to act cultured so that we didn't bother her peaceful journey, but as soon as she said hello and started asking questions, we were able to crack open the beers and engage in conversation. She immediately fell in love with us.

It was the best train journey ever. We had our own compartment similar to a Harry Potter train or something from the Victorian era. We told the woman our story and she hers, that she was going back home after visiting her grandchildren, and is enjoying her retirement from being a nurse. Her English was remarkably good and at one stage, once the alcohol had taken its full toll on me, I got in an argument with her about what was the better sport, football or basketball. Arguing with a retired Lithuanian citizen about the finer points of football whilst extremely inebriated was one of the highlights of my life. It was surreal, I was drunk and I was talking about football. After agreeing to disagree on which was the better sport, we came up with a remarkable excuse for me to carry on drinking that I ended up taking far too seriously, down to the letter.

It turned out I wasn't drinking to drown my sorrow at being in a part of Europe where it was evident that I wasn't going to make it as a professional footballer. I was drinking to aid my performance in my impending trial. All geniuses have a vice, and drink was to be mine. Throughout football history, even in the modern game, all the greats have vices. Zinedine Zidane smoked and had a temper, George Best drank, Cristiano Ronaldo has vanity and Diego Maradona had all three. Perhaps I was rubbish at football because I wanted it too much. We levied that with alcohol to relax me I could release the genius part of my brain and become the legend on the football pitch I'm destined to be.

When we arrived at the train station we said our goodbyes to our travelling companion. If you got on a train in England drunk, with one other person for company, there wouldn't be a chance in hell that we'd have conversations like the ones we'd just had, if any at all, but I was finding Europe, and Lithuania in particular, to be an incredibly agreeable country. We also said goodbye to Justina as she returned to her student life. I was extremely thankful for all she had done, travelling all that way just so she could translate for us when meeting Solus, and also giving us her bed (or giving Tristan her bed and me her floor).

Our hotel was situated directly opposite the train station, which was a massive blessing. We dumped our bags down in our ample and comfortable room and immediately made our way to the 'old town' for a night of debauchery, alcohol, nightclubs and dancing, all under the smokescreen that it was for my football career.

A cheap meal in the square whilst drinking the amusingly named 'Horn Beer' led us to talk to an extremely pretty waitress who recommended a bar and nightclub that the tourists don't know about, and is only frequented by locals. Describing her as a pretty waitress doesn't really differentiate her from any other girl in Vilnius. As soon as we stepped off that train every other girl we saw was an astounding beauty. Perhaps it was something in the water, or the alcohol we'd consumed, but all of these women seemed to be incredibly good-looking and all we could do was shake our heads in wonderment.

The nightclub, Avitstai, was a mix of how I imagine Manchester to be in the 80s, and every great thing ever. Beautiful women, awesome dancers, cheap alcohol and good music resulted in us being very satisfied by the waitress' suggestion. Surrounded by Eastern European 6ft-tall cube-like men hovering around girls I attempted to dance and did myself no justice, but it was all for the football, all for the football.

During some not so awe-inspiring dance moves in the middle of a Michael Jackson medley, Tristan grabbed my arm and we went to the bar and drank consummate amounts of our new favourite Lithuanian vodka and talked about the trip, and how we felt I could still make it, if I applied myself correctly; and boy was I applying myself. George Best would have been proud.

'This stuff just doesn't give you a hangover, it's amazing!' said Tristan enthusiastically as he downed his drink and ordered another one from the barmaid by clicking his fingers. It was quite impressive.

'Let's get wasted!'

Waking up the next morning I had entered new territory in the hangover stakes. I opened my eyes and blearily made out the remains of a McDonalds meal on the floor. Memories of waiting in line at the drive-thru part of the 'restaurant' and not actually going inside were coming back to me. My tongue was so dry it could have been used as sandpaper. My temples were visibly throbbing; my arms and inner core were shaking and I couldn't speak in sentences, merely groans and grunts. Lithuanian vodka, according to Tristan, may not give you a hangover but it will make you want to kill yourself. Standing up hesitantly my legs shook like an elderly dog taking a dump.

Through my bleary eyes I could see outside onto the green suburbs nearby and there I saw a small boy tightrope-walking no more than 3ft above the ground. I was sure I wasn't hallucinating.

Turning away from this bewildering sight and seeing an empty bed next to mine, I made haste downstairs to the breakfast area. I'd had just three hours' sleep. My ears felt as if they were bleeding, and were still echoing the music from last night as I made my way down the spiralling spinning corridor towards the lifts. Legend has it George Best famously scored a hat-trick after an all-night bender where he hadn't even gone to bed at all. I fast discovered that I was not George Best, nor would I ever be.

Turning the corner to the breakfast area, I saw Tristan, who only looked better than me by virtue of him wearing shoes. I was barefoot and wobbling in the hotel lobby. Unable to muster any dexterity in my paralysed fingers I stood at the meat plates of the breakfast buffet and threw pieces of ham at my open mouth; whatever stuck in there would be my breakfast. I exchanged a couple of grunts with Tristan who informed me he'd managed to book us an extra night in the hotel in order to recover. Staying in hotels wasn't the cheapest or best option for my ever-decreasing budget, but in this scenario I really had no choice. I returned to bed hoping that the hangover I was suffering would unlock the potential in my brain and make me a world-class footballer, but I began to doubt it.

Six hours later and having drunk four litres of water, three carrot juices, seventeen coffees and two fruit smoothies I finally felt ready to brave the outside world and see Vilnius during the daytime. Tristan managed to leave the hotel room before me and make his way to do some sightseeing, leaving me in bed to sweat out the night before.

If Kėdainiai was pretty then Vilnius was something else. Huge white stone churches and a cathedral that was bigger than Malta itself were just some of the highlights of this remarkable old town. It felt old but new, clean and vibrant and beautiful with its women and architecture. No wonder it's twinned with Edinburgh in Scotland – it's more than a match in its marriage of old beauty and modern structures.

It was a crisp, sunny evening, buskers were in the street and everyone was strolling around slowly and contentedly. I was hung-over, and with my brother, and that kind of took the romance away a bit. At the start of this trip the idea was to become a professional footballer, but what I was doing in Lithuania was almost like a holiday, one in which I could have easily come on without the distractions of football. With these thoughts the stakes increased in my mind and the idea of failure made me wonder if I should have just gone away sporadically rather than all of this football desire. But then I remembered I never would have gone to this most incredible of places were it not for football. Before my quest I had no desire to go to Lithuania or any Baltic states, but football had brought me here, and so for that I was grateful. As I sat there listening to a nine-year-old girl busking with a violin playing the most beautiful music I realised that seeing this country was the first major victory I'd had on this journey, even if it wasn't a victory in the football terms.

Returning to the hotel room for an early night, I looked out of the window to see the circus boy still practising his tight-rope walking under a dim 40-watt bulb. If only he knew all he needed to be become exceptional in his chosen field wasn't hard work and practise, but just a copious amount of Lithuanian vodka.

The next morning I was still tremendously hung-over. We had agreed to get the train at 9am back to Kėdainiai but our in-built recovery systems had made us sleep through our alarms, and we were having none of it. Well, we didn't exactly sleep through the alarms, more like we woke up and battered them into submission before passing out again.

Our initial plan gave me six hours to prep for the evening trial once we had arrived in Kėdainiai, but now having woken up at midday we had no plan. This time I managed to remember to put my shoes on, and made a mad dash to the train station across the road. Now, the Eastern European public transport system is a bit lacking it seems, and Justina and Solus were surprised that we could even get a train to Vilnius from Kėdainiai, as buses were the done thing, with the train lines being reserved for freight passage. Even so, I couldn't have envisaged the problems that lay ahead.

As I ran through the huge glass doors and made my way to the giant 'I' in the sky that signified 'information', my ears tuned in to a man speaking English to a young woman behind the counter. After being told by some very stern looking female staff – who fully represented what I thought all women in Eastern Europe to be like (i.e. sour) – that the only person who spoke English was the woman at the counter already engaged with the aforementioned man, I joined the queue.

This man ahead of me clearly wasn't English. He was wearing an all-denim ensemble and a baseball cap that no sane Englishman would wear without dying of embarrassment. There are only two nations in the world where people wear all-denim ensembles to my knowledge: America and Germany, and this man certainly wasn't American.

'And when is the next train to Dresden?'

Did I just hear him right?

'Sorry sir?' said the young girl behind the counter.

'Dresden, in Germany. When is the next train there?'

'I'm sorry sir, I've never heard that city.'

'Dresden in Germany. The train, when is it?'

'I don't think there are any trains to Germany. You need to go to the European travel office over the road, they can help.'

The man then slammed his fist into the counter, turned round and gave me a look to say 'unbelievable!' and moved off. What was unbelievable was the man's sheer arrogance in believing he could simply hop on a train across three countries at the drop of a hat.

'Next please,' said the smiling, round-faced girl behind the counter, who was wearing a tad too much blusher. It looked like she had two beetroots for cheeks. Her happy, red visage could not have more contrasted my miserable, gaunt white face.

'Hi, do you speak English?' I don't know why I asked that question, she clearly did, as she had addressed me in English and I'd just witnessed her conversation with the German. In my defence I was still hung-over.

'Yes, I speak English.'

'Great, I need to get to Kėdainiai for 4pm today, when is the next train?'

'Kėdainiai?' she questioned.

'Yes, Kėdainiai,' I said, knowing it existed.

'Kėdainiai? Sorry, I don't know a city called Kėdainiai.'

Did this girl know any cities?

'I need to get to Kėdainiai.' It was like the Andorra tourist information office all over again.

'But I do not know Kėdainiai, I think no trains go there.'

'But Kėdainiai!' I pointed at it on the overly sized map of Lithuania and its train routes which was conveniently situated over her shoulder.

'Oh, you mean *Keh-dye-knee?*' she said, turning back towards me with a roll of the eyes, as if to say: *why didn't you say so?*

'Yes Kėdainiai!'

'You mean Kėdainiai?'

Oh for crying out loud.

'Yes! When is the next train? I need to get there for 4 o'clock.'

'Oh sorry, I not know word, erm… day before Wednesday?

'Pardon?'

'What is name of day before Wednesday?'

'Tuesday?'

Smeg. That's tomorrow.

'Yes Too-es-day. The next train is Too-es-day.' Her face beamed as if she was happy that there was a train once a day to take people just 100km. I too slammed my wrist into her counter on my way out and as I left I saw the German consulting a train timetable. To my surprise trains did eventually go to Dresden. He must have just been saying it wrong.

Cursing the Baltic region's poor rail network I ran back to our now grotty hotel room in an extreme panic and I told Tristan of the predicament.

'What do you mean Tuesday? It's Monday today. You mean to say there's only one train a day?'

'It seems so.'

'What a backward country. When does the bus get us back?' asked Tristan sat stationary on his bed idling flicking through his camera inventory again.

'I don't know.'

I made a mad dash to the bus station, which was adjacent to the train station, and thank the lord there was a bus that would get us to Kėdainiai an hour before the trial. We'd only need to sit on a bus for three hours. I had been moving about for only 20 minutes, but my hangover was causing sweat to drip from my forehead, and I panted heavily. All this effort just to make sure I could have the bloody trial. Slowly moving my way back to the hotel and bedroom I opened the door and told Tristan the good news, but we had to get a move on.

'Well that gives us plenty of time. I saw a Eurolines office yesterday; I think we should go there and sort out our travel to Riga and then Estonia. It'll be cheaper to do it now than later.' He made a face as if to say *what's all the fuss about?*

'Okay, probably a good idea, from what I saw on Saturday I don't think I'm going to impress too much.

'From what I saw in Malta and Andorra I agree.'

'Well great work this morning getting everything arranged,' I said sarcastically. I didn't like his tone so thought I'd get him back.

'Thanks, I've seen some of the footage and you are admirably making a twat out of yourself, so lets move on and get this travel sorted.'

'I meant with the trains and buses and getting back to Kėdainiai. I was being sarcastic.'

'I know you were slag.'

'Shut up slag.'

'Great putdown.'

'Come on, we don't have time for this… you sweaty slag.'

Throughout our stay in Lithuania I had been constantly on the internet emailing the clubs who I still had potential trials with, so that there could be no repeat of the Andorra situation, where we were sat on our arses with nothing to do. With it being Monday and having a trial with Nevezis in a couple of hours it was looking likely that we would go over the border to neighbouring to Latvia to have a trial there on the Wednesday, followed by a trial in Estonia on the Friday as a backup to the backup. In Malta I'd made a promise to myself that I wouldn't under any circumstances have two trials in three days again, but it now it seemed I was going to have three trials in five days: an insane amount for a man who was still so hung-over from a night out two days previously that even when sat down I got alcohol cramps in my legs.

'What about the trial in Sweden?' asked Tristan, back into super-organisation mode in the Eurolines offices that run buses and ferries across Europe.

'What do you mean?'

'Well I've got a mate, Lars, in Sweden we could stay with, and you said you may have a trial in Sweden yes?'

'Possibly, but I haven't spoken to them since we left. Anyway Sweden is ages off.' He wasn't making much sense to me.

'Well we could leave Estonia on a boat and go to Sweden for a couple of days for a trial. Ring them.'

'What?'

'Ring them.'

'They're not going to remember who I am.'

'They will, how many shit English footballers are they going to get an email from asking for a trial with no football CV. Ring them.'

With Tristan staring me down in a sort of animal kingdom Stag mode, I reluctantly tried but there was no answer.

'Why are you so desperate for me to ring them?' I said.

'Because the earlier we book the ferry the quicker the cheaper it will be, plus I don't want to be sat around again like in Andorra.'

'But we may have to hang around in Latvia or Estonia for a couple of weeks yet, they may want me to stick around.'

'Ralf, look at me, what are the chances that that's going to happen?' He had sincerity in his eyes and put both his hands on my shoulders, either to add weight to his comment or for balance from his heavy bag.

'The chances are not great I grant you that,' I said.

'Well let's book the ferry to Sweden now then,' he slapped my arm in a gung-ho fashion.

'But it's still not set in stone.'

'No matter, they've said yes, it will go ahead.'

Tristan was right, the Baltics weren't likely to offer me anything if the game I saw Nevezis play is anything to go by, but a semi-professional club in Sweden might.

'Okay, let's book it.'

With no trial confirmed for Sweden, we booked our boat from Estonia to Stockholm for £30 each in an overnight cabin. We had the next week planned and for the first time in two weeks we were almost organised. If one of the clubs asked me to hang around to potentially play a game, it would throw a spanner in the works. But for that we needed my football ability to be up to scratch and the chances of that happening?... Hmmm.

Checking into the Kėdainiai hotel with my 48-hour hangover retreating at last, I got ready for my fourth trial. The bus journey itself was almost like a train – slow, rickety, overcrowded, with more than a few dubious smells. It was just like being at home. The bus even had a conductor to check our tickets, and also go around with a basket to all the passengers in a trolley service. I had to sit next to another delightful older Lithuanian female citizen, but unlike our friend on the train out to Vilnius, this one spoke no English and had few teeth, but the language barrier or lack of dental work didn't stop her talking to me constantly throughout the journey, smiling at all times. Either she was a bit mad or 'I'm English, I don't speak Lithuanian,' translates perfectly into Lithuanian as something hilarious and thus makes me a bit of a hoot in this part of the world.

Once we finally reached our surprisingly cheap and clean hotel room in Kėdainiai, I went through my pre-trial brief checklist.

Ankle protector on?

Check.

Football boots in hand?

Check.

Kit on?

Check

Butterflies in the stomach?

Check.

Briefs crushing my genitals?

Check.

I was ready. With five minutes to wait until Solus arrived to pick us up I stared at the white wall facing my bed, seriously regretting consuming more alcohol two nights ago than I had done in my entire life. I felt horrendous. George Best and all other great football-playing drinkers obviously had two things I didn't: an abundance of talent and a strong liver.

Stumbling downstairs to greet our host, I did my best to put on my happy face, although I think he read it immediately and blatantly didn't care. I imagine he was happy to have guests visit his club and show an interest. He laughed and simply pointed at my sunken, ghoulish face and said: 'Vilnius, vodka, hahaha.' I didn't think it was very amusing.

We jumped in Solus' car and I looked at Tristan, hoping he'd have a heart attack or something so that I didn't have to have the trial, but the selfish moron stayed in fine health and just laughed at my nervous expression.

The training session was taking place on the same pitch I'd seen the team play their game on. The pitch was in poor condition with holes, bumps, and all manner of divots in the ground making me think that the only way anyone could impress on this pitch would be if they were a world class player who can play on any surface or just your average bruiser. It was not an average technician's pitch as the bumps and holes made the passing side of the game difficult to accomplish without an exceptional amount of skill and talent that I clearly do not have.

As each player turned up I couldn't help but notice how young they all looked. Solus explained that they were the reserve side and some were as young as 16. What embarrassment lay in store for me?

Standing there at the side of the pitch eagerly anticipating my introduction I felt a tingle in my groin, odd considering I wasn't moving. Another tingle moments later, this time on my buttock, then another on my thigh, then again in a more 'delicate' area. Before I knew it my entire crotch wasn't just tingling, it was on fire. It didn't take long for me to deduce what had happened. The deep heat that exploded in my bag obviously found it's way to the new pair of briefs I'd put on in preparation for the trial. My balls were on fire and my eyes watered with the pain. A quick peek whilst no one was looking by stretching my shorts elastic revealed red raw skin everywhere. But it was too late, as I was looking at my testicles, a wiry man approached us in a full blue Nevezis tracksuit. Being caught staring at my nuts was not the best way to start.

The coach introduced himself to me and asked if I spoke German. I in return asked if he spoke English. Both questions were met with a 'no'. He may have even asked 'Why were you staring at your penis with young boys present?' but I wasn't to know. Without Justina there to guide us, our communications with Solus and everyone else was proving difficult. My 'translator' for the training session, Kielson, was one of the club's youngest players, and his knowledge of the English language was not of the same calibre as Justina's. It may be the case that they won't want to sign me, but they'd have no way to tell me. The best thing was the fact that the climate was similar to an early English spring evening but this in no way cooled my crotch. I was in agony, and this time before I'd even started running. The coach himself was not like Patrick at Santa Venera, or Joey with St George's, or the rotund Francois at FC Lusitanos – all these men were strong-looking figures. This man had more of an Arsene Wenger appearance about him. He was thin, unshaven, pacing up and down the pitch, eyeing his players as they chatted and idly kicked a ball between them.

With a quick clap of the coach's hands and a circling motion with his wrist we began running, and to my relief it was brief. Just a short warm-up – three laps of the pitch – was exactly what the doctor ordered to get rid of my lingering hangover. And then we stretched. And then stretched, and then we stretched some more. 10 minutes later I was wondering if this was going to be a yoga session. Thankfully by now by crotch had cooled so I could concentrate on the task in hand, however I couldn't see any footballs, and no member of the reserve squad even questioned the length of the stretching session. On and on it went until finally from nowhere a mass of balls appeared that had been hidden amongst some bushes from the last training session, canny. The sun had set and out came the mosquitoes – and not just any old mosquitoes. Massive mosquitoes. They were the size of my thumbs, and were there were hundreds of them. And every last one of them was swarming around Tristan.

'Get off you bastards. Ahh, slags… Ahh, piss off!'

Sixteen Lithuanian teenagers, Solus and the coach all stared at my brother as the bluest of profanities, some of which I had never even heard before and that won't be written here, came hurtling from his mouth. His limbs flailed in all manner of directions. He began to use his camera as a swatting device, punching the air, yet not making a dent on the health of the mosquitoes swarming around his person.

'Get off me you *BEEP BEEP BEEP*. You little mother *BEEP BEEPS*. I'm going to *BEEP* show you the meaning of *BEEP BEEP* pain. I hate you. you little *BEEEEEEEEEEP*!'

A collection of schoolchildren from Lithuania had been introduced to some of England's darkest swear words, and although they didn't know the true meaning of them, they knew they weren't very nice. Tristan stopped and looked at me.

'They won't leave me alone the little shits!' (Sorry, the little *BEEPS*). 'Look at the size of that bite,' he said pointing to his hand, which was host to a bite as big as a VW camper van.

'I have to play football now Tristan. Please stop making me look bad.'

We split into pairs. I was with Kielson whose English was still sketchy, but eventually, through a series of mime and examples, he managed to convey to me what we needed to do.

First was passes to each other. Easy, back and forth, back and forth. Then, however, we had to pass to each other, spin 360 degrees on the spot, receive the ball back, pass again and then receive it. It looked odd, it felt odd and I had no idea what the benefit was, but for the watching coach I did this without question and admirably.

Following the simple passing exchanges was heads and volleys to each other in the air whilst moving around the open pitch, all the time making sure we kept the ball airborne. I was actually doing well, with the ball staying in the air more often than not. An occasional lunge was needed to keep it going, but by and large we did well. Could it be that alcohol actually does have some mystical powers to make you play football well?

We then played a game of football, once again seven-on-seven, with small goals and no goalkeepers. This was obviously a very light training session for them, and I was a bit annoyed. I had requested a trial, but instead I was having a training session with the reserve squad, the vast majority of whom were aged 16-18. Again, my standard wasn't disgraceful and I played well, but without playing with the first team I'd never know how I measured up. Not that it mattered really, because in all honesty I wasn't up to scratch compared to even some of the 16 year olds, so it was apparent I wasn't about to be given the V.I.P treatment and ushered straight into the first team. I needed to run the show for our side in this small game, win every tackle, make every pass and score a hatful of goals; but I didn't score a goal, I misplaced far too many passes and I didn't put any tackles in. I was average. Don't get me wrong I didn't disgrace myself, but I didn't stand out so much that Solus and the coach would want to fork out a 2,000-Euro registration fee to sign me. They had seen enough, and I hadn't done enough.

'For you to be a professional footballer would be difficult,' said the coach, through my translator. 'You have a bit of skill and understand the game, but your technique is not strong enough and your aggression and physical presence is not good enough. He says that after erm…'

My young translator then slapped his thighs to illustrate the word the coach was looking for.

'After being a teenager?'

'No, it's erm…'

He slapped his thighs once more.

'After puberty?'

'No erm…' Again slapping his thighs. 'After being ten you didn't erm…'

'I didn't grow after being 10?'

'No, erm…' The slapping continuing.

We weren't getting anywhere and I called a halt to proceedings as I already knew I couldn't make it. If only Justina was there I may have known what he was on about and could have improved for my next trial, but as it happens she wasn't and so I had no idea what my thighs did or did not lack, or if my thighs had anything to do with it in the first place. I rationalised it for myself, as it was pretty obvious – I'd heard it all before at the three trials previous to this, and throughout my life. I had half-decent technique, but I'm not strong enough or aggressive enough to warrant a closer look, let alone a contract. Once the translator and coach left me to my own devices Solus approached.

'Vilnius!' he said with a smile.

'Yes, Vilnius; it ruined me.'

He laughed. Although I don't think he fully understood my words he certainly understood my body language. He then lifted his nose as if a smell had caught his attention, I was in no doubt that smell was the deep heat emanating from my briefs.

Solus drove us back to the hotel and we went out to dinner, where he talked to us about football, his love of Tottenham Hotspur and what it was like to grow up in the Soviet Union. It was difficult to understand everything but what I did get was that he was, and everyone was, a much happier person now than when under a communist regime. When we returned to the hotel, we presented him with a bottle of Red Lithuanian vodka, the stuff that had shaped our last 4 days. It seemed an apt gift to give him although he deserved so much more for all his efforts and incredible hospitality. We hugged Solus a fond goodbye.

Lithuania offered me little in the way of footballing opportunities, which made me sad, but that was purely down to my own shortcomings. It did, however, introduce me to an incredibly kind people who were cheeky and hospitable beyond what I deserved, and I saw two amazing cities in Kėdainiai and Vilnius that I will never forget. Saying all that, despite the fast accruing lifelong memories I was getting from this trip, I would trade them all in at once if it meant being professional footballer. Then I could be done with the whole thing and get on with the rest of my life.

CHAPTER 13: 4 MINUTE WARNING

Budget Left: £500

Situated further east along the Baltic ocean and bordering Russia ,
Estonia and Belarus as well as Lithuania, Latvia was the next target.
I say 'target'; I hadn't exactly targeted the country. I didn't think to
myself 'Latvia has a history of being rubbish at football I'll try there'
– far from it. Latvia has a decent history in the sport and is the only
country of the Baltic states to have competed in the European
Championships, with an appearance in the 2004 competition, but
with my options now fast dwindling, and given its geographic
closeness to Lithuania, I had no choice but to hop on the three-hour
continental bus service between Vilnius and Riga in order to
potentially embarrass myself further.

Similar to Lithuania in its language, culture and geography,
Latvia is reminiscent of Northern England, with open fields and farm
equipment everywhere. With a population of just over 2 million – a
million less than Lithuania – I was naively pinning my hopes on the
million missing being those who were good at football. The first we
knew that we were passing into Latvia was when we drove through
quite possibly the most relaxed border control barricade in Europe.
Two policemen sat in cars each facing each other at a right angle to
the arrow-straight road all day, with binoculars staring at swathes of
traffic passing in and out of the respective countries. What a boring
job. I imagine the only vehicles they would stop would be those on
fire or those carrying banners saying 'Death to the Baltic region!'

Having slept on the coach and feeling groggy, I stepped off the
bus in Riga and found the temperature was even more biting than in
Lithuania with the smell of the now ever-present navy blue Baltic
sea reminding me of visiting Blackpool as a kid, in the sense that it
was cold, smelt weird, everything looked off-colour and I didn't
want to be there. I needed a rest, badly. I still wanted to be a
professional footballer, but a two-day sleep without travel or football
would have been appreciated at this juncture.

The trial I arranged in Latvia was through an agent, Andrejs, via
email. My initial correspondence must have bounced round a few
people before ending up at his desk, and his response offered me a

trial with FC Daugava. He is the first agent I have had the misfortune of coming across. I acknowledge that having an agent would have made this whole experience a lot easier for myself, and seeing as most agents lack any sort of moral compass they could have lied bare-faced to all of these clubs and I could have pulled off a con, of playing in a game without training, with the agent taking his healthy 80% cut – but I am not one to do that. I wanted to succeed or fail on my own merit.

A lot of high-level clubs only deal with agents now, who can wax lyrical about a player and be able to understand contracts, which many modern-day professionals can't be bothered to do, or simply don't have the ability to do in the first place. They hike up wages and appearance fees, and this has a negative effect on the perception of the sport. I realise that they're only doing their jobs, but I imagine most sports agents would sell their mothers to the devil if it made them a few quid. Andrejs, I am sure, is looking at some sort of financial gain from this arrangement if at all possible, even if it's only to take 70 cents from my 1-Euro payment.

Thankfully FC Daugava are based in Riga, Latvia 's capital city. They are in the second tier of Latvian football and are based only a mile out of the city centre. They are named after the Daugava river, which runs through Riga and used to be the city's main artery, much like the Thames to London. Although visiting Kėdainiai had been an excellent experience, it had been difficult to get there seeing as Lithuanian's themselves didn't seem to know where it was. Travelling there on an archaic public transport system after our night out in Vilnius where few understood English was tricky. At least now with Riga our bus would pull into the terminal and everything would go swimmingly well, you would hope.

Using Tristan's best friend (his trusted internet phone, not his penis), we booked a nice, clean hostel amidst the cobbled streets of the old town and went out to explore. Riga, like Vilnius, was gorgeous. Gothic spires, pedestrianised streets, ridiculously talented buskers, open aired squares and beautiful women (although not in the same league as Vilnius), offset only by the fact that it was now less than 24 hours to my trial and Andrejs still hadn't contacted me to confirm it.

He had confirmed to me in previous emails that a trial would definitely go ahead on a Wednesday evening, but despite repeated attempts to call him and email him, he was proving elusive. Had stage fright got the better of Andrejs? Was he beginning to question why an Englishman would travel so far in order to become a professional footballer when places such as Malta and Andorra had already turned him down? In fact, I reasoned, that's exactly what he was thinking. I decided there and then that I would no longer tell prospective clubs where I had already been, as that provides a great amount of evidence towards me being crap at this game. I don't like misleading people, but sometimes it doesn't pay to be so truthful, and with Andrejs I fear I might have been just that.

With a similar situation to the first day in Andorra unfolding, I was a bit annoyed. Granted, I was in a beautiful city surrounded by beautiful women but that's not what I set out to do (and I never thought I'd catch myself saying that). If Latvia was going to fall through I would have rather gone straight to Estonia where the trial was definitely going ahead, and spent a couple of days there, perhaps even a couple of days training, heaven forbid. Unfortunately due to the agent I was in a state of limbo with nothing to do but to go out and look at beautiful women and beautiful architecture and watch the world go by.

That evening we settled for a meal in one of the outside restaurants situated in one of Riga's many squares with a view of the Dome Cathedral, which ironically had no dome. We conveniently stationed ourselves next to a patio heater and awaited service. Although the heater probably caused more damage to the ozone layer than China's last ten years of industrialisation, it's warmth was most welcome.

'What are we going to do then?' asked Tristan, who for once did not have any of his bulky camera equipment on him.

'I don't know. I'm losing the will with this in all honesty.' I truly was. We were in Latvia with no trial, running out of money and I felt like I wasn't going to fulfil my dream. Not in the Baltics anyway.

'Well we can have a nice night tonight, and then do touristy things tomorrow. You know we still haven't had a full-on tourist day yet? Let's see… some churches, and then get pissed tomorrow, yeah? Then we'll give Estonia what for!' While Tristan was trying not to agree that all was lost at this point, I could see it in him. I think he was just being a big brother rather than a mate or director, by not allowing me to get too despondent about the whole journey.

'Okay then,' I concurred at last, 'we'll do touristy things and appreciate everything we've done so far, and then get drunk and bitch about agents who break their promises.'

'Groovy.'

After finishing our meals we wandered the streets until midnight, and it was inspiring. The Old Town had a glorious medieval feel to it, but without the Black Death or corpses in the street, which I imagine would have put a dampener on things. The narrow streets, tall buildings, and a café culture that lasts until the wee small hours were all majestic and, well, foreign. Many have said that Riga is being destroyed by the 'stag' scene of European tourists who are there simply to get drunk on the relatively cheap alcohol and visit the abundance of strip clubs (I only know this due to second-hand knowledge, honestly) but what I found was quite the opposite, and like Lithuania we felt like we were aliens in a foreign land, which is an increasingly difficult thing to do in an ever-interchangeable Europe. It may have helped that I was there on a weekday, but it felt like I was an adventurer.

Looking at my phone to find no correspondence from anyone, let alone Andrejs, my mood sank. However, we then chanced upon a small narrow street from which the faintest orchestral music was resonating. Taking a chance on walking down an unlit alleyway in the early hours of the morning, something we wouldn't ever do in London, the music grew stronger and clearer and out of the dark shadows two stationary seated figures appeared before us. As our eyes adjusted to the darkness we saw that the figures were sat in an oversized stone archway of a church, and both were playing cellos, which before this event I've always seen simply as a violin for people with chubby fingers. I was wrong. My classical music knowledge is not so great, but there were some recognisable melodies that warmed us to the core despite the arctic temperatures. The dynamic was that the less-talented partner played the simple bass-lines and the man who was obviously infinitely more talented launched into piercing melodies. As several more people filtered through to listen to the music, I took a seat just three metres in front of them on the street floor and listened intently. Music for the first time had made me speechless. I sat there for an hour, and as other tourists came and went due to the cold, and even Tristan eventually bailing out, I remained there to the very end with a numb bum, shaking with cold, but it was worth the discomfort to listen to the simple deep reassuring music that rose high into the street in the natural acoustics of the surroundings. It was mesmerising. When it finished I paid them a handsome busker's fee and thanked them. I returned to the hostel to find Tristan in bed but not asleep. He greeted me by passing wind. I'd gone from the height of Continental European Culture to the depths of English humour in a matter of minutes.

'I think we should go the Latvian War Museum,' I said, chewing an overdone breakfast omelette in the hostel's restaurant.

'Really?' asked Tristan. He looked worried. Clearly he didn't want to go.

'Yeah, the guidebook says it's really good and I'd like to see it. It's free!'

'Alright then, but if it's boring I'm blaming you. Have you heard back from that chump agent yet?'

'Nope.'

'Have you tried emailing?'

'Yes.'

'Have you tried phoning him?'

'Yes. No answer.'

'What a chump.'

'What a chump indeed. Come on, let's go and do something with our day so it's not a complete waste of time.'

I 'dropped out' of a history degree when I was 18, citing that there was too much reading to do, before foolishly doing a Journalism degree that required just as much reading and a whole lot more writing. Not only did you have to read things, but the majority of the time you had to create the content as well. Planning, I hope you can now appreciate, has never been a strong point of mine.

I've always found history interesting but the degree-level was too much, so I tend to just watch documentaries on television about history, thereby letting the producers and researchers decide what's interesting and cutting out the boring stuff. It's a much more colourful and exciting way to view history than my imagination could ever give me from dusty old textbooks written by one too many a historian with a double- barrelled last name, such as Laurence Basil-Farnley or James Monkton-Tomlinson. Museums have pictures and stands and objects from the past, so although reading was required, I felt I could brave it.

I highly recommend the museum, and particularly to those like me who were born in peacetime in Western Europe in latter half of the 20th century. The privileges afforded to the majority of us, such as food, clothes and water, really are taken for granted. The trial was supposed to be taking place that evening. However, that seemed unlikely now given Andrejs lack of consideration for a man who has travelled over a thousand miles to a foreign country at his behest. Feeling despondent, we went for a beer.

'So what do you want to do now?' asked Tristan, writing a post card home.

'I wouldn't mind finding somewhere really good to eat tonight and stuffing ourselves really. A kind of commiseration.' I said as I polished off my third beer that was placed before me merely 30 seconds beforehand.

'Great. I can't believe that agent you know. What an arse!' Tristan was right on the money.

'I know! What a dick. Yes you can have a trial. Yes you can have a trial. Yes you can have a trial. Come on this day, come on this day, come on this day… that's all he kept saying. Well I'm here on this day and no trial! There's three things I can't stand about people and that's arrogance, ignorance and inconsistency and this guy has been inconsistent to the max. I wouldn't have minded him simply saying no, I accepted it from the other thousand clubs, but this winds me up. I don't like hanging like this, the least he could do is answer his phone but obviously he's running scared and is too good for that.' The beers really had hit home, and now I'd got a taste for it, and for complaining.

'You want another beer?' Tristan motioned towards the waitress who had served us just a minute before.

'Yes I definitely want another beer. You know what REALLY annoys me about this guy is that—'

And then I was interrupted by my phone buzzing to tell me I had a text message.

*From: Andrejs *******

14:37

*Hi Ralf. Sorry I have been so late in getting back to you. I have been
driving for a day. You can have your trial tonight. It starts at 6. Get
the number 8 bus out of the station at 5 to the last stop where player
Igor will collect you. It will cost you about 80lvs.
Andrejs.*

Bollocks. For the second trial in a row I would have alcohol very
present in my bloodstream.

'Tristan, I've just got a text message,' I said despondently.

'Yeah?'

'The trial's back on.'

'What?'

We quickly downed our fourth drink (I'm not one to waste
money) and jogged back to the hostel to get changed.

The beers had made us both very sleepy and I wasn't feeling the
need to run around a field for two hours any more than Tristan
wanted to run around a field for two hours filming me. Unable to
find access to the internet I couldn't do any research on the club until
I met the coach, whoever that may be. A short bus journey was
followed by a long wait, until what was now becoming a far-too-
familiar scene on this trip, a silver BMW pulled up alongside me
with an open window.

'Ralf?' asked a man with a well-worn, leathery face.

'Igor?'

Trial number five was around the corner.

Round the corner it was, quite literally so. Unlike Nevezis in
Lithuania, this training pitch wasn't adjoined to the stadium's
ground, nor like the ones in Malta was it part of a training complex,
astroturf or otherwise. In actual fact it was a park – a normal park
you would find anywhere, and didn't look like a semi-professional
operation, much less a professional one. The pitch was sandwiched
between a scrap yard and another small pitch that had Latvian
primary school kids honing their skills en masse, all kicking each
others shins more than they actually kicked the ball. They all had
regimented haircuts, and some of them even had mullets. Tragic.

I learned from Igor that he used to be a professional footballer in the Ukraine, and was one of the only full-time players for FC Daugava, and judging by the size of his forearms – which looked like home-made loaves of bread – I figured I was already out of my league here. He was coming to the end of his career but he still looked incredibly fit and strong; not much taller than me, but broad, with an uncompromising look to his face that dispersed fleetingly whenever he smiled. His English was broken but he was able to hold a conversation, not that I got real chance to have one once we had arrived as he bolted for the wooden shack next to the pitch masquerading as changing rooms. In my brief time with Igor I had learned that Daugava was a club with little money and a team that concentrated on youth development, with Igor the oldest player by over 10 years. The idea being that anyone half decent would be sold on to help with the running costs of the club. I was to be training with 18-21 year-olds again.

Already kitted out (having been mindful to avoid dousing my privates in deep heat again), I didn't feel the need to go into the changing rooms but with Igor in there and seemingly my only ally as I had no idea who the coach was, I decided to try and meet up with him again. However, he didn't seem too interested and was more keen on talking to the players in the dilapidated changing rooms. I did my best to integrate with the players, but without anyone present to introduce me, I felt like a geeky kid at his first day at school desperately trying to make new friends. Thankfully one young man, Arthur (pronounced *Art-cha*), took pity on me and spoke to me in fluent English. He was only 19, and the spitting image of Manchester United midfielder Michael Carrick, the only difference being that he classified himself as a striker. It was from him I learned that the coach wasn't going to be here today, and that Igor would be taking training as he was by far the most experienced player. This was the first time in all of the trials I didn't either have a proper representative of the club there to introduce me to everyone or show some hospitality. The faceless agent was probably merely sat by his phone waiting for Igor's verdict on whether I would be worth his precious time in drawing up a contract.

Walking out onto the pitch with the rest of the players it was business as usual in terms of the questions asked of me: 'Where had I been?', 'Where was I going next if I failed in Latvia?', 'Did I have any trials in England?', etc. This time, however, I was far more cagey with my answers, still thinking that being honest about not being good enough in Andorra probably isn't the best policy in a country that has 40 times the population. Igor gave me a brief shout out to all the players, explaining what I was doing and explaining why Tristan, wrapped in about 16 layers, was stood with a film camera the size of King Kong. It was cold, but I didn't care so much – I had a beer coat on and soon enough I was sure I would be sweating and feeling like I wanted to die.

Twenty minutes in and we were still doing sprinting, jogging and stretching. Igor was obviously a big fan of stretching, and it's probably because he knows players who stretch correctly can get another couple of years added onto their career. Although he was a professional, I doubt he will have earned enough to retire on, so you can understand why he'd want to stretch for ten minutes longer than what was probably necessary for everyone else.

Some of the stretches we were doing, it has to be said, were insane. We formed a large, spaced-out circle around Igor, who at one stage had us all lying on our fronts with only our bellies touching the ground, before systematically lifting all four limbs in the air to almost touch one another above the spine. It was something I had never done before, and my body was telling me as much, with twinges and twangs in my back, and the feeling of cramp coming on in muscles I never thought I had. Other stretches were more standard: groin, hamstring, arms, quadriceps, etc, but again lasting far longer than I had experienced before, even during the yoga session that passed for a warm-up in Lithuania. Just as I thought we had done stretching he had told us to sit down and more limbering-up ensued. Another one I had never seen before, as Igor sat down with his legs stretched out and then bent the knee in his right leg and brought his foot to rest flat on the ground next to the top of his left groin. I didn't really see what muscle this would stretch and attempted it, only to find that it did in fact stretch my right arse cheek to smithereens, I was certainly going to have a sore gluteus maximus for a while, and we still had to do it on the other side. Attempting to avoid damaging the left side in similar fashion to the right, I took a more laidback approach to this one and didn't try to raise my knee as high, so as not to stretch the muscles so much. However, on concentrating so fervently on not over-extending my left bum cheek, I inadvertently kicked myself in the testicles when bringing my left foot to rest next to my groin. Masking kicking yourself in the nuts as a foreigner amongst natives during a football trial is difficult to do, but I managed on virtue that I was in so much pain I didn't actually make any noise. When you see someone get kicked in the shins they scream, but when you see someone get shot in movies they often don't make a sound due to the shock. I was in both shock and pain, and my stomach and testicles were aching in such a manner that I would have quite liked a lie down and a hot water bottle nuzzled between my thighs for a few hours in order to recuperate.

With bruised testicles and a torn right arse cheek, the trial and training was about to begin proper. If that was the warm-up, I was dreading the training session. Before the stretches started, Igor had spent a good few minutes placing cones around the pitch. In that time the rest of us took it upon ourselves to play keepy uppy with a ball in twos and threes. I was with Arthur and his friend who, of course, were roughly 27 million times better than me. They were stretching and lunging to keep my below-adequate passes under control, whereas I stood stationary, not moving a muscle to control any ball as each one they volleyed, kneed or headed to me was pinpoint in its precision. My return passes were often shinned or sliced and required the other players to go fetch, and this was before I'd kicked myself in the balls and torn my arse cheek.

With the cones remaining redundant for now Igor instructed us in pairs or threes to 'ping' the ball between each other over great distances, 40 yards and beyond. This I could do, I thought, and thankfully Arthur and his friend let me join in with them.

Drilling and lofting the ball high in the air isn't a very good way to determine if anyone is good at football. I know this because it's a skill I actually possess. Passing it high and long in a triangle I looked good, seeing the pass and my target and perfectly delivering it to the feet of my team-mates. Things were going well; the testicles had come back out to play and were no longer cowering after I had treated them so harshly, and my bum, although feeling gammy, was warming up and would be okay for the next few hours I was sure. Just as I started to develop a certain swagger, even playing passes first time with one touch without controlling the ball, Arthur sent a long and high pass to me that approached far to my right, at high velocity, and at a height that would fall in my midriff. Igor was watching and would surely report back to Andrejs and the coach. Great players wouldn't be flustered by a ball travelling like this, they would simply move quickly and control it with either their head or chest, or would stick out a telescopic leg to tame the miss-hit pass, control it and then send it on its way back to the source or another team-mate. In those split seconds I couldn't decide how to control the pass. Was I going to head it? No way – I have a very fashionable hair cut. To chest it down wasn't an option either, as the ball was moving away from me and I worried I'd just divert the ball even further from my grasp. There was only one thing for it. With Igor watching, I would have to run to my right, jump in the air, stick out a leg and hope I caught it right and brought it down to ground level with me. I lunged with all my might, rose high into the air, stuck out my right leg, and missed the ball completely. In fact, I misjudged the flight of the ball so much it went over my head. And just to put a cherry on the top of proceedings I pulled my right groin muscle in the attempt. Igor turned away from me to watch players who warranted his time more than I.

Then the proper football started, and unlike other countries where we had nice exercises of attack versus defence, or seven-a-side, this time we did something that I still don't fully understand. It was a game, I know that much, with four small boxes created by cones situated in each corner of the pitch. Each box had an occupant, two boxes had players wearing white and two wearing black (my team). I think the idea of the game was that the men in the middle had to get the ball back to their team mate in one of the boxes and then swap over with them in a capture-the-flag scenario. I was pretty sure it was that, but then something would happen where players didn't swap. I simply had no idea, not that it mattered, and I think in the half-hour duration of the game I must have touched the ball six times. Boy, were they good, both my team-mates and the opposing team. There was slick passing, constant dialogue between one another, and small touches of brilliance and flicks of inspiration. As soon as I got close to the ball or a player, it or they were gone in a puff of the pitch's dry turf. The only thing of note I did do was get a cut eye when a flailing hand caught me, but it was minor and I continued with the blood soon drying thanks to my congealed sweat. I ran round in circles, saying 'Hep hep hep,' which was my new universal word for 'Yes!' whenever I wanted the ball. However, no matter how much I shouted 'Hep!' the ball rarely came to me because the positions I had taken on the pitch seemed to be too elementary, or I was unable to shake my man. I considered for a while that 'Hep' might be an insult in Latvian, but stuck to my new word tenaciously. Whenever the opposition was in possession my team-mates would yell at me 'Stay with a man, stay with a man,' but they were so quick in thought and feet that it was like trying to keep up with racehorse. I wasn't about to roll off the pitch to be sick, but the speed and acceleration of the players did me in. It was incredible, and I wasn't. They were doing things that in the most part I could do – it was simple passing and movement – but done at ten times the speed that my skills or physique allowed.

At one stage I saw how serious the training session was to Igor, who was constantly shouting words of encouragement or abuse (I worked this out by his tone of voice) to the players. At one stage he even stopped play and shouted at a mullet-haired boy who was, in my opinion, one of the better players on the field. He did so with ferocity for 3 minutes, with the player a safe distance away. At one stage it seemed Igor was just ranting to himself, as he wasn't making eye contact with anyone and simply dawdled with the ball under his arm, with no one daring to make a move, before locking his gaze on the culprit once more. The mullet-haired boy's crime was choosing not to head the ball and turning his back to it, something Igor then demonstrated as being wrong by shouting a lot in his face. Of course all of this was in Latvian, but you didn't need to be fluent to know what was going on. The mullet boy entered a momentary sulk before the game was back up to speed.

With the full-time whistle blown after 45 minutes I was informed by Arthur that our team had lost and needed to do press-ups, twenty of them, as punishment. Still not understanding the rules of the game I had just played for 45 minutes, I thought twenty press-ups was a fair punishment, and I'd rather not question how we'd lost or ask 'how do you score a point?' I did the press-ups – something my light body is naturally half decent at – and we moved onto a version of attack vs. defence.

Seven players vs. seven players; one goal, one goalkeeper. One side starts as attack, the other defence. Once the defence has completed five passes and returned the ball to the other end of the pitch, they become the attacking side and the opposition switches to defence. First to five goals wins, losers do 20 press-ups.

I ended up doing 20 press-ups.

During the hour-long game you could count the touches I made on one hand. That's less than one touch every ten minutes. Shameful. Again I was outdone by the pace and movement of the players and whenever my side were in possession I couldn't keep up with them. If they ever did pass to me I would slow them down in their move. I wasn't so much a third wheel because I was making up the numbers, but I was certainly a wonky one. I was doing a job, just not as efficiently as everyone else and so they naturally gravitated to using each other rather than me.

It was up to me to impose myself, show them that I can play, that I should be paid to play football. I figured if I can't be the flair I'll be the engine, use my one attribute, the one thing I actually trained before the trip begun: I decided to run and run and run. I still felt surprisingly fit despite sore testicles, a pulled groin and a strained arse, and so I chased everything with all my might. Head down at a constant pace I chased everything, harassing everyone, and yet I still didn't get anywhere near the ball as they sprayed first-time passes to whoever was in space. The closest I got to the ball in my ten-minute role as 'the engine' was during a 50-50 challenge with the mullet boy who had been on the receiving end of Igor's frustrations an hour earlier. With the ball equidistant between us, we both lunged for the ball. He got it and I got his shins with an almighty clash. He wasn't wearing shin pads, as most players don't in training, and the reaction in his eyes which flared with rage suggested that my testicles may be in for a rougher ride yet. Thankfully, all my football expertise got me out of any harmful retribution. I extended an open-palmed hand to him which he slapped in acknowledgement of my apology and made his way past me to continue to embarrass me on the football pitch.

Our team lost the game 5-2 and I had no involvement in any of the goals, either for or against. I wasn't anywhere near anything decent we did, and was too far from the action to make any costly mistakes. It's often said by many football pundits of a striker who is continually missing easy chances that 'at least he was in the position to miss' – the now-retired Andrew Cole got that often during his Manchester United and England career. This was something I never really fully understood until that night. I was barely noticed by anyone really, simply because I couldn't be in the right place at the right time to do anything right or wrong. For the first time ever I felt my football brain had let me down, not my physical or technical ability. I didn't do anything good to impress but I didn't do anything bad either to make a lasting impression. I was beige, and no one likes beige.

A final warm-down exercise of free kicks took place, with each player taking one free kick and the team that scored the most out of seven attempts winning. The losers again do press-ups.

Stepping up, I casually stroked the ball into the bottom corner and scored from 20 yards, something the majority of players failed to do. Ironic applause was given to me. I looked over to Tristan, who was whispering profanities to himself once more, as he'd failed to capture the one good thing I'd done yet again. It was far too little, far too late and I wished I had managed to do that in Andorra during the free kick session there, where I'd had the slimmest of chances. Here it was clear all hope was gone.

'Igor, thanks for letting me train with you tonight.'

'Hey it's okay.' Igor's face was cheerful again, rather than menacing.

'Do you think I'm good enough to be a professional footballer in Latvia?'

Igor laughed, and then looked and me and realised I was serious.

'It's difficult to say. Although you have some technical ability you are lacking mentally and physically, but because I was playing too I couldn't see everything. If a coach was here he would be able to help more.'

Igor was trying to spare my feelings, it was clear; he knew and I knew that I wasn't good enough, but I wanted confirmation from a professional.

'Do you think I could even get paid one Euro for one minute in a game in Latvia?'

I asked, rephrasing the question hoping it would result in a finite answer.

'No, not if they were taking it seriously. But like I say, it's difficult because no coach is here.'

'Thank you Igor.' I had heard everything I wanted to hear, it was becoming increasingly apparent that it wasn't going to happen, not in Europe anyway; there were only four clubs left in Europe willing to give me a trial, and they were all arguably in better footballing countries than the Baltic states.

'You know,' said Igor in a casual way as we drudged off the pitch, 'our young players dream of 1 million Euros, you dream of one; that is a beautiful dream.'

Later, Igor drove us back to Riga. I had spent a little over two hours with FC Daugava and it was clear that I wasn't going to make it in Latvia.

'Where's your next trial?' asked Igor as we exited the car.

'In Estonia, Tallinn. FC Levadia.'

'Levadia? Top division – very, very good.'

That's not what I needed to hear.

From Andrejs *****:
Hi Ralf,
How did the trial go?

Hi Andrejs,
It didn't go well. Definitely the best standard I have encountered so far so I am going to Estonia to try my luck there.
Thanks for the trial.
Ralf

Although I didn't get to be a professional in Latvia, at least I embarrassed an agent. A minor victory.

CHAPTER 14: WONDERKIDS

Budget Left: £300

We'd spent just two days in Latvia and we now had to hop onto another bus to Estonia's capital city, Tallinn, where I had arranged, yes you've guessed it, another football trial.

I wasn't in the greatest of moods though, and it wasn't just heavy bags containing camera gear we were still yet to use that was weighing me down, it was the research I had now done on FC Levadia in Tallinn that was really worrying me.

'So how good are these guys then?' said Tristan, drinking a cup of brown water from the on-board coffee-making facilities as we pulled out of the bus station.

'Very good,' I said. I was resigned to the knowledge that I had in all probability wasted hundreds of pounds to get the Baltic states and stay there for a week, knowing that in football terms I never should have gone.

'Yes but how good?' Tristan said as he slurped his coffee. 'Are they better than Lithuania?'

'Yes.'

'Better than Latvia?'

'Probably.'

'How do you know?'

'Because this morning before we left I looked at FC Levadia's website and they are Estonia's Manchester United. They play in the top division, and have won six league titles and five Estonian FA Cups. And they've only been in existence since 1998. These guys are proper footballers. In Andorra they were by and large sheep herders or tourist operators.'

'Ah,' said Tristan, continuing to drink his questionable coffee before getting one last look of Riga as we pulled away from the city.

'Oh, they also played Galatasaray this year in the Europa League.'

'Who are the Galagays?' asked my brother.

'They're quite a good football team from Turkey... it doesn't matter.'

I was on a bus to Estonia preparing myself for my third trial in five days, already knowing the outcome. My pulled groin and strained arse were feeling remarkably okay after the previous day's exertions, so at least I wouldn't be feeling sore and achey like I had in my second trial in Malta with St Georges FC. It seemed my muscles were once again used to the rigours of playing football, but only after five football trials, and I seemed to be going up in standard with each club I went to, another failure of my planning. I should have arranged it so that I went to the best ones first to get my fitness right, get used to football again and get the agility back before going to the Maltas and Andorras of this world, where I actually stood a chance.

Riga was beautiful but I wasn't sad to be leaving. I felt I saw all that I wanted to see in the city in our morning of sightseeing when we were bitching about the agent not following through on his promise, only for him to make us feel a bit guilty afterwards.

This time, I had a contact with FC Levadia who answered his phone and emails, and an address and arranged time to meet and then train. Our next back-up after this was a semi-professional outfit in Gothenburg, Sweden.

The transport system in the Baltic states certainly needs some work, or at least some trains. The English train network gets a lot of bad press but if you wanted to take a train anywhere in the Baltic states, it appeared you would require a timetable several months in advance to plan your trip, the ability to speak fluent Lithuanian, Latvian or Estonian, and the blood of a badger cub. It was impossible. Travel was done by bus in these countries and so we were forced to ride aboard a slow, gas-guzzling coach for five hours until Tallinn. Without doubt the worst coach journey I have ever had the misfortune to be part of. The coach company thought it would be pleasant for the passengers if they installed TV screens on the bus. They'd be correct only if they were willing to show films that people could choose to watch and listen to using headphones. Instead they chose to play bad – truly bad – western music videos from the 90s that you had no choice but to listen to as the speakers on the TVs were on all the time, for five hours. And after 1 hour and 45 minutes the tape they had started again for the torture to be relived. Why couldn't they have played classical music? Everyone likes that surely? It may be boring but it doesn't offend the ears. Instead they chose to take me to the depths of my soul with 90s pop drivel. There are many things I can think of that I don't want forced upon me when I'm a thousand miles away from home, nervous about a football trial against some of the best footballers in Eastern Europe, and one of them is being forced to listen to Lou Bega's Mambo Number 5. Music, like many things in civilisation, can be beautiful. However, when it's been arranged badly it can offend like nothing else; like an ugly building, an ill-poured pint, or appointing Steve McClaren as England manager.

My mood sank from despair to suicidal on that coach journey, the only respite being when we passed through the border between Latvia and Estonia, when guards got on the coach and demanded to see our passports and seemingly said 'This shite music gets turned off whilst we do our jobs – you can inflict it on them again once we've buggered off.' I didn't bring my own MP3 player with me on the trip, reasoning I'd be too busy organising or making new friends, but I vowed I would never leave the house without one again so that I can always be saved from the savage Ricky Martin song 'She Bangs!'

Whilst on the coach I tried to distract myself by trying to learn some Estonian phrases so that I didn't seem completely ignorant when I met my hosts the next day. The language barriers so far hadn't been too bad by and large, apart from in Andorra when ordering a taxi. I've got nothing against people having their own language or own culture and history, it makes life and travelling all the more exciting, but I couldn't get my head round why Lithuania, Latvia and Estonia all felt the need to have their own language and currencies. They all get on and share a history with one another. The Scots hate the English but it doesn't stop them speaking the same language as them or using the same currency. The Baltic states seem to be well acquainted but still it appears they want their own identity. Perhaps it's me just being typically English but I thought it would be far easier for them if they all got together and said: "This is the plan, we'll speak Lithuanian on Mondays and Wednesdays, Latvian Tuesdays and Thursdays and Estonia can have a long weekend of it, then hopefully it will all mix together as one. What do you say?"

Although, now I have said it, my theories are starting to sound very Stalinesque. He wanted to lump them all together too. Perhaps I should move on and just learn to appreciate the uniqueness of these nations.

Off the bus with our souls destroyed by some of the worst music mankind has ever produced, we stood in a car park experiencing temperatures colder than the depths of English winter. Immediately everyone moved on, knowing where they were going before the bus too departed, leaving us stranded. We looked around to see just a small newsagents and a metallic, modern-looking hot dog van advertising all sorts of fancy looking products and the latest TV shows .

We had booked accommodation for the evening once more through deals on the internet. As I commandeered us a hot dog each, Tristan hailed a taxi. Our first taxi in the whole trip. Incredible when you think of all the miles we had to cover, and the random football training grounds on the outskirts of towns we'd had to visit. I suppose the fact that this taxi was our first is testament to the hospitality we had received from everyone across Europe and also to the fact that it was so cold that me and Tristan couldn't face walking with heavy bags in the wind and chill to our next lodgings. We were getting soft.

As we raced through Tallinn's city centre it all looked shinier and more modern than I'd anticipated – anonymous and very Western. If it weren't for the foreign advertising hoardings in a combined English and Russian alphabet, this could have been anywhere in Europe. When we first agreed to shoot off to Eastern Europe I was expecting grey, regimented buildings and not shiny, modern affairs. However, it's now nearly 20 years since the Berlin wall fell and these countries gained freedom from communist regimes, and it was clear that none of the three countries were as they once were even ten years ago.

As we drove through the city and out towards the sea our lodgings came into view. The hotel is a concrete block overlooking the Baltic Ocean, where we could see huge ocean liners coming into dock before setting sail to Finland and beyond. Having checked into the hotel we walked the miles of corridors to find our room. This place could not have been more different from where we were in Latvia. In Latvia we stayed in a small building situated on a delightful cobbled street where there were no more than 20 rooms. This hotel was almost city–sized, and was garishly decorated with red, yellow and green walls, with steel doors. It was supposed to be trendy, like an IKEA showroom, but it made me feel sick. The communists wouldn't have allowed such disgusting décor as this, that's for sure. The room was nice enough, and our window overlooked the ocean and the impressive ferry docks.

' I'm getting sick of this bag! It's getting heavier, I'm sure it is,' said Tristan in a grump.

'Tristan, what's the name of the boat we're getting on if we're not hanging around here?' I asked, peering out the window.

'The *Baltic Queen.* Why?' asked Tristan, checking his camera equipment.

'We can see it from our room. Look.'

It was massive. We'd done planes, trains, automobiles and taxis, and soon we'd be on a ferry – but first I needed to confirm if I was good enough to play in Estonia or not. We could see our escape route; I just needed to find out if we needed it.

The next day was simple; we were certainly hitting our stride when it came to balancing tourism with trials.

We ventured once more into the old part of town, and again we were taken aback by the beautiful architecture. The stones used to build the houses and churches were the size of caravans. Tallin's walls and churches were a brilliant white and that, combined with the constant biting wind from the sea, gave the town a distinct, fresh feel, something that had been sorely lacking in Malta a couple of weeks previously.

Having had a bit too much perspective delivered by the Latvian War Museum, we decided not to visit any more museums but simply wander the streets and look inside churches and get a feel for the city. The Old Town is a two-tiered area, unlike the flats of Vilnius and Riga, and because of this it has a more unique character and atmosphere. It seems absurd but a church looks much nicer when you have to scale a quite steep incline to get a proper view of it rather than just chance upon it around a corner, and this was no different. The Alexander Nevsky Church constructed in 1900 was a glorious building, a Russian Orthodox church of unique design. The locals initially wanted it torn down because of the animosity they felt towards the Russians, but they couldn't afford the demolition costs and so the church remained, eventually becoming a tourist attraction.

Despite its unique white, red and gold appearance the highlight was inside. Enter any church and you feel compelled to be silent and appreciative of the area, even if you yourself are not religious. Looking around hearing people's footsteps and whispers echo throughout the massive open structure that soared above, I saw a donations box, typical of most historic sites – but this one being was here for a slightly unusual purpose.

Above the box were several translations of the Estonian original text, giving reason as to why you would want to part with your Estonian Kroon, and the English translation read simply as:

'Donations for Church reraping.'

After reading that I certainly wasn't going to give any money; I don't condone the raping of architecture, never mind the repeated act of 're-raping' it. I sniggered and tried to hide my juvenile sense of humour as best I could given the surroundings and made my way out of the church.

With time creeping up on us I drank an expensive, lukewarm coffee and made haste to the pub where I had a bite to eat and ordered a taxi to the club's headquarters. I didn't have a beer this time; I needed all my football playing attributes to be at their peak.

As we arrived at the training facilities at FC Levadia I gulped an almighty gulp. The training area was situated a short drive from the city, in an area of woodland. On arrival I was thinking that perhaps it would be once more a bumpy grass pitch like Latvia, but this was in fact a training 'complex'. Complex meaning 'a conceptual whole made up of complicated and related parts'. There wasn't just a football pitch in the middle of a park like in Latvia, or an ageing astroturf pitch like in Malta – this was massive. There were several fenced-off football pitches and overlooking offices, with football nets and all manners of other equipment. I even noticed on the horizon a giant metallic Adidas football. What on earth was that there for? Certainly not to play football, but more to do with endorsement from Adidas. This was a proper sponsored team! I was going to make an idiot of myself.

There was no one to greet us at the gates, but we were definitely on time. As we waited I could see one of the junior sides training, and I saw a kid doing consecutive headers in the air to himself over and over again, a sequence of 50 or so, and he was no older than 10. The most headers I can do is about three and this kid seemed to have the ball on a string. I began to think I couldn't even make the under 10s team here.

Nervous and shaking from the cold, we waited at the metal gates, being tortured by the view of primary school kids in green FC Levadia training tops who could do things with a football that would make a grown man weep, that man being me. I felt like crying – I was prepared to pull out, simply to save myself the effort and embarrassment of playing against adults of a standard higher than those kids.

'You're really nervous about this aren't you?' Tristan picked up on the telltale signs of me chewing my fingernails, pacing and general fidgeting.

'Yes.'

'Why?'

'Because I'm going to make a tit of myself that's why!'

'It's no different to the other places.'

'Yeah but at least in those countries I only marginally failed. This is going to be a titanic failure.'

'You need some confidence mate, you're not that bad at football.'

I stopped pacing and looked at him. We both knew how ludicrous that statement was.

We were interrupted as a huge black Land Rover pulled up alongside us, with FC Levadia badges and advertising plastered all over it. A man leaned out of the window.

'Ralf?' he said, and I nodded. 'Good to meet you. I am Sergey. I will park over there and then we'll talk.'

Crikey Moses, was Sergey big! Huge, hulking in fact. Not particularly muscular or tall but very 'set'. About 6ft 2in, in his mid-to-late 20s, he looked like a remnant of whatever communist 'superior being breeding programme' had been in place before Estonia regained its independence at the beginning of the 1990s. He was the marketing manager, and he was more than happy for me to visit and talk about the club. I found it odd that I was dealing with the marketing manager, seeing as he had said yes to me having a trial before I had even mentioned we were making a film.

'We have so much difficulty breaking the market of ice hockey and basketball. Everybody loves it here. I've tried free hot dogs, free tickets, discounts on shirts – and yet we still only get 350 people to our biggest games and we've only sold about 50 shirts'. Sergey's English was excellent, probably as a result of spending six months on a marketing degree in London, and he even threw in swear words when they weren't needed, much like a native Englishman.

'Really, 350 people? So how can you pay for all of this? Are you professional or semi-professional?' I asked.

'We are professional. We have a chairman who is very generous and loves the game, and he subsidises the project.'

Sergey was extremely enlightening about the problems which a football club faces in a country where ice hockey and basketball have always been dominant. What was even more interesting was hearing the rumours that many people refuse to support the club because the owner and manager were Russian, and because of the animosity many Estonians feel towards Russia and their previous Soviet Union regime they would rather take their business elsewhere than support what they see as a Russian club. Sergey added that they do plenty in the community, like free after-school classes to try and hook the youngsters early, but it's more often than not that the allure of ice hockey, which unlike football is shown on terrestrial Estonian television, prevails.

'So why did you say yes to me coming to visit today to have a trial?' I asked, still wondering why I was dealing with the marketing manager.

'Because you said it wouldn't cost us anything, and you are English and you could be our David Beckham,' Sergey laughed, uproariously like only massive men can. Was he laughing at how he was over the moon of having a marketing ploy like me potentially on the football books, or laughing at the preposterous nature of his remark? 'Maybe if you are good I will get the contract sorted out and sign you up straight away?'

'Erm…' I said, worried that they might be thinking I was their financial saviour.

'Don't worry, our sports team got your email first and weren't willing to give you a trial because you lack a football background. But they passed it onto me. Seeing as it isn't costing us money we thought we'd help you out in your quest. You're only training with the reserves, the majority of them are under 19 so you should be okay, but of course if you're good we can look into something permanent.' Not if that 10-year-old I was watching was anything to go by. 'Our coach is very experienced and he will talk to you about your skills at the end.'

He flashed me a pearly white smile and led me into his offices. The offices themselves were just a series of temporary shelters, but they were still a step up from anything I'd experienced so far.

As I drank a coffee looking down on the training complex outside, I spoke to Sergey about my quest, thus subtly letting him know that I was rubbish at football. I learnt more about him and the club and he was a top bloke. Regaling us with the time he had spent in London as a student and his hopes for the club now, he was a very easy person to be around. Like Justina in Lithuania, although he worked in football he said he didn't really care for it as a youngster, and preferred Judo of all things. I was then introduced to Sergey's protégé, Nikolai, who was there on an internship programme. He couldn't have looked any more different to Sergey. A black leather jacket zipped to the top, long cigarette at the side of his mouth and thin-rimmed spectacles. He looked like an assassin, or French Philosopher, or both. He too spoke fluent English and, like Sergey, didn't mind swearing or making jokes about getting drunk, or the obstacles the club was facing. It was taking a massive investment and so far the financial rewards had not been forthcoming for the club despite all its success on the football pitch. Time ran away from us and before we knew it I was late to get changed for the trial. I had to say a fleeting goodbye to Sergey who was unable to hang around as he had to attend a friend's birthday. It was now just me, Tristan and Nikolai, who I had only met minutes previously.

I ran downstairs and into the changing rooms below and was greeted an alarming view.

A collage of penises.

Quite a few of them with owners too.

Several naked men and boys ranging in age from 16-24. How do you broach this situation? They looked at me in horror, they obviously hadn't been notified I was arriving on that day so to them all that was happening was that a man, fully clothed in a Zippy from Rainbow t-shirt, had run into the changing rooms of a football team and then stood there rooted to the spot. I desperately tried to rack my brains for the small amount of Estonian I had learnt in our European guidebook on the bus but unfortunately all it came out with in my mind were the Estonian words for hello, goodbye, thanks and please. There was nothing my brain was offering me by way of Estonian that could convey 'Don't worry boys, I'm a footballer like you, and I am here to have a trial. I am in no way a pervert. Your penises are safe with me.' Instead I did my best with a very geriatric English 'Hello', with an army salute, sat down on a changing room bench and then began to unpack my bag, with a penis mere inches away from my face. I don't know why I saluted, probably nerves but I've no doubt it made me look like an idiot. As I unpacked my football boots, socks, shorts, briefs and training top I was hesitant about getting changed. These guys, however, loved it – so much so in fact they seemed to prolong the experience as long as they could. If that were me I'd be quick as a flash. It takes quite a bit to shut me up, but being naked in public is one way of doing it. During the rare occurrences I am naked in front of other men I keep my eyes down and try and get changed as quickly as possible, but these guys were idly stood around with their tackle hanging out, chatting. What they were discussing I don't know, probably something to do with the weather, or that foreigner sat on the bench staring at their cocks. I got changed quicker than you can say embarrassed-about-his-manhood and followed the players outside. It was here that it occurred to me that I could potentially be playing with youngsters who have represented the youth levels of Estonian national football, given that they were part of the academy of one of the best clubs in the country.

Nikolai spoke to a well-built, middle-aged man who looked serious. He was wearing a huge coat, had a discerning look and he had his arms linked behind his back, all great attributes to have when you want to look intimidating. He looked like the type of coach I'd been dreading meeting on the trip – someone who may actually push me beyond my limits.

'Ralf, I have spoken to the coach and he is happy for you to train and will talk to you afterwards. I have also got a player called Zhany to translate everything that happens on the pitch so you know what exercise is going ahead.'

'Excellent, thanks Nikolai.' I was a whiter shade of pale through nerves and the temperature.

'Hi Ralf I am Zhany. I am the captain of the reserve team and I am going to translate for you what happens today on the pitch, so just do as I say okay?'

'Okay!'

I liked Zhany; he said things in a friendly manner and I felt like I knew him already. The fact that I had seen his penis probably helped break down the barriers. Perhaps from now on I should be naked in front of every new person I meet in order to make them feel at ease. It wouldn't work really though would it? Probably would result in a court order or some such.

Zhany was ginger, but I didn't hold that against him. As we did the customary several laps of the pitch in warm-up he asked all manner of questions about the trip and life in England and I was enjoying chatting to him, it was taking my mind off the fact that this warm-up was nearly killing me. The pace was far quicker than anywhere else so far. It turned out Zhany himself had tried to become a professional footballer but never quite made the grade, so he decided to be a full-time student and play football on the side for free as captain of the reserve team, helping the youngsters' progress. Looking at Zhany was like looking at an inverted image of myself. He was now a student and I was a professional footballer, sort of. After the warm-up the coach then introduced me to all the players in one grand sweeping motion with his arm and said a sentence in Estonian that finished with a familiar sounding 'Ralf'. The majority of the players were no older than 20 and they looked slim, fit and small. Obviously physicality in this side is not seen as a pre-requisite for success unlike the brawling in Andorra.

Unfortunately we didn't start playing football immediately after this, but instead started agility sessions of pace, hopping from side-to-side between cones, lifting our legs high in the air and shuffling in between objects in a sort of rapid sidestep movement. It was like the first trial in Malta all over again with Santa Venera on that plimsoll day.

I had trained in lung capacity by running on a tread mill for two months prior to the trip, I hadn't actually done any running with changes of direction or pace, or hopping or shuffling. All this was now required of me as we began racing against one another.

Three cones were set up directly in front of a queue of players in a straight line – three sets of the cones and three lines of men in total.

The movements varied; sometimes we hopped side to side then sprinted, and then other times we would simply shuffle through the cones as fast we could in a snaking formation. Before each new exercise, the coach demonstrated it himself, moving his huge frame at impressive speed whilst talking, most probably about the benefits of doing that particular action. After winding through the cones he then instructed us that on completion through the cone maze we would have to sprint to the finish line ten metres beyond. As I had done in all other previous trials I hung around at the back of the queue to assess how good my rival players were before it was my turn. The first of the agility tasks involved no cones and was a mere sprint to a line 10 metres ahead, against two other people.

Judging how fast people are when you watch them is difficult without a frame of reference. We only know Usain Bolt is ridiculously fast because we see him run 100 metres in nine and a half seconds. Without the time there ticking away to judge him by or the other runners struggling to keep up with him we wouldn't realise he was breaking world records. I couldn't time the sprints ahead of me so I had no idea if they were fast or not, I would only find out when I myself took part in the activity. One by one more sets of threes did the sprint against each other over the 10 metres, the third set, the fourth set, the fifth and then my turn.

I got on my marks and looked at the coach who was ready to blow his whistle. With my money fast running out and my patience at these clubs wearing thinner I knew I had to perform, even if this was the best club I had visited thus far. As I put my right foot on the starting line and squatted into my starting position everything stopped. Things were going in slow motion. It was like I was in *Chariots of Fire*. I became very aware of my heartbeat and even my eyes blinking made a shattering sound as they closed. I was in *The Zone*. Everything was crystal clear. I was ready. I stared down my 10-metre track ready for the whistle, my vision distorting the final cone to make it look closer than it was. As soon as I saw the coach's chest and cheeks exhaling the air into the whistle I told my body to move, sharpish. I could see the air going into the whistle but the sound hadn't reached us yet but I didn't care, I was off. Every ounce of strength I had in me went into my lunge at the start and although I was putting my soul into my run I felt like I was still in slow motion, and I was. Pumping my arms from side I moved into a full stride, but by then it was already too late. My two other competitors had already finished the sprint. I had just lost a 10-metre race by a whopping 6-metre margin. I'll repeat. I lost a 10-metre race by a 6-metre margin.

That's unbelievably bad. There were looks of disbelief from the coach and the assorted staff around him. Did they just see someone lose a 10-metre race by six metres? They had indeed, and then they saw it again and again and again throughout each of the agility runs. I looked at Tristan and he laughed at me. I looked at Nikolai and the ever-present cigarette in his mouth nearly dropped to the floor, along with his jaw. I was way out of my league. These boys were thoroughbred greyhounds and I was a mongrel.

I hocked up an almighty mouthful of phlegm and shot it through the pitch's perimeter fence whilst no one was looking and told myself to get my act together. I was experiencing an altogether new type of fatigue in Estonia, suffering from the cold and what felt like thin oxygen I couldn't get enough air in my lungs. It seemed in hindsight that the conditions that had suited me best so far was Lithuania – unfortunately I'd decided to poison my body with alcohol and set my balls on fire with deep heat, thus rendering those ideal playing conditions useless. Things were about to get even worse.

Sidestepping between cones. Who needs that in life? No one, not even sports people. Perhaps football linesman need to sidestep, as their profession is one great sidestep up and down a touchline with their eyes fixed on a game, but footballers? No, we don't. But the coach didn't seem to care, and instructed us to sidestep through the cones and at speed. We had to spread our legs apart to form a triangle with the ground and then bring them back together quickly, making sure we did at least one step in between the cones. It was fast becoming a dance class and I was fast running out of steam. The other players looked fresh and sprightly, but I looked tired, sweaty and deathly.

More sidesteps followed, and then disaster struck. During one rapid sidestep I lazily went to bring my legs back together and trod on my own ankle, my left ankle, my good ankle, the ankle that wasn't wearing an ankle protector. As my right leg dropped all of my body's weight onto the skinny slim-line joint an almighty crunch was heard and I felt an immediate pang of muscles saying 'Erm, do you mind not doing that?'

It hurt; not so much that I yelped or fell to the ground, but it hurt. I managed to keep my balance and complete the exercise, ironically the last one before the footballs were introduced into training.

My ankle was throbbing. It didn't appear to have swollen up, but it did feel weak, like a tree trunk that was 90% sawn through and was ready to timber. I made the decision to carry on, I would run it off. No one had noticed the injury as I was at the back of the running pack when it had happened. I would run and hopefully the adrenalin would make it okay. Coming all this way to have a football trial but to duck out after 30 minutes wasn't an option – a bit of pain was worth the chance of a shot at a dream.

The warm up was over, thank god. It had proved to be a nice gentle exercise session for them, and what felt like the beginnings of a stroke for me, with a crocked ankle to boot.

Possession football followed, nine against four, with a maximum of two touches allowed. The nine men had to keep the ball, the four had to win it. Simple, and I made it look so as I unbelievably played out of my mind by dictating tempo, playing passes at all angles and threading one-touch nutmegs through people's legs. I was at last the conductor of proceedings and these boys were taking it seriously, you could tell with their lunges, bursts of pace and constant chat, and all the more impressive was that I was getting nods of approval and compliments, albeit in Estonian. This wasn't just a simple training session to them, they were either trying to impress the coach or the film camera, but it was me who was impressing the most, but Christ my left ankle was killing me. I was playing better on one foot than I ever had with two in the entire trip, I was awesome. It was like Steven Gerrard had just taken over my body. I followed my passes, made myself easily available for return balls, and sprayed the ball to my team-mates on the other side of the pitch when things got tight at one end, all the while whilst my ankle was in agony. This was a captain's performance of the highest order. Why couldn't I have played like this in Malta, or Andorra, or Lithuania?

For fifteen minutes during this game I felt like I was one of the better players. Zhany, obviously more accomplished than the rest due to his age and experience, was prominent too, and we were – what is described in football terms and is totally platonic – 'having it off' at one stage, helping each other run rings round our opponents. I was incredible, awe inspiring, and although I clearly lacked the pace of the other players my speed of thought for once was making up for it. Things were going great, if it wasn't for my ankle! Attempting to run off the pain wasn't working, it was there to stay, and it was getting worse. I cursed under my breath. Just my luck to play brilliantly but have an injury.

During a water break Nikolai came over to me.

'What do you think Nikolai?' I asked, doubled over with hands on knees whilst everyone else stood and sipped from their water bottles.

'You're good,' he said in his Eastern European accent with a hint of the laidback philosopher about him. 'Your technique definitely matches up to the other players here, the only difference was the pace at the start during those runs but that's expected if you haven't played regularly for a while.' He lit another cigarette, inhaled and exhaled the smoke from the side of his mouth like a movie star would. 'Keep it up.'

I moved off to join the rest of the team for shooting practice. Brilliant – I wouldn't have to use my left foot, I could just use my right, with the ankle that still hadn't fully recovered from the injury in England several months earlier. It was still in far better nick than its counterpart, which was screaming for mercy.

'Here we are going to shoot, yes?' said Zhany.

'Yes, that's fine with me.'

'We will line up. Take turns to shoot at goalkeeper, everyone will shoot with right foot and then after we will use our left foot.'

Nut-sacks!

'Okay,' I said despondently.

It wasn't okay. No way did I want to be hitting a football with that foot, let alone with enough pace and accuracy to make it look good.

When it came to my turn I put the ball on the floor and struck it with my right foot. The ball went sailing over the bar. Everyone else was slamming their shots in the top and bottom corners with ease and skill that belied me. The wind had gone from my sails. Steven Gerrard no longer inhabited me – I was back to being Ralf.

My turn again, this time with the left foot. I ran up and hit it as hard as could and bit down on my bottom lip hoping the pain wouldn't be so bad but it was.

I didn't exhibit the pain to anyone, I just winced as I struck the football high and wide. I felt sick, the pain was unbearable, but I didn't want to give up. I had to shoot again, this time with the right and this time forcing the keeper into a full stretch save to prevent the ball going into the top corner. It made him look great and me mediocre. The following left-footed shots from my counterparts started to fly in. I stepped up again to take my second left-foot shot and this time it was curtains. I hit the ball as hard as I could manage with the ankle bordering on death and I didn't even bother to see where the ball ended up, my ankle and determination had given way. 'Right that's it, I warned you didn't I?' my ankle shouted at me. 'I'm now going to be buggered for the foreseeable future and you've only got yourself to blame.' I broke down into a full-on limp, my ankle had timbered, the throbbing in my crocked joint was visible even through my sock. The trial was over.

With balls still flying all around me towards the busy goalkeeper I hobbled over to Zhany who was waiting in line for his next shot and explained my predicament. He nodded and escorted me to the side of pitch. With Nikolai busy on the phone it was up to Zhany to take action for me.

'You are lucky, the physiotherapist is here today, he only comes to see the reserves once a week. I will get him for you, wait here.'

As Zhany moved off the coach shouted something at him and Zhany responded in Estonian whilst jogging backwards with a smirk and a shrug. The coach then smiled at me as I hobbled to my feet to speak to Tristan. I still don't why the coach had smiled at me, either out of a mute commiseration or at the fact I was having to give up. I was so frustrated, I had been playing well, better than I had anywhere else and even though I was probably not good enough on that form to play for Levadia, a performance like that could have done it for me somewhere like Sweden or Norway, Denmark or the Faroe Islands; but it appeared any chance of that happening would be a long way off now.

'Unlucky mate,' said Tristan, sounding as sad as I was feeling. 'You seemed to be playing really well. What happened?'

'I trod on my own ankle during the warm-up, I tried to run it off but it just got worse. It's killing.'

We shared looks of anguish. Was this the end of my football dream?

From the changing rooms, a dark-skinned young man emerged, sporting a stylish ponytail and trendy beard you would expect to see at an indie gig in a funky New York bar rather than a football pitch. The only way I knew was the physio was because he was wearing an FC Levadia tracksuit.

'Hello Ralf, my name is Marius. Follow me,' he said in a staccato accent, accentuating the consonants in the words.

'Is my brother allowed to come?'

'No I am sorry he is not.'

We entered the physio's office and closed the door on Tristan.

I sat high up on the Physio table with my foot in Marius' face while he prodded, probed and rubbed at my ankle. After a while it was clear where most of the pain was – right up the back of my Achilles tendon, going all the way up my calf, and it hurt a lot. Other movements didn't hurt at all, however, so it was at least a relief that the pain itself was isolated and perhaps not as bad as first feared. Sat there I found it amusing that in England I had Coop to look after my bad right ankle and now I had an Eastern European version of the same man, ponytail and beard to match, doing the same thing on the opposite ankle. I had only ever met two physios, and both had beards and ponytails. In medieval times no one would have batted an eye lid at this, but in the 21st century the beard/ponytail combo is a rare breed.

'I see what you have done here,' said Marius. 'I don't know word in English. You have erm…' He reached for a piece of paper and held it against the back of my ankle and then tore a small centimetre line into it.

'I've torn it?' I said.

'Yes, torn muscle but no so bad, only small. I am going to put cool gel on and tape it but that's enough for today, no more football.'

I could still hear the shouts of the coach from outside and the sound of footballs being kicked but here I was on a sickbed. Marius began to massage the painful area with a cooling gel that once on your skin was like an ice pack. I was glad I hadn't met Marius earlier naked in the changing rooms with the others, otherwise this could have been seen as homoerotic. As he began the lengthy process of tearing pieces of plaster tape into small chunks and moulding it round my ankle to form a temporary cast, he idly chatted to me.

'So you want to be a footballer ya?' He had a very easy demeanour about him.

'Yes that's the dream but I don't think its going to happen now. Not through skill anyway, only through pity.'

'Pit-tee?'

'Yes, someone would feel sorry for me and let me play. I think that's the aim now.'

'Okay, are you not good at football?'

'It doesn't seem so. I thought I might have a chance in different countries to England because in England too many people play the game, but I underestimated how good people are around the world, and overestimated how good I was.'

'Where are you going next?' said he asked, focussing on my ankle with the plaster taking shape.

'Sweden, Norway, Denmark and then maybe the Faroe Islands, but I am running out of money fast.'

'You are paying for this yourself!?'

'Yes, sadly and when it runs out, it's over. How long will it be until I can play football again?'

He sucked in a breath through his teeth and then exhaled, wobbling his head from side to side.

'With injury like this, hard to say. I would think maybe four to fourteen days.'

'What about three days?' My next trial was potentially in Sweden in just 72 hours.

'I don't think so, it would be risk. See how it feels in the morning. Here take this, as a gift.' He held out the plaster tape towards me. 'You just watched what I did. Take this off your ankle tonight to let it breathe and then tape it up tomorrow for support. Are you doing lots of walking tomorrow?'

'It looks like I'm getting a ferry to Sweden. I don't think FC Levadia are going to want a crocked Englishman hanging around.'

'Well try and rest it when you can, and no dancing tonight.'

I thanked Marius. Just as I was leaving one of the younger players came in, and Marius made the noise 'Ai-yai-yai'. Obviously a regular customer.

I hobbled outside barefoot in the icy temperature, and moved towards Tristan and Nikolai, both of whom looked concerned.

'It's not bad but it could be worse,' I said, my bottom lip out in a sulk. 'I'm out for 4-14 days.'

'Shit happens,' said Nikolai. The philosopher was right on the money.

Shit does indeed happen.

CHAPTER 15: THE BALL ACHE QUEEN

I woke to the garish décor of our hotel room, which didn't make me feel any better. The red blinds covering the window filtered the sunlight to make the room look like Jack the Ripper had been in town. Opening the curtains to bring some natural light into proceedings I looked down at my injured ankle and there was a small purple bruise on the joint from the day previously. Why did I have to stand on my own foot? The term 'shooting yourself in the foot' comes from when soldiers in war-time would do so to injure themselves and ensure a journey home away from the horrors of war. Had it happened merely because I was unfit and ungraceful and didn't know how to sidestep properly, or had I subconsciously stood on my own foot in order to cut the trip short?

I was still having a good time despite the injury, the heartache, the homesickness, financial ruin and embarrassment I had brought upon myself these last three weeks. I was enjoying exploring Europe. I had drastically underestimated the scale of the task before me. But I was here, and I was still giving it a go.

It was Saturday morning and I had a slight hangover after me and Tristan had gone for beers the previous night to numb the pain. After grabbing a word with the coach at the end of the trial he'd said: 'Your standard isn't good enough here. You are too slow and your technique wasn't quite up to scratch with the players here today, and they are the reserves and they are not paid. I think your dream is possible, but unlikely.' We decided to leave Estonia as soon as possible – with no one else willing to give me a trial, I needed to move on.

I had £250 left. I don't think that's enough for a plane ticket to New Zealand, Kenya or Canada, or anywhere in Asia, so unfortunately they're out but, deep down, I knew that already. In Tristan's bag were two overnight tickets to Stockholm on the *Baltic Queen* ferry. My next trial was with Varslunda IK, a semi-professional club in Gothenburg, on the other side of Sweden, on Monday night, giving me 60 hours to get there. I hadn't yet done any research on Varslunda IK, and wouldn't have the chance to do so before we reached Sweden as the next 18 hours would be spent on a boat.

The ankle was gammy but I could walk on it. I'd have to take it easy though. After Sweden there was still Norway and Denmark with confirmed trials, if I could string out the budget. That's three opportunities, and I knew that if none of those clubs wanted me I would have to accept defeat. I would like to go to the Faroe Islands, but that realistically was out. £250, three countries and three trials remained. It seems impossible.

That morning we went downstairs to discuss our options over breakfast. I was missing the UK a little, but not the breakfasts. That's another of many things Europe has over the UK. The cheek to have meat and cheese every morning for breakfast on a baguette is admirable. Yes we have a 'Full English' but how many of us have that every day? Meat and cheese morning, noon and night is the norm here. Estonians also seem to be fans of meatballs and jam for breakfast, as was I. Several helpings later, we had our meat intake for the entire year sitting in our stomachs. We were sure Tallinn had more to offer, but we'd seen so many Old Towns in the past week that sleeping, albeit in a grotesque room, didn't seem like a bad idea.

Hours passed, and with my ankle taped up by my own hands (looking like I'd aimlessly swung the tape round my ankle, which I had) we boarded the boat. I was asked at border control if my trip to Estonia was business or pleasure. 'Business,' I said. When they asked what type of business, I told them I told them I was a professional footballer, I showed them my boots and I put that down as a minor victory.' Actors seem to be able to get away with it when the majority of them are out of work, so it so why can't I?

Me and Tristan had thought it would be a good idea to get a boat on this trip because it was cheaper than flying and would add to the romance of it. We'd travelled across Europe using all every different type of transport now, and with the cost at £30 I wasn't about to argue.

I wish I had.

Naively, I was expecting a boat like the Titanic, decked out with classy chandeliers and butlers in waistcoats serving margaritas, but what we found was a wave of Eastern European chavs wheeling crates of lager around on trolleys, amidst a backdrop of horrible décor that was much like our previous hotel. This was hell.

Mental Note: Ralf you get seasick, you can already feel it rocking, and having a hangover doesn't help. Never get a boat again.

It was too late to get off this tin monstrosity. It was a booze cruise between Tallinn and Stockholm, a night out for most, not a way of transport. The deck plan, situated atop every staircase of the ten-floored beast, gave details of where you could buy even more duty free alcohol or get drunk in a number of terrible bars that were ridiculously expensive to boot. The steak restaurant on board cost £30 per head, and the buffet £20 a head. We also found that there were no cash machines on board, and we had no Swedish or Estonian currency. We were to go hungry it seemed.

We ditched our bags in our shared cabin with a young Russian man called Volvo or some such, and were relieved to see he was travelling alone and wasn't on a drinks-fest like the rest of the passengers on the boat, meaning that perhaps a good night's sleep could be had on this floating horror show.

With the sleeping quarters cramped, and in desperate need of a lift, I went up on deck to ring the contact at Varslunda IK to confirm the trial. Like most of the people I had arranged trials with I had only spoken to them via email up until that point, reasoning I only needed to spend money on my phone bill when absolutely necessary. I dialled the number, my hands shaking from the biting cold.

'Hello?'

'Hello is that Sven?' I shouted. The connection was weak and the wind was distorting the sound in my earpiece but outside was the only place with signal.

'Yes.'

Another gust of wind distorted his response so much I couldn't hear his response.

'Hello, its Ralf, the English footballer who wanted to visit your club to have a trial. I was wondering if it was still okay to have the trial this week?'

'I'm sorry Ralf the team…'

Another huge gust of wind lifted me of my feet.

'I'm sorry Sven can you repeat that. Can I have a trial?'

'No!'

'Pardon?'

'The club is currently bottom of the league and we need to concentrate all of our efforts on the team, not new players. I'm sorry, perhaps when we have settled a bit you can but not until the new season.'

'When's that?'

'Next year. Our season starts in January. I'm sorry to disappoint.'

'Okay.' It wasn't. 'Thanks Sven. Bye'

I hung up and stared into the ocean. I wanted to swear but I couldn't muster the right expletives. Even with Tristan's tutelage over the past week I had nothing in my vocabulary that could bring any sense to how I was feeling. I was devastated. My trial in Sweden had fallen through in the space of a 30-second phone conversation. As put my phone back into my pocket the ship's engines roared into action and we started to move out of the harbour and into the Baltic Ocean. Unable to turn back I was on a one-way trip to Sweden, for no reason whatsoever.

Chapter 16: Decisions

'What do you reckon we should do then?' asked Tristan, after I broke the news to him inside one of the ship's hideously decorated bars.

'Well I think I need help summing this up.' I replied and slurped a coffee.

'Okay.' He replied earnestly.

'We've both pissed a thousand pounds of our own money up the wall, I've had six football trials and dismally failed in them all.'

'Correct.'

'We're on a boat, with no money, on our way to Sweden for no reason.'

'Correct.'

'And my ankle is fucked.'

'It does appear that way.'

'Good, well at least I'm not going mad.'

'Doesn't improve our situation though does it?'

'Not really, but I'm looking for positives at the moment, and sanity is one of those. I don't have any ideas. You?'

'We could play bingo.' Tristan shrugged his shoulders.

'Bingo?'

'Yes.'

'Right, well that is quite possibly the worst idea in the history of everything, more so than the Matrix sequels, the Star Wars prequels or even Hitler's attempts to invade Russia. But it's the only one we've got. Bingo it is.'

'Any ideas now?' whispered Tristan as he marked number 48 from his bingo card in the 'Starlight Lounge'. He clearly didn't want to interfere with my adventure, wanting me to make the decision.

'I don't know. I reckon if the ankle isn't better by tomorrow then maybe we should look into flying home, assess the damage to our bank accounts, let my ankle get better and then I may fly out to Norway for a trial there if I can get a cheap flight.'

'Number 36,' said the caller.

We both marked our cards.

'Staying in Scandinavia is going to be expensive.' I said as I marked another number. 'I think if I go home and plan a couple of countries in advance, say Norway and Denmark, I'd have a fighting chance of getting there wouldn't you think?'

'It'd help if we won this jackpot,' said Tristan licking his lips at the prospect.

'How much is it?'

'Close to £250.'

'Whoa.' £250 didn't used to sound like a lot of money, but to a man with no job and a dream all but dead and buried it seemed like a lifeline.

'Well let's do that then.' said Tristan 'We'll stay with my mate for a night and look into how to get home. It's definitely cheaper to fly home for a week and then fly back out to a trial than hang around in hotels in Scandinavia. Plus it gives your ankle chance to recover and that's the most important thing.'

'Cool, we'll do that then.'

'Number 67.'

'BINGO!' shouted the man to our right.

'Bollocks,' we proclaimed in unison and to the shock of the faces of mothers and daughters around the room.

I'm glad I hadn't budgeted that £250 prize money into my plans otherwise that would have sent me further into despair.

We both decided on an early night so that we could be awake and fresh for our jaunt to Stockholm. There was no trial there but we had free accommodation and a guide to the city. Being fresh for that was better than staying up on this booze cruise with the dregs of Europe playing Bingo and drinking vodka. However I couldn't sleep. The sleeping quarters were adequate and my bed comfy so I couldn't complain on that front. What was keeping me awake was anxiety, as well as the two-tonne Lithuanian in the bunk opposite me snoring so loudly that any chance of sleep was nigh on impossible. When we had first dumped our belongings and Tristan's mobile production unit into our room it was just us and the quiet Russian, Volvo, but as I bedded down for the night the steel bedroom door swung open, light shone in from the corridor and then it was gone again in a flash as the frame of the person opening the door perfectly obstructed anything that was heading in. He was huge. He asked Tristan his nationality, then Volvo's and then me last. He then stated 'Me, Lithuanian,' before climbing on his bunk above Volvo's and passing out instantaneously. I had never seen anything like it; a man fully clothed, collapsing onto his bed and snoring so loudly the thin walls of our cabin shook. I thought he was taking the piss, but he wasn't.

As the hours passed we all tossed and turned in a manner so as not to make too much noise and disturb the others in the room, which was a flawed concept given the snoring coming from the only man who was sleeping. Volvo clearly needed to do a rather loud disgusting phlegm-like cough, but rather than do it all in one loud clearance of his throat he tried to do it in 30 separate pitiful clucks and fast exhalations of air rather than just letting rip. The monotonous back and forth of the Lithuanians sleeping could have put me into a hypnotic sleep eventually if it weren't for Volvo's over-politeness in the close sleeping quarters. In the bunk two inches above my face I could hear Tristan similarly rolling endlessly side to side as Volvo's hocking and the Lithuanian's snoring kept us awake.

Lying there with my thoughts for company I cast my mind back over the trip. Had I really had six football trials in three weeks? Well, yes I had, but boy had it gone by in a flash. I came to the conclusion that it had gone by so quickly because my brain, in an act of chivalry, had decided to blank out any embarrassing memories to protect my feelings. Unfortunately, those moments accounted for 95% of the trip. Just the previous week alone had been manic. Three football trials in five days? Three football trials across three countries in five days? That's insane, surely no one else had ever had three football trials in five days for different clubs, let alone in three different countries. It then dawned on me, perhaps I'd set a world record without realising it, without wanting it. How many people break world records by accident? I wager not a lot; I must be in a small band of merry men. I should be ecstatic with this thought, but no one would want this world record. I've got this record because I am shit at a game I love. If I were any good at it, as is my wish, then I wouldn't have broken it. Breaking a world record for being rubbish at something you love is an odd feeling. The only way it could get any worse is if I had been awarded the 'world record for most consecutive amount of times that during intercourse with your partner you have failed to give pleasure'.

Now on a boat to Sweden for no reason, an injured ankle, no money, starving, unable to sleep and a newly crowned world record holder, anger washed over me before I finally managed to get some sleep.

Morning broke. The other two occupants of our room were absent, so me and Tristan did what all Brits do about a situation that has annoyed them, and moaned about it after the fact.

'What a dick!' Tristan could not have summed the situation up better. 'What sort of knob snores *all* night? I feel hideous now and the boat arrives in Stockholm in an hour.'

'Lets not forget we're going for no reason with the trial falling through.' I gave a sarcastic double thumbs up. I felt that heaping on the misery may have made me feel better. It didn't.

'How's the ankle?'

'Not good. It feels worse than it did yesterday. It's a good job there's no trial because I wouldn't be playing in it.'

'Probably should get a bit of this on camera.'

Tristan removed his bag from the overhead storage compartment and dropped it on his head in a Groucho Marx slapstick fashion and proceeded to film me looking severely pissed off about the entire situation whilst he himself looked pissed off about the entire situation behind the camera.

With the footage of me looking suicidal racking up and having done another woeful job of applying my taped bandage to my ankle we made haste for the deck of the boat.

Walking the green carpeted corridors of this chintzy behemoth I had a far more pronounced limp than when the injury had occurred one-and-a-half days ago. It was bad. The ankle was black and yellow, and I don't think my amateur bandaging techniques aided proceedings though, my tendency to do all jobs in a half-arsed way was highlighted perfectly as a trail of medical tape leaked out of my sock and trailed behind me up to the deck.

The long decks that hugged the side of the boat all the way round, and on several floors, were occupied by a great number of hung-over Eastern Europeans having a cigarette to make them feel all the more refreshed after a night of debauchery on the newly christened 'Ball-Ache Queen'. I'm glad I didn't witness the boat at night-time, instead choosing to listen to the dulcet tones of a hippo-sized

Lithuanian snoring for several hours. Despite the hoards of shaking individuals looking decidedly worse for wear, I think I stood out as the one person that these people were glad they weren't. I hadn't slept, was pale, seasick, had a prominent limp and looked like I was ready to throw myself overboard at the smallest injustice against my British personage, such as someone not holding the door open for me. If the crew attempted a rescue operation, I suspect witnesses would have stopped them in their tracks and said 'I wouldn't bother, I don't think he'd thank you for it.'

As it happened I didn't throw myself overboard and stayed out on deck to breathe in the weird mix of fresh sea air and cheap cigarettes. With an hour to go before we were due to arrive in Stockholm, my mood was lifted in the unlikeliest of ways. Sailing through open water we were suddenly passed by a small island no bigger than a small park flower bed, or rather we passed it, and then another and then another before it became ten, then twenty and then all of a sudden hundreds of them all varying in size. And these grassy hilly rocks, some no bigger than a Bus, weren't bare – some of them had houses on them, planted in the middle overlooking the ocean. Some islands were in fact just a house on a rock with a boat attached to it. My mind boggled at the insurance costs, daily commute and quality of the TV reception before I gave myself a mental slap across the face for being such a geek, and reminded myself to simply enjoy the beauty of this dotted island landscape sat amongst some of the stillest water I had ever seen.

Stockholm is built on over 2,000 islands, an impossible figure to comprehend in your mind until you actually see the beginnings of the city from the ocean perspective. Hundreds of islands stretched out in front of us as the boat made its way to the mainland, where we could see blue skies over the city. I was mesmerised by the image, it was like something out of a film, or how you'd expect the lost city of Atlantis to look. Everyone else had obviously seen this before and found it no more unusual than getting the tube in London but this to me was special, and lifted my mood when I needed it the most.

Finally disembarked and outside we dumped our bags, gave our two customary manly grunts of relief, consulted a map in the fresh, crisp air of Stockholm's docks in the surprisingly warm sunshine, reloaded and headed for the underground station nearby which would take us to meet Tristan's old University friend Lars. After that we had no idea what we were doing. I now only had two or three trials left it seemed, little money and an ankle that wanted to rest for a significant period of time.

Stockholm is a refreshing city. Described as the Venice of the North it has a complicated network of waterways that give it a remarkably fresh feeling that you wouldn't normally associate with a capital. Eastern Europe had provided a refreshing change financially from the expense of Malta, Barcelona and Andorra (which had surprised us so much that we had to stay in a tent for a week). In Estonia, Latvia and Lithuania we could eat drink and be merry, but Scandinavia now brought us back to earth with a bump. Anything that did take our fancy, such as a plastic Viking hat or steak in a restaurant was bypassed due to the inflated price-tags. I should have appreciated Stockholm's beauty even more, but I just wanted to sit down and have a sandwich, which given Scandinavian prices, was pretty difficult. Lars – a lovely man – met us at the station and showed us the sights of the city. He had the look of former Aston Villa defender Olof Mellberg about him, which made me like him even more. We dumped our bags at his apartment, booked flights home in 24 hours' time which left my budget at a paltry £40. I could go into debt to keep going, but I promised once it was done, it was done, and if nowhere could promise me a game and a fee, then perhaps it wouldn't be worth flying out there at all.

We went to the pub and drank a £6 pint of flat beer that, if it weren't for Tristan's naivety in stating that he'd get the round in, would have shrunk my budget even further, and I watched on TV Michael Owen score the winner in an epic Manchester Derby where United triumphed 4-3 in the dying seconds over their closest rivals.

Seeing Owen's goal reminded me of his wonder-strike for England against Argentina at World Cup '98, in the same game David Beckham infamously got sent off for a kick on Diego Simeone who made a meal of it, it was the best goal I had ever seen from a player in an England shirt. At the time I was on a school-organised week-long camping trip, aged 12. I had my arm in a sling after spraining my wrist playing football in a field hours beforehand, which rendered my participation in rock climbing, bike riding, sailing and all the other fun things impossible. It meant that I spent the week doing orienteering over and over again, ironic considering my complete lack of direction skills. That day when I sprained my wrist punching a football turned out to be the worst day of my life, barring bereavements. I sprained my wrist away from home, threw up on the way to hospital through travel sickness, latterly found out it was the same day my dog was put down, and England were knocked out of the World Cup. Witnessing that goal against Argentina was the only highlight of a very shabby day and should have inspired me to train hard during my teenage years but instead, after that goal, I descended into laziness, not pursuing anything with determination. The irony wasn't lost on me that despite all of my recent hard work I still couldn't make it, and here I was seeing Michael Owen score again 11 years later, as the dream I had risked everything on seemed to have come to an end and with another injury. The next morning at the bus station I hugged Tristan goodbye as we were departing from different airports. We shook hands and agreed I would call him once I had recovered from the injury, rearranged a trial and found flights that we could afford. We were both rather shell-shocked by the course of events over the past 24 hours. It wasn't the end, but it sure as hell felt like it.

CHAPTER 17: 1P

On returning to England I spent an inordinate amount of time sat around my flat with nothing but my own thoughts. My ankle was still sore but was well on its way to a full recovery. I looked at jobs and trawled the internet trying to find cheap flights that would warrant another assault. There was now a significant hole in my CV. It should have read: 'Office Worker, February 2008-September 2009; Professional Footballer, September 2009 onwards', but sadly the latter never came to pass. I kept thinking of how I had played in Estonia, the best of the whole trip but injury took any chance of further participation with them or another side in Europe away from me.

Spiralling into depression I spent hours on end sat at my computer looking for a job that may suit my skills as an office dogsbody, while still trying to find a flight to either Copenhagen or Oslo that would give me another chance at the dream. But with fees, airport taxes, transport to and from the airport, and accommodation, it all looked unlikely. Hours turned into days and days turned into weeks. Two weeks doing sod all doesn't do a lot for the human spirit. However, something simple saved me from the metaphorical clouds above my head. A tiny envelope appearing in the corner of your computer monitor signalling a new email can work miracles on your mood.

'RYANAIR SALE, 1 MILLION SEATS **FREE**. HURRY!'

And boy did I hurry. Rushing to the Ryanair website my palms were sweaty. Were Ryanair giving away free seats to destinations where I still had clubs willing to give me a trial? YES THEY WERE! Oslo!

'Get in!' I exclaimed, throwing a punch into the air that opened my bathrobe to reveal my naked self to passers by in the street.

Oslo is in Norway, and Norway meant Mangelrud Star, who'd said yes months ago! Mangelrud Star is a semi-professional football club, a club that pays, a club that has foreigners, a club low down the football pyramid in Norway. My ideal club, my niche market! Perfect! A chance, one last chance! Hang on, why would it have to be my last chance? Could I have another trial as well as Oslo? Could

I have another two? Does Ryanair fly to Kenya? The answer to that was no. Bollocks, they don't fly to Denmark or the Faroe Islands either, but I don't care. Just one more chance to do myself justice and achieve the dream.

Now, technically speaking the flights weren't free, they were 1p, and then there were charges for using cards that weren't Visa Electron to pay, up to £5 for a 1p flight, but luckily I have a Visa Electron card! Ha-ha, screw you Ryanair!

'Would you like to book a bag onto the flight for just £10?' asked the website.

'I'll just take hand luggage thanks. Ha-ha screw you Ryanair!'

'Do you require travel insurance?'

'Nope, as far as I can remember my legs are still insured for £10million. Ha-ha, screw you Ryanair!'

I successfully avoided all the extra surcharges and so all I had to pay was 1p there and 1p back, and if I wasn't going to make it in Norway after my trial I could get a plane home the same day, thus avoiding hotel costs. It was perfect. The only problem was that I didn't know when I could have a trial and so I block-booked seats for me and Tristan on all of the flights for a fortnight between London and Oslo, hoping that on one of those days Mangelrud Star would be able to accommodate me. In total it cost my Visa Electron card 56p to do all of that. The coach from the Airport, that was by no means anywhere near Oslo, would cost me £30 for a return ticket, and that pretty much maxes out the budget, but let's be honest now, I am an adult, and I have credit cards and an overdraft and an ability to go into debt if it was required for me to stay in Norway for a month to become a professional footballer, regardless of the no-doubt paltry wage they would pay me.

I emailed Mangelrud's chairman, Kjell Roar Kaasa, and immediately received a response.

Sender: Kjell Roar Kaasa
To: Ralf Haley

Hi Ralf,
Yes you can come next Tuesday. Training is at 16:00 on an artificial pitch. Come before 13:00 and we can talk your trial here and about the club.

Here is my phone number xxxxxxxxx
Call me when you get into Oslo.

Kind Regards,
Kjell Roar Kaasa

I fumbled with my phone manically, failing in excitement. Finally after going round some options on my phone I never thought I had, I got there. I pressed call and the phone rang once, twice and then thrice before the answer.

'Alright Slag,' said Tristan. 'How's the ankle?'

'Tristan, we're going to Norway next Tuesday!'

'Eh?'

'Oslo baby. One more trial. I have one more trial. I got flights to Oslo for us for 1p and we can do it in a day trip! I can't turn that down! One more club, one more trial! I'm going for a run and I'll speak to you later.'

I left Tristan dumbfounded, stuck on my trusty red plimsolls and left the house for the first time in three days, pounding the tarmac towards my local park. My desire, something that had been on a continuing downward spiral since trial one, was back and higher than ever. 'I am going to be a professional footballer, I am going to be a professional footballer,' I kept saying to myself as I ran. 'I am going to be a professional footballer, I am going to be a professional footballer.'

I ran down the hill to the park, with phlegm building up in my mouth and chest ready to burst. I ran and ran until I realised I was lost in the green outskirts of Manchester with the M60 ring road the only sign of life in the distance. Doubled over, hands on knees struggling for air I began an extremely slow walk home dreaming of being a professional footballer once again.

5 days later I reflected on my three-point action plan that I'd drawn up at the start of the trip.

1) Pick the countries well, you have NO money – Manglerud Star, third Tier in Norway, has money, my perfect niche club.
2) Pick a position and stick to it – Who gives a shit.

3) Be in the best physical condition you can be otherwise you're up dump creek without a boat never mind a paddle – I am fitter than I have ever been.

Height: 5ft 7in
Weight: 10.25 stones
Fastest Mile: 5:00 (5 miles in 33 minutes).
Sit ups done in a row: 150.
Press ups done in a row: 150.

Come on Norway! Let me be a professional footballer, I'm desperate!

Chapter 18: Glory

Me and Tristan were both happy for me to have one last trial, mainly because he wanted an end to his film, and me because I don't think festering in an empty flat eating yoghurt using only my hands shouting abuse at daytime television any longer was a healthy way to live my life. I simply needed 'closure'.

Now I know what you're thinking. I've already failed at the minnows of Andorra and Malta as well as Eastern Europe, managed to injure myself and have trial cancelled in Sweden. So why did I pick Norway as my final destination? Well it's simple, because they said yes and the flights were 1p. If you require further convincing as to why I should go to this club, it's confirmed when you to the club's webpage. They have an abundance of foreigners as well as Norwegian players. They pay money, are eligible to sign me, are in the third tier of Norwegian football and are in the midst of their season, looking for new players. I reckon their standard equates to approximately the 9th or 10th tier in England, and when you consider how well I was playing in Estonia until my ankle gave way, I think, given my fitness and experience from all the past trials, I could make it there. It's my perfect club.

I do realise that out of all the countries I have visited, Norway is no doubt the best in terms of football ability, infrastructure and history in the game, but this really is my last hope, a penny flight is too good an opportunity to turn down, and for the first time ever in the entire year that this quest has encompassed I felt that things were going right for me. All I needed to do was play, and all they needed to do was pay.

It was a simple plan, fly to Norway at 6am and arrive at 10am, meet chairman at 12 noon, trial at 16:00 and then either a) stay in Norway at considerable cost for extra training at the request of the club before signing and being a pro footballer, or b) return to England at 21:00 to arrive in London at 22:30 and end the longest day ever and put to rest this ridiculous quest.

I am quietly confident. The stadium capacity is just 2,000, which is smaller than most the clubs I have visited, and although it's in the third tier of Norwegian football it's been beset by a wave of financial problems over the years, but the level of support for football in

Norway, the national sport, means that there should be enough to finance these clubs sufficiently so that I can get paid.

Our flight to Norway took us over the coastal city of Sandjeford, way outside the city of Oslo. The birds-eye view we had of the islands dotted around the ocean with small houses and harbours spread along the crystal sea was beautiful. Lush forests rolled over into the horizon and all that there was to interrupt this most amazing landscape was a few slaps of road intersecting the woodlands. Touching down and stepping of the plane, my genitals, who had endured so much pain during this trip, decided that the weather in Norway was too cold for them and thus retreated inside of my body with the sign-off 'We'll see you when we get back to England.' It was only the beginning of October but it was ridiculously chilly and was only just above freezing.

After coasting through passport control and to the airport shuttle bus to Oslo that cost 3,000 times the amount of the flight itself, we set ourselves up on the back seat of the coach to drink coffee and sleep. People who don't fly with Ryanair need to realise that Ryanair often don't fly to the most convenient airport that a city has to offer because that would be too expensive for them in airport charges, so we sat at Oslo Torp airport, which is over 100km away from Oslo itself, waiting for our coach into the city centre.

Drawing out of the small airport and onto Norway's roads, the view was like the front of a postcard. Everything seemed fresh, green and with the sea clearly visible from the window I was almost tempted to stay awake to see this unconventional tour of Norway's backwaters, but the early start had gotten the better of me, and my eyes slowly shut several times before welding themselves closed.

Waking up with drool all my face pulling into Oslo I was dazed and confused and was lost momentarily as to what was going on until the Norwegian road signs reminded me I was on the final leg on my tomfoolery quest.

Before flying out I trained and trained at home. I didn't rejoin the gym, I didn't want Marvin to see what a sorry state of affairs I had gotten myself into. Instead I just did it on the mean streets of south suburban Manchester, Rocky style. Running every day for an hour, stretching methodically and actually doing some work with a football this time around to improve my touch and technique was the order of every day of the last week in the build up to this trial.

Having learnt from my mistakes I was on a crash diet of living, breathing, and eating football. Before, I merely thought about the training part and did some running around at the gym for a while. This was the club I was physically and technically best prepared for and this was my last chance. I was ready.

Tristan foolishly trusted me to get us out of the shopping mall-come-bus station as he concentrated on his gear while eating an overpriced soggy sandwich. 40 minutes later we found our way out of the mammoth sized central station. I really do have an awful sense of direction. Tristan knows this; why he let me lead despite there being no signs in English I do not know, but I ended up leading us into the same outside smoking area twice in ten minutes. We were literally walking in circles. Finally, after much bickering, we found an exit that was far too obvious and made me look like a fool.

'I told you it was here you idiot!' said Tristan in annoyance.

'No you didn't, you just ate your sandwich and shouted insults at me, like you're doing now!' We were both tired and nervous.

A quick walk to the cathedral resulted in my lungs freezing over, and by that time our tourist activities were completed and work had to commence. I rang Kjell, who answered immediately, and transportation was arranged – he was going to pick us up in a mere five minutes. I sat at the foot of the statue of George IV, whoever he may be, looking at the almighty building of the cathedral while waiting for Kjell. Tristan had a camera three inches from my eyes filming every worried frown and expectant look on my face. I was anxious, but it was a feeling I was used to – it showed I still wanted this. One more trial to go, and if it doesn't happen it's quits. The next six hours were to determine the rest of my life.

'That there is our Parliament and that down there is our treasury office,' said Tom from the passenger seat as we passed through Oslo in the back of Kjell's people carrier.

Tom was stereotypically Norwegian. If he wasn't so slight of build he could have entered the European Stereotypes competition. His hair was blond, spiky and thin, whilst his face was home to rimless glasses first made prominent on British shores by Swede Sven Goran Eriksson. Kjell, on the other hand, was broad, tall and stocky with a full head of thick, curly hair, and possessed of a deep booming voice. When you think of chairmen you think of spindly fellows interested in balancing the books, but this guy in his sharp, open-shirted suit was quite the opposite. He too looked very Scandinavian, but more of the Viking kind rather than the 21st century type.

More monuments passed us by as Kjell explained to us he wanted to take the scenic route before showing us the training ground and the club offices. I was ignoring most of the words coming from his mouth as I mentally prepared myself, imagining flying over a player's slide tackle, taking a penalty, and delivering short, sharp passes. I was trying my hardest to get my mind in the right frame. I had no idea why Tom was there. It was said he was the club treasurer, which by his studious looks was easy to believe, but I think he was there for security as much as anything else in case we were knife-wielding maniacs. But why would we travel all that way, spend months in correspondence via emails to get this window of opportunity in the back of a man's car only to do that? Surely there are easier ways to mug people without a stringent six-month planning operation duping them into believing I wanted to be a professional footballer. He was either there for security, or was merely getting a lift to work.

Once our 15-minute tour of the city was complete, we headed for the ring roads that would take us to the district of Mangelrud. Tom and Kjell explained to us that the area is one of the roughest and poorest in Oslo. I presumed that probably meant it compared nicely to an English park district, and lo and behold I was right. If this area was rough and poor I'd love to see the affluent areas of Oslo's suburbs.

From where we had parked we could see the club ground, or pitch to be more accurate, with floodlights installed to boot. This didn't make me panic – we had seen floodlights in Malta and Andorra and in those countries they were only marginally better than me. Floodlights didn't alarm me in the slightest. What did alarm me was the sight that was presented to us as we slid our way out of the tight car-parking spot Kjell had drawn us into. A gargantuan metal construction stood front of us. It looked like a Jetsons aircraft hanger dropped in from the kitsch future. It was massive and dominated the skyline.

'These are our offices and training facilities,' said Kjell about the aforementioned building.

'What? This?!' I asked, sounding like I was insulting the size of the place, but in reality I was worried about how good they were based on the size of the building they train in.

'Yes, we have it in partnership with the community, there is an ice hockey rink inside and also our artificial pitches.'

At least we were training inside, it was absolutely freezing. But on the downside, we were training on an artificial pitch inside. Inside! This club had money, too much of it probably – my heart sank and my bottom lip started to stick out as I felt a sulk coming on.

In Latvia during my trial with FC Daugava I touched the ball about 12 times in a three-hour training session, cut my eye and kicked myself in the balls. They trained outside on a bumpy park pitch next to schoolchildren and a scrap yard, and here I was about to play in a proper training complex. Stepping through the glass doors of this modern building I immediately regretted coming to Norway; why hadn't I gone to Denmark instead, or the Faroe Islands, or even Kenya? But then I remembered my financial situation, and the constraints I was under.

'How much did this place cost?' I asked Kjell.

'The structure originally was just the Ice Hockey rink but we added our training ground and facilities for about 4 million Krones (£400,000 to you and me).'

Inside the building there was a club shop up ahead of us, stairs to our left going up to offices and down to changing rooms, and to our right a glass wall that provided a view of the full-sized indoor astroturf pitch beneath a 50-metre high metallic curved ceiling. Not a soul was on the pitch, but as I looked at it I think mine left my body. I had come a long way from my first trial in Malta where they trained on a half-sized old dusty pitch that couldn't accommodate proper studs, and I'd come all this way without meriting it. It wasn't as if I had moved through the ranks of professional football up to this incredibly advanced and modern structure, I had simply written to people begging for a trial, and this was the fruit of my labour, not the result of my talent.

Kjell showed us the pitch, and I felt like I was walking out on Wembley. It was only a football pitch, but the grand structure around and above me made me feel even more nervous. My stomach was on a heavy cycle as Kjell gave us the tour. Things got worse when we could see a gym through another glass wall only visible and accessible from the pitch.

Throughout all of my trials, some clubs took me seriously and others simply wanted to do a jovial English boy a favour, knowing I wouldn't actually make it with them. However, it felt as if I had a realistic chance of getting a game if I impressed Kjell. We entered the gym so Kjell could show me the facilities they had on offer to the players. Again without anyone around, bar my brother with his camera lens fixed on our faces, I investigated how good I needed to be, using the gym as a gateway to the inquisition.

'It's good a gym,' I said, trying to sound nonchalant, so as to not give the game away about how intimidated I was by the place. I folded my arms and nodded my head, thinking that would make me look relaxed. 'Are there any specific physical traits or attributes a player needs to have?'

'What do you mean?'

'Well does a player need to be able to run a certain amount of distance in a certain amount of time to make it into your team?' I said, thinking back to the five miles in 30 minutes that Jamie had set for me all those months ago, which I was just about able to do now, but only at risk of coughing up a lung along the way.

'No, not really, as long as they are fit and are able to perform then we don't tend to monitor the levels.' This was music to my ears. All I needed was talent. Oh hang on, I don't have that. 'The gym is situated like this overlooking the pitch so that players coming back from injury still feel involved and get a feel for what the coach wants, rather than training in a gym in a different building.'

'I recognise a couple of these machines from my training regime back in England before I came back out here, I like to think I am pretty fit now.'

Why did I say that? It was only going to bring trouble to me.

'And what about your playing career, you said you were scouted as a junior?' said Kjell. Tristan looked alarmed behind his lens.

I had gone all the way round Europe and not one club had raised my little white lie in my original email to me about being scouted (or my friends were at least) by some of Yorkshire's bigger clubs. I had to be careful with my words.

'I was watched by them, but never made the grade,' technically true, 'and then everyone got bigger than me,' definitely true, 'I got injuries to my ankles,' true also, 'and I never kicked on like everyone else.' All true, in a manner of ways. Kjell raised an eyebrow and we moved on.

We were then showed us the ice rink for the Mangelrud ice hockey team. I thought about asking for a trial with them, but Kjell informed me they have no partnership with the hockey team and simply share a building. The hockey rink was awesome – I'd never seen one up close and it had a thousand seats surrounding it for spectators. I thought about the pace and physicality of ice hockey and imagined what it would be like to be a professional in that sport; that would be some adrenalin rush. Skating on ice at high speeds in a game where possession of a solid metal disc is paramount and where violence is encouraged, with or without using a big stick. I would be crap at ice hockey. As I thought that, a torrent of what I thought initially was midgets, but turned out to be small young children, flew past me onto the ice, decked out in protective gear ready to kick the shit out of each other during training. Valuing my shins, I made a hasty exit.

'What made you choose our club for your project?' asked Kjell, once again posing questions I didn't really want to be answering.

'Well you fell into my niche market of being a lower league club but still professional or semi-professional, and you said yes.'

'And how many clubs did you write to?'

'Quite a few.'

'How many exactly?'

'One-thousand-and-forty-four.'

'One hundred and forty-four?' asked Kjell, hearing me incorrectly.

'Roughly yeah.'

The tour continued, taking in the changing rooms, chairman's office and manager's office. I began to feel more and more confident. Sure, this club had training facilities that would put some League One and most of League Two teams in England to shame, but in Malta at St Georges they'd had good facilities, a grand history and floodlights, and I was only marginally off the pace there. This club was everything I had hoped for. Granted I was hanging my hopes on not judging the book by its cover, but if I were to go on appearances then I was going to get myself ready for an arse kicking.

The final part of the tour involved Kjell showing us the boardroom, used for meetings and general hospitality. As he swung the heavy varnished wooden double doors open I gulped. A room the size of my flat back in Manchester with leather sofas, a huge rectangular oak table with high backed chairs and flipchart put the 'VIP' area Solus showed me in Lithuania to shame.

I was feeling nervous but ready. I played the best football of my entire life in Estonia with a team that regularly competes in the early rounds of Europe and didn't stick out, and since returning to England to recuperate from my ankle injury I have only got fitter and also improved my technique marginally. I was hoping my old-school training would pay off for me. Kjell had to leave us and attend to some important work. He didn't seem like a normal chairman and when I asked how he got involved in football I found out he used to be a player for Rosenborg and had trials all over Europe, including England with Bristol Rovers, set up for him by an agent, but he never made it. Saying he 'never made it' is a bit of an exaggeration – someone who was once top goal scorer of the Norwegian Premier League and also had played against World Cup Winners Marcel Desailly and Frank Lebouef of Chelsea in front of 40,000 people at Stamford Bridge in a UEFA Cup game certainly 'made it' to me. He explained he was a bit of a celebrity and he was the face of the board, not the money-man like so many chairmen are. I asked if he ever got close to the Norwegian national squad and he remarked that he nearly got involved, but there was always two or three, including the likes of Ole Gunnar Solksjaer and Steffen Iversen, ahead of him in the queue. I liked Kjell, and I think he liked me, but could sense that he wasn't expecting much from me, especially after all the disclaimers I gave him in the gym about my ability. He left us in the players' lounge, which was a cafeteria really, with a tea and coffee maker, sandwiches aplenty and a Playstation 3 and plasma TV screen in the corner. Okay a posh cafeteria. Tristan, still visibly tired from our early start, made a dash to the coffee machine but I was now alive and awake from adrenalin.

'Do you want one?' he asked, trying to decipher the Norwegian translations of the buttons.

'No thanks mate, think I'll be sticking to water. Trial starts in an hour.'

'How are you feeling?' This was the first time Tristan had asked me this without a camera in my face.

'Nervous, but strangely confident. I mean Estonia went well. '

'Did it?' Tristan interrupted.

'Yeah, I thought it did. Well apart from the negative feedback from the coach and the fact that I injured myself by treading on my own ankle. Anyway I was playing well, and these guys won't be as good I don't think; they're not as high up the league pyramid.'

We sat in that room for half an hour and it was like waiting for an exam. No one was making their way through the players' lounge, and so I was pacing around manically. I had taped both my ankles up so much that they were barely able to move. I wasn't going to let them get in the way of me performing to my best, even if that meant sacrificing mobility.

Finally people started to emerge – well some children did, and one man. The man was the coach for the after-school club run by the club and the children were energetic, lively and chatty, everything I wasn't. As Tristan showed the kids his camera and they played up to it, the man approached me. He was no older than 30, had a sweeping dark wet-gelled fringe and perfect teeth. With toned legs shown off by shorts that were all-too-small for him, he looked like a model, and for this I didn't like him. He knew immediately we were English and began speaking to me fluently.

'You're going to play football?' he asked, obviously referring to me wearing a kit whilst swigging on a bottle of water with my ankles taped halfway up my shins.

'Yeah, I have a trial. My brother is making a film about it, about pursuing your dream; I think this is my last chance.'

'Where have you come from?' he said without stopping to think about the camera.

'England.'

'Oh okay. I thought so. You had trials anywhere else?'

'It's a long story,' I said, shaking my head. 'What do you do here?' I asked, trying to change the subject.

'Well I train these kids and I also play for the team.'

'Really?' I had a chance to gauge how good they were.

'Yeah, the club I was with was having problems so I came here because I knew one of the players. I managed to get a job doing this a couple of hours a day and play football as well.'

'And how much are you paid if you don't mind my asking?'

'Me, I get about 20,000 Kroner a month,' he said shrugging.

'So that's about £2000 in England,' I said tensing every fibre in my body.

'Something like that yeah. Anyway I'm going to get changed and I'll see you down there.'

£2000 a month! I looked at Tristan and he at me. His jaw hit the floor and mine went through it. This was the last club we were visiting and by my reckoning was by far the wealthiest, and that really could only mean one thing – they were amazing. I went to the toilet and I was sick. I pebble dashed the porcelain and wiped the sweat from my brow. I am not a religious man but I have to admit I offered a small prayer up to the man upstairs, asking him for my dream to come true, I just hoped that if and when it did he didn't expect me to get baptised. I considered crossing my fingers whilst having a word with the big guy, but I thought with him being almighty and all powerful that he'd probably cotton on.

'Dear God, big guy, dude in the sky, holy one, whatever your preference. Please please please please please let me be a professional footballer. Please let me play to my ability so I can be a footballer. Actually, scratch that last bit, please make me better than I actually am so I can be a professional footballer, just once will do. I know you're probably busier with disease, famine and wars right now, but if you could go out of your way for me that'd be great. I've tried really hard but it just doesn't seem to be enough, so I need your help. Yours truly, Ralf Haley.' I didn't disclose any other details about myself, I'm pretty confident he knew who I was. The trial was in 15 minutes.

I delayed my introductions to everyone until I couldn't wait any longer. The coach had yet to make an appearance but I decided to walk through to the pitch as some of them were there playing impossibly good long passes to each other, controlling the ball and laying it off to one another before getting on with tying their boots up or chit-chatting. The majority of the squad, however, of which there were about 15, were sat on the floor wobbling their legs from side to side in readiness for training. I walked through and introduced myself to everyone, bracing myself for the most important two hours of my life. I shook hands individually with them all, got all their names and immediately forgot them like I had at all my other trials. There was a rich ethnicity to the group with all manner of skin tones; the majority typically looked Scandinavian but a couple had an Eastern Europe glumness about them. I took solace in knowing that foreigners could sign readily. Each player had their own squad number on their shorts and that small detail filled me with even more dread – this was my first club to assign short numbers. How can such a small detail strike fear into someone?

Then, amidst all the questions about the trip and the camera, came the coach, who was very friendly towards me, but to everyone else was a short, angry man. His name was also Kjell, and so for storytelling reasons will now simply be known as 'the coach'. Chairman Kjell followed the coach, in his sharp suit and loafers, to wish me good luck. I was going to need it.

As the squad took off on a gentle jog around the pitch, I sprinted to catch up with them, tagging onto the back of the pack. They were no mountains of questions fired at me this time once we had started running like in Malta or Andorra, this was strictly business. I was left to my own devices and thought about what lay ahead, telling myself to do the things I am bad at – like aggression and pace – as best I could, and then really show off the things I could do, like reading the game, movement and passing in a straight line, making sure I was 110% accurate each time. The physical presence of the players didn't worry me and they didn't seem to be as honed or toned as I was expecting from a predominantly Scandinavian team, which was a relief. But then I thought back to Lithuania and, despite the fact that they were only 16, they were still as good as me. I was a nervous wreck.

After just two minutes of jogging round the pitch the coach called us over. We hadn't even broken into a sweat – this was great for me. There was no agility sessions like in Malta or Estonia – even better – and hardly any stretching like in Andorra or Lithuania. This trial and the result of it would come down solely to my ability with a football, not whether or not I can hop in between cones on my left foot three times every seven seconds. Bibs were distributed, and the coach and his assistant set up a small coned area in the shape of a rectangle on the pitch. Another game of seven-on-seven, blacks versus orange – keep the ball, with only two touches allowed. If the ball goes out and the team not in possession didn't actually claim it (i.e. it merely ricocheted off their knee), then the coach would return the ball at speed to the team originally in possession. Basically, the rule was: don't lose the ball.

I was in orange, and with no banter between us like there had been in previous trials I felt out of place. Our team won possession and I made myself available in all kinds of positions, offering an easy pass here and an easy pass there, but always they chose a different option. Were they intentionally not passing to me, or was I putting myself into positions on the pitch that they didn't warrant worthy of a pass in the greater scheme of things? I thought it was probably the latter. I continued to make myself available when we had the ball and closed down the best I could when we didn't. I didn't touch the ball for the first five minutes, but I didn't think I was doing too badly, it just hadn't naturally come to me yet and my fitness was just about bearing up. Finally, when the ball did come to me by way of a generous team-mate I put my foot on it to use one of my allowed two touches. With the ball dead on the floor I had two Scandinavian athletes bearing down on me. Shit! I froze, they both lunged, I tried to loop the ball in through a gap between them both to anyone but them but I woefully scooped it into the opponent's lap. He laid it off to his colleague who had aided him in closing me down and before I knew it they were gone down the other end of the pitch, keeping the ball between themselves and their team-mates.

'F**K!' This was the first time I had sworn during any of the trials.

'Come on Ralf!' yelled Kjell at the top of his voice. He looked the part, assessing his employees, judging each and every movement they did shouting words of encouragement or disapproval. His shout to me was a bit of both I felt. Head down, I ran for the ball, trying desperately to get it back, but in doing so I was drawing myself out of position, I wasn't marking one particular man, thus bringing the balance of the team out. I was desperate and it was affecting my decision-making. Normally I would stick to a man, but here I followed the ball, which meant that there was always a man free for the opposition, the man I should be marking. I could feel Kjell and the coach's disapproving glowers in the side of my head but I didn't have a choice, this was my last trial. In the first five minutes I had touched the ball once, the best players had touched it dozens of times. If my ratio of minutes to ball contact were to stay like this then I was in serious danger of only touching the ball 24 times in a two-hour training session, and no one has ever impressed anyone with just 24 touches of a football, even the world's greatest would struggle to do that.

'Come on Ralf.' The shout was given again and I tried, I desperately tried, but the tempo was too fast. They were only using one touch most of the time and at speed and with accuracy to boot. They were definitely the best team I had trained with, regardless of league titles and standings.

Desperately lunging left to right, back and forth to get the ball my breathing grew heavier and deeper. But all of a sudden the ball came to me once more by virtue of another team-mate, who would soon learn not to pass to me again. The ball was coming towards my feet along the ground at pace, and although my eyes were solely focussed on the ball I could see two more players following it towards my trembling legs. I'd identified an escape route for the ball though, a team-mate available, all I had to do was play the ball first time on the floor through the eye of the needle to my team-mate, thus spreading the play and setting my team up for a prolonged period in possession. with the ball still coming towards me I prepared myself – if I pulled this off I would start to look good – I'd look like an intelligent footballer, like Dennis Bergkamp or Franz Beckenbauer. The ball arrived at my feet and I played the pass. It went straight off the pitch. I had dragged it metres wide of the gap where it should have gone.

'F**K!' I swore louder than I've ever sworn before and kicked at the plastic turf in disgust at my inability to do the most simple of passes. As so often my mind knew what I wanted to do but the ability just wasn't there.

'Come on Ralf!' came the shout once more.

It takes a quick mind to see those sorts of passes and I certainly have one of them, but if you can't do it then there's no point having the mental ability in the first place. Like knowing how to speak French but not liking the French people, a conundrum for many around the world.

I gritted my teeth and raised my game. I finally started to put some challenges in but it came at a cost of my physical wellbeing. This was meant to be a simple warm-up exercise but I was going at it all guns blazing to get on par with these people and even then I couldn't do it. My dream was slipping away from me and I was getting torn apart inside.

After 20 minutes the coach called a halt to proceedings and called for a drinks break. I had left my water bottle upstairs, so I made a desperate dash for the bottles on the floor adorning the name of the club's sponsor. To my horror even these each had squad numbers on them so that each player could identify it as their own. I needed liquid but what could I do? I quickly scanned the playing squad's shorts and noticed for whatever reason their number three was not present and I grabbed the corresponding bottle and necked half a litre of water and spat half it out as a way to clear the spit building up in my mouth. The rest of players began to move off towards the middle section of the pitch and I began to follow, breathing deeply and loudly. Hands on hips and sweat dripping down my face. I was interrupted in my recovery by an approaching Kjell.

'How was the warm-up for you then Ralf?'

That was the warm-up!?

'Okay. It was a good fast pace. Although I am annoyed with myself. That's the worst I've played in years but I'm feeling good,' I lied, and Kjell nodded sympathetically, knowing I was lying.

I decided my tactic of taping my ankles up so much that they couldn't move was a bad idea and so began to tear both the tape and ankle protectors off from skin in a rapid fashion to bring dexterity back to my legs, which ideally is needed if you want to play football. I joined the rest of the squad and the coach approached me and smiled, and explained we were to play the same game again, except on a much larger area spanning what would normally be a third of a football field. He then handed me a yellow bib. Everyone else was wearing either black or an orange bib but I was going to be wearing yellow. Why? I could see a plentiful amount of orange bibs just metres away from him, why was I wearing yellow?

'Ralf, it's the same game as before but this time you will be wearing yellow and the person wearing yellow is always on the team with possession. So never close anyone down, just always be available for a pass and remember who you need to pass to until the other team wins possession and then it's your job to switch sides to help them out. Okay?'

'Okay'

I understood clearly but I couldn't understand why I was being asked to be this floating player always on the side with the team in possession. Was it so the coach and Kjell could take a closer look at me? It must have been. The last year of my life had led to this moment. I was going to be at the crux of proceedings, the man always looking for the pass, in the playmaker position, not having to worry about tracking back or closing down. This was my time to shine in a role that suited me brilliantly. It's as if the coach had heard me speaking to myself earlier in the day saying not to get involved doing stuff I can't do like aggression or sprinting and just concentrate on the stuff I am good at. It was like he was reading my mind. I tried my best to telepathically tell him I was the spirit of Zinedine Zidane's now retired footballing soul, but he didn't seem to pick that one up.

The game started and I was everywhere, offering easy options to everyone, constantly running in the direction of the ball pointing at my feet begging for it to be put there so I could then lay it on to another player. Every pass I received I dispatched to a team-mate with ease. The larger pitch space that playing in this area afforded me time and space to knock the ball into, pick my pass and launch another delightful lofted ball to spread the play or simply lay it off to bemuse the opposition. I was exceptional and exhilarating. I was thinking about signing the contract there and then. I was playing well, seriously. I was playing really well. No, seriously, I was playing *really* well! Every time the team in possession lost the ball I simply transferred to the other team and offered my services to them as the man in yellow always ready to receive a pass. The space I was finding myself in and the amount of passes I received made me feel like Frank Lampard, directing play with ease and standing out as a good player. Of course some passes were mislaid, but so were other people's; some were shinned, sliced or dragged, but for the majority they all went to their intended targets. I was having a stormer. I'll go one further, I was having a *barnstormer*! The only problem I had was the sheer athleticism of some of these players. They were short and agile, always able to stick out a telescopic leg to bring a ball under control, make a pass and then make a mad dash into space to receive the return ball. I was playing at a far more pedestrian pace, picking my runs wisely like Teddy Sheringham in the latter (and the early) part of his career. I wasn't wasting energy needlessly but I was still playing well, really well.

Sadly though as the minutes ticked by my level began to drop because of fatigue. I felt like a boxer on the ropes – this I was sure was the fittest I had ever been yet still I was struggling, breathing deeply, fighting the urge to put my hands on my knees for a small breather so as to not show weakness to Kjell and the coach who were both still watching intently. As the noise in the football cathedral echoed around the metal shell I started to get sloppy. My passes were going wider and wider of their marks, I wasn't getting into positions where I could readily receive the ball from my colleagues and I was so out of breath I was struggling to raise my voice to get their attention to let them know I was free. My chest got heavier and my heartbeat stronger and louder, I could almost feel it bursting it out my chest. I was getting frustrated with myself. My level wasn't so far from these guys and yet my fitness couldn't get me to the areas on the pitch where I needed to be. I fast became the game's passenger rather than the conductor – no one was playing to my tune and that's exactly what this yellow jersey was for, to make me stand out from the rest, to show the world that it was me who should be always involved, but alas I wasn't. My floppy, curly mane was stuck to my face and I could taste the salt from the sweat on my upper lip seeping into my mouth as the full-time whistle went. 45 minutes of the trial down and it wasn't good enough. The players made their way to the corner of the pitch for another water break and I began to follow, but then the coach grabbed my arm.

'I'm sorry Ralf it's not working. I'm going to have end your involvement in the training session. You are affecting my players and I have a big game to prepare for this weekend. If you want you can warm down by taking some shots at our youth goalkeeper over there, but the trial is over. I'm sorry.'

He smiled sympathetically, his hand on my shoulder, and I did my best to shrug it off.

'Hey it's okay, you have to do what you have to do,' I said, my voice quivering under the immediate onrushing emotions.

He smiled again even more sympathetically this time and made his way off to talk to his players. Emotion welled up inside me, like a bubble ready to burst. I could feel tears in my eyes and taste the choke in my throat.

It was over.

Chapter 19: Acceptance

I stood at the side of the pitch watching the training continue. The coach offered some kind words, but none of them made me feel any better.

'There is no way you could be a professional footballer. You don't have strong enough technique to be able to succeed at a level where you would get paid, and you lack any strong physical attributes such as strength pace or height in order to counter act your shortcomings on the pitch. Some of our best players here don't even get paid.' I had now heard this almost word for word from seven different coaches.

'You don't think it could happen, anywhere in the world?' I asked, pleading one last time.

'No, I am sorry. There are plenty of other careers out there where you can make plenty of money, so I advise you to do that. Football, I'm afraid, is not for you.'

The coach then had his attention distracted by antics on the pitch and he shook my hand and went about his business. Kjell, who was present during my chat with the coach, smiled at me and I at him. He didn't now that this was my last opportunity, I hadn't told him as much. I had broken a world record for the most trials in a week, and now it seemed I had broken a world record for the shortest football trial ever, lasting just 45 minutes before rejection ensued. Of all the trials this was the most spectacular failure, and of all the feedback it was fittingly the most concrete – I couldn't be a professional footballer.

At all the other clubs when they said no I was upset, but okay about it, because it meant I could carry on my adventure. But as each club slipped by I started to really want it, but it wasn't to be. I felt like I had suffered a bereavement, like I had let down the 10-year-old boy inside of me who I had promised as an adult, as a big brother-type figure, that I would be a professional so that I – we – could be proud. Alas, I'll never be able to use my line of 'You know I used to be a professional footballer?', but I gave it my all. Tristan did his duty as a big brother admirably, putting an arm on my shoulder followed by a big hug that would have looked odd to the players still training. We shared a wordless conversation as he gave me a look to say 'We knew this would happen' and I returned it with one that said 'But still... I'm pretty upset.' I tore off the boots that I'd worn across Europe – which I have vowed never to wear again – and hobbled off to get changed.

Kjell, ever the gentlemen, drove us to the bus terminal and shook our hands. I thanked him for his time and we boarded our bus back to the airport. The plane carried us over the North Sea and back into London. We had got up at 4am and were touching back down at 10:30pm the same day, and in the course of those 18-and-a-half hours my dream was laid to rest in a metal training complex a thousand miles from home, in one of the most affluent countries in the world.

The next day I woke up in Tristan's flat and we had breakfast in almost complete silence. He looked at me and there was a long pause before he broke out in a smile.

'It's been a laugh hasn't it, even if you didn't make it?'

'Yeah definitely. If I could I'd do it all again, but it's time to accept defeat.'

'Okay.' Tristan exhaled a huge breath that added a footnote of despondence and sadness. It wasn't my journey any more, it was ours. Another man hug that lasted an eternity ensued as I said goodbye and his door shut behind me.

I travelled over 4,000 miles to eight different countries, had seven football trials and spent £1,500 pursuing a fantasy that sadly never came to fruition.

My football dream was exactly that, a fantasy.

EPILOGUE

So there you have it; that was my story, a story that occurred over four years ago, at the time of writing.

The quest itself almost feels as if it didn't happen, that I had wasted this time in my life and that I could have spent the time and the money on something a whole lot more worthwhile.

If you weigh everything up in hindsight, you could say it was a foolhardy idea. Realistically if I was good enough an athlete I would have been noticed long ago rather than having to dupe myself into the belief that there was hope on foreign shores.

Working and living like a monk for six months to save up in pursuit of a boyhood dream that was likely never going to happen probably isn't everyone's picture of sanity, but to me it made sense and still does.

Yes I tore my ankle ligaments, broke two world records I didn't want, and embarrassed myself around Europe. I had trials with seven teams and had my dreams quashed on more than one occasion by an inability to do anything right on a football pitch. But I did meet some amazing people and was reminded of how beautiful a game football is without the corporate juggernaut behind it, inspiring good in people and breaking down language and cultural barriers through the simple love of two nets and a ball. I visited some of Europe's most beautiful cities and actually tried to achieve my boyhood dream.

It was a choice to spend all that money, a choice to leave a comfortable job and a choice to continue when all hope had gone, but I wouldn't change a thing. My dream was sadly and ultimately out of reach. But at least I found out.

When I started this trip I didn't think I'd want a cheesy moral at the end of it. I just wanted to be a professional footballer; no 'happily ever after', no 'message'. But there is one feeling that I can't ignore and should share. It is simply this:

If you have a dream, go for it.

Fair enough, we've all heard it a thousand times, but how many times have you followed that age-old advice?

Don't wind up regretting something you never did. If you want to be an artist join an evening art class, if you want to be an actor join an amateur dramatics society and try to write a play with you as the star, and if you want to learn to play the piano… well, do it, don't just watch soaps in the evening, do something to change your life. The philosopher Alan Watts once said 'It's better to live a short life full of the things you want to do, than a long one filled with nothing.'

If you're wondering why it's taken so long for this story to be typed and told it's because Tristan and I have been busy. My elder brother has become a father, so any production on the film is slow due to the fact that he has greater priorities in life, although if you do want to see some of the footage you can do so by visiting my website, ralfhaley.com, from there you'll find photos of the trip and a collection of trailers that me and Tristan edited together whilst slightly inebriated during a viewing of all 27 hours of footage that Tristan admirably filmed. Alternately you can YouTube 'beautiful dream teaser trailer'. Tristan's still working in the film industry and is still forcing me to drink too much.

As for myself I've spent the last three years working at Manchester United's in-house TV Channel, MUTV. A job I adore because I get to work in and around football all day, and a job I'm told wouldn't have happened were it not for the planning and production involved in the trip you've just read about.

It is here in my job that I have found a happy ending for the quest as it's given me a career that will last longer and reap more rewards than my vocation as a 'professional' footballer ever would. Because of this, hopefully someone somewhere will take courage from my story and just go for it, whatever *it* may be. I can't guarantee that if you pursue your lifelong ambitions in life you will ultimately end up in a job you love; all I can say is that if you don't go for it, some part of you will always have a feeling of regret.

Dreams need to come true for some people, and that person may just be you.

THE END

Thanks for making it all the way here, if you enjoyed the book then I'd appreciate it if you could spare a moment to write a short review on Amazon or Goodreads as self - published authors rely on your reviews to spread the word. If you didn't like the book, well, best not to.

If for some unlikely reason you'd like to ask any questions about the trip you can do so at ralfhaley@yahoo.co.uk, and I'd be happy to answer any queries you may have.

Acknowledgements

My wife Hannah & Tristan are the main reason this actually happened so they deserve massive thanks. Mum and Dad are the reason I happened so thanks for that, the rest of my brothers deserve a nod as well and Mark Latham for his contributions helping getting this over the line. However my biggest thanks must go to all the football clubs who wrote back offering a trial and giving me the confidence that it was possible, I'm sorry I couldn't afford to get to you all. On top of this I'll always be grateful to all the representatives from Santa Venera Lightnings, St Georges FC, FC Lusitanos, FK Nevezis, FC Daugava, FC Levadia and the sadly no longer running Mangelrud Star, in my mind you're the greatest clubs in the world.

www.ralfhaley.com

Printed in Great Britain
by Amazon.co.uk, Ltd.,
Marston Gate.